S0-BAM-214

READINGS ON EQUAL EDUCATION
(Formerly *Educating the Disadvantaged*)

SERIES EDITOR
Edward P. St. John

MANAGING EDITOR
Phyllis Kreger Stillman

ADVISORY PANEL

Walter Allen, University of California – Los Angeles
Deborah F. Carter, University of Michigan
Steve Desjardins, University of Michigan
James Hearn, Pennsylvania State University
Donald Heller, Pennsylvania state University
Don Hossler, Indiana University
Sylvia Hurtado, University of California – Los Angeles
James Kaminsky, Auburn University
Martha McCarthy, Indiana University
Luis Mirón, Florida International University
Michael B. Paulsen, University of Iowa
Laura Perna, University of Pennsylvania
William E. Sedlacek, University of Maryland
Scott Thomas, University of Georgia
William Tierney, University of Southern California

READINGS ON EQUAL EDUCATION

Volume 22

CONFRONTING EDUCATIONAL INEQUALITY

REFRAMING, BUILDING UNDERSTANDING, AND MAKING CHANGE

Volume Editor and Series Editor
Edward P. St. John

Managing Editor
Phyllis Kreger Stillman

AMS PRESS, INC.
NEW YORK

371.96
E 23
v. 22

READINGS ON EQUAL EDUCATION

VOLUME 22
Confronting Educational Inequality
Reframing, Building Understanding, and Making Change

Copyright 2007 by AMS Press, Inc.
All rights reserved.

ISSN 0270-1448
Set ISBN 0-404-10100-3
Vol. 22 ISBN-10: 0-404-10122-4
Vol. 22 ISBN-13: 978-0-404-10122-0
Library of Congress Catalogue Card Number 77-83137

All AMS books are printed on acid-free paper that meets the guidelines for performance and durability of the committee on production guidelines for book longevity of the Council on Library Resources.

AMS PRESS, INC.
63 FLUSHING AVE – UNIT #221
BROOKLYN NAVY YARD, BLDG. 292, SUITE 417
BROOKLYN, NY 11205-1005, USA

Manufactured in the United States of America.

VOLUME 22   **CONTENTS**

CONTRIBUTORS' NOTES

MICHELLE ASHA COOPER is the Deputy Director for the Advisory Committee on Student Financial Assistance. Her research focuses on issues of college access, persistence, alignment of P-16 educational standards, and financial aid, particularly for low- and moderate-income students and racial/ethnic minorities. Dr. Cooper received her B.A. in English from the College of Charleston, M.P.S. in Africana Studies from Cornell University, and Ph.D. in Education Policy and Leadership from the University of Maryland, College Park.

AMY S. FISHER earned a B.A. in History from Brandeis University and an Ed.M. in Student Personnel Administration from Teachers College, Columbia University. She is currently a doctoral student in the Center for the Study of Higher and Postsecondary Education at University of Michigan. Her research interests broadly include access to and persistence in higher education from both policy and student development perspectives with narrower foci on middle- and low-income students and working students.

TERRY G. GESKE is the J. Franklin Bayhi Professor of Education at Louisiana State University. Professor Geske has published extensively over the years in the areas of the economics of education and education finance policy. Professor Geske's current research efforts are concerned with state broad-based merit-aid scholarship programs, and also school choice issues.

SHOUPING HU is Associate Professor of Higher Education at Florida State University. He received a B.S. degree in geography from Peking University and earned his M.S. in economics and Ph.D. in higher education from Indiana University. Dr. Hu's research interests focus on postsecondary access and persistence, college student experience, and higher education finance. He is a recipient of the emerging scholar award from the American College Personnel Association (ACPA) and an editorial board member of the *Journal of College Student Development*. He has consulted for the Bill & Melinda Gates Foundation, MGT of America, and the U.S. Department of Education, among others.

MASAMICHI INOUE is Associate Professor of Physical Oceanography in the Department of Oceanography & Coastal Sciences and Director of the Coastal Studies Institute at Louisiana State University. Professor Inoue took a year's leave from Louisiana State University to study higher education at the University of Michigan-Ann Arbor and was granted a M.A. degree in 2006. His primary interest in higher education involves issues of access and equity including desegregation of higher education.

KIMBERLY KLINE is Director of Institutional Research and Planning/Associate Professor of Social Sciences at Hilbert College. Her research interests include social justice issues, moral and cognitive development, well-being and reflective practice. Her most recent article on social justice practice, co-authored with Megan Moore-Gardner, is titled "Envisioning new forms of praxis: Reflective practice and social justice education in higher education graduate programs" in the journal *Advancing Women in Leadership*.

LUIS MIRÓN is Dean of the College of Education at Florida International University. He is a member of the International Network of Philosophers of Education and the Philosophy of Education Society. His work seeks to weave insights from cultural studies, aesthetics, and the humanities into the understanding of schooling, particularly equity issues and the possibilities of establishing deep democracy in inner city schools serving large numbers of students of color. Dr. Mirón has a Ph.D. in Politics and Policy in Education from Tulane University.

PENNY A. PASQUE is an Assistant Professor of Education Leadership and Policy Studies in Adult and Higher Education at the University of Oklahoma. She received a Ph.D. from the Center for the Study of Higher and Postsecondary Education at the University of Michigan and M.S. in interpersonal communication from Syracuse University. Penny's work has been published in books, journals and monographs throughout the field of higher education and her book *Understanding and Achieving Higher Education for the Public Good* (Pasque, Bowman, & Martinez, Eds.) will be published later this year.

LAURA W. PERNA is Associate Professor in the Graduate School of Education at the University of Pennsylvania. She is a member of the technical review group for the GEAR UP and Upward Bound evaluations, the technical review panel for the National Postsecondary Student Aid Study, the external advisory committee for the National Council of Higher Education Loan Programs, and the Lumina Foundation for Education's Research Advisory Committee. In 2003 she received the Promising Scholar/Early Career Achievement Award from the Association for the Study of Higher Education.

EDWARD P. ST. JOHN is Algo D. Henderson Collegiate Professor of Education at the University of Michigan's Center for the Study of Higher and Postsecondary Education. His research focuses on the effects of public on equal opportunity and moral reasoning in professional practice. His recent books include *Education and the Public Interest: Education Reform, Public Finance, and Access to Higher Education* and *Action, Reflection, and Social Justice: Integrating Moral Reasoning into Professional Development*.

WILLIAM G. TIERNEY is University Professor and Wilbur-Kieffer Professor of Higher Education and Director of the Center for Higher Education Policy Analysis at the University of Southern California. Having spent over two decades conducting research on college access for underrepresented youth, Dr. Tierney is committed to informing policies and practices related to educational equity. Tierney's work has appeared in numerous journal articles, book chapters and books.

KRISTAN VENEGAS is an Assistant Professor of Clinical Education and a Research Associate in the Center for Higher Education at the University of Southern California. Dr. Venegas's research agenda focuses on access to college and financial aid. She has published and presented her work for policy, practice and research audiences and served as a consultant to the College Board and the Advisory Committee on Student Financial Assistance.

ONTARIO S. WOODEN is Director of the Velma Fudge Grant Honors Program and Academic Success Initiatives and Assistant Professor of Education at Albany State University. He serves on the editorial board of the NASAP and is a reviewer for Scientific Journals International. His research interests include school reform, college access and choice, higher education policy and finance, and multiculturalism and diversity in higher education. He holds a Ph.D. in Higher Education from Indiana University.

INTRODUCTION

Edward P. St. John

The fact that education public policy emphasizes *excellence for all* over remedies to inequality is beyond dispute. Policy rationales that espouse the value of reducing inequality are typically framed as arguments for educational excellence, including the framework provided by *No Child Left Behind* (Pub. L. No. 107-110). More recently, state and federal officials have used the excellence paradigm to reorganize high schools to improve college preparation and advocate for accountability schemes within higher education. The logic that policies that emphasize excellence dominate in the framing of strategies to reduce inequality in opportunity—or gaps in achievement tests—have an underlying logic that is too seldom questioned by academics or policymakers. The condition of inequality in educational opportunity is not only saddening, it is also ironic, given that so many of the policies used to organize and fund education in both K-12 and higher education were originally rationalized based on arguments about equity, as evident in the phrase "no child left behind." It can be argued that we need to learn better how to contend with inequality—and take steps that could ultimately reduce it—in policy work that overtly emphasizes improvement in educational success.

Rather than argue for reasserting equity as dominate in educational policy, an argument that has often been made, the authors in this volume of *Readings in Equal Education* take a collective step toward reframing the problem of inequality in educational opportunity. The papers solicited for and contributed to this volume illuminate paradoxes of inequality in American education policy. The labeling of three sections of the volume—reframing, building understanding, and taking action—is not meant to imply a uniformity of thought among the authors. Rather, the authors worked on bits and pieces of the problem in specific ways. The chapters in Part I address problems with theory in education policy and the need to reframe it. In Part II, the authors uncover problems with respect to the reproduction of inequality, but these researchers did not necessarily focus on inequality at the start of their work. In contrast, the authors in Part III are fundamentally concerned about inequality and how to engage in new practices that better contend with the pervasive set of policy and behavioral forces which reinforce and, indeed, reproduce inequality in educational opportunity. By looking across these chapters it is possible to gain perspective on strategies for contending with inequality in policy, practice, and research.

Reframing

The three chapters in Part I address different aspects of the theory problem, an aspect of the inequality paradox. One focuses on a very specific problem—access to and use of information on student financial aid by low-income high school students—that requires more careful thought and research. The second provides a review of the extensive literature on the public good in higher education, but with an explicit focus on the reasons why inequality tends to be overlooked in arguments for public funding. The third considers how the study of college students who have their financial need met through last dollar scholarship aid can help us retheorize equal educational opportunity.

First, in "The Cultural Ecology of Financial Aid Decision Making" (Chapter 1), William G. Tierney and Kristan Venegas develop a compelling theory of early awareness of college affordability, one that is situated in the contexts of the lived lives of students, their families, and their schools. They develop a cultural theory of information and awareness that can inform a future generation of research on high school students. Initially this theory has been explored through qualitative research (e.g., Venegas, 2006) but it can also be examined in quantitative studies. At the very least, qualitative studies exploring these culturally situated arguments about awareness and preparation merit the attention of researchers framing quantitative studies of student preparation and enrollment behavior.

Next, Penny A. Pasque's "Seeing More of the Educational Inequalities Around Us: Visions Toward Strengthening Relationships Between Higher Education and Society" (Chapter 2), contributes a substantive literature review, focusing on the ways the public good is framed in the literature on higher education. She examines how the literature views social, economic, and academic aspects of both public and private good. In addition to observing the well-documented shift to arguments about private benefits of higher education, she notes the relative silence about financial inequality within this discourse. She notes how arguments for public funding of higher education usually do not include arguments for equal financial access for low-income students as an integral part of the funding rationales that are put forward.

In Chapter 3, "Students' Voices and Graduate School Choices: The Role of Finances in the Lives of Low-Income, High-Achieving Students of Color," I examine focus group interviews of student receiving Gates Millennium Scholarships (GMS) to build an understanding of the ways financial aid enables students to expand their thoughts about graduate education opportunities. With the heavy emphasis placed on academic preparation for college, it is important to also consider the ways that adequate financial aid creates and expands educational opportunity. Easing the financial burden of paying for college by work and borrowing enables high-achieving, low-income students to dream beyond current expectations, as was evident from interviews with students who received generous scholarships after they enrolled in colleges. This study develops a refined set of hypotheses about the role of financial aid.

In combination these chapters provide a basis for thinking critically about the discourse of inequality in higher education. Tierney and Venegas speculate about how we might bring the voices of low-income students into the discourse on access, while Pasque ponders why these voices are so frequently left out of policy advocacy for higher education, and I explore how students' voices help us to retheorize the role of finances in creating and expanding educational opportunity. These chapters also illustrate the role of theorizing in the process of building understanding of methods for confronting inequality in educational opportunity.

Building Understanding

While the authors did not necessarily start out with this intent, the chapters in Part II help build an understanding of how policies evolve that undermine equal opportunity in education. The four chapters examine different aspects of the problem of inequality.

In "Improving Educational Opportunities for College Students Who Work," Chapter 4, Laura W. Perna, Michelle Cooper, and Chunyan Li provide a comprehensive examination of college students who work using the National Postsecondary Student Aid Survey of 2004 and other information sources. With the decline in the purchasing power of Pell grants in recent decades (Advisory Committee on Student Financial Assistance, 2002), many low- and lower-middle income students work long hours to pay for college. They examine the consequences of working long hours for college life and consider how colleges can reduce barriers for working students. Perna, Cooper, and Li build a student profile that can inform efforts to improve educational opportunities in colleges that serve large numbers of working students, as well as raise issues for consideration by policy makers.

Chapter 5, "Seeking Equal Educational Opportunity: Desegregation of Higher Education and the TOPS Scholarship Program in Louisiana" by Masamichi Inoue and Terry G. Geske, examines the simultaneous implementation of two policies affecting college opportunity. They focus on the contradictory effects of a merit scholarship program and desegregation plans for public higher education in Louisiana. They uncover the ways that the merit aid actually undermined the court ordered plan to desegregate public higher education in the state. Their analysis offers an alternative explanation for the rise of merit grant programs in the southern U.S. (Heller & Marin, 2002), one that is certainly less compelling than the economic arguments that are so frequently made (Dynarski, 2004).

In Chapter 6, "State Valuation of Higher Education: An Examination of Possible Explanations for Privatization," Amy S. Fisher examines possible explanations for the declining percentage of educational costs subsidized by state funding, returning to the topic of the public good. She develops a measure of state support that is the weighted average public tuition charge by colleges in states, divided by the sum of a weighted average public tuition charge in states plus the weighted average state appropriations for student. This represents a relatively accurate measure of the percentage of costs covered by tuition, controlling for the distribution of students within state systems of higher education. One surprise is that, using this outcome measure, the overall student share of educational costs did not rise as fast as we would expect from other studies that have not weighted these measures per student in public systems. She presents two forms of regression analyses—ordinary least squares and fixed effects methods—using multiple years of data on states to examine how demography, political ideologies, taxation, and other actors influence the share costs paid by students. She finds that per capita tax rates provide the best explanation for declining public support of higher education.

Finally, in "There's an Alarm at the Gate: The Role of High School Tracking in Determining Success for African American Students in a Georgia High School" (Chapter 7), Ontario S. Wooden takes a fresh look at the role of tracking in undermining the cultural tradition of uplift among African American students. For a century before school desegregation, the deep belief in cross generation uplift enabled African Americans to persevere in the face of discrimination. In depth interviews with high school students and administrators in a southern urban high school reveal how the sorting mechanisms within high schools undermine opportunity and deny opportunity to students who have discarded the college dream.

Making Change

Taking action to reduce educational inequalities may involve departing from traditional conceptions of teaching, research, and service. The three chapters in Part III focus on using research as an integral part of action.

In Chapter 8, "Activist Research, Post-Katrina: One Tool for Renewal," Luis Mirón examines the lessons learned as an activist researcher who was engaged in planning for the redesigning of schools in New Orleans after Hurricane Katrina. Some argued that the near demolition of a great American city created a new type of school system, one that valued market forces over traditional methods of organizing education. Yet some educators and researchers were confronted by basic challenges to their values as they collaborated with public officials who were committed to this new vision of schools. Mirón reflects on how researchers can engage in discourse in support of general public good even when they have discontent for the direction of public policy.

Chapter 9, "Professional Development in Student Affairs: From Learning about Diversity to Building Just Communities," Kimberly Kline presents an action research study of a student affairs class on professional development. She examines how a pedagogy focusing on reflective practice can enable students to overcome prejudices about diversity, formed from prior schooling and professional experience. Her study focuses on core issues related to building just learning communities in higher education.

In "School Reform, Scholarship Guarantees, and College Enrollment: A Study of the Washington State Achievers Program" (Chapter 10), with Shouping Hu, I examine how the association between the major program features of Washington State Achievers (WSA) program— aid guarantees and school reform—relate to changes in college enrollment. While the earlier paper (St. John & Hu, 2006) found that the initial year of awards improved the odds of college enrollment by participants, this study also reveals that school reform—including the creation of small schools within large high schools—was associated with preparation and enrollment.

Confronting Educational Inequality

While these chapters address a wide range of topics in educational policy and practice, they deal with a common underlying question: how can practitioners and researchers contend with inequalities in educational opportunity, given the devaluation of this goal within most discourses on education? The conclusion builds on understandings researched from these chapters, recent volumes of *Readings on Equal Education*, and other recent research, to focus on this critical question.

References

Advisory Committee on Student Financial Assistance (2002). *Empty promises: The myth of college access in America.* Washington, DC: authors.

Dynarsi, S. (2004). The new merit aid. In C. Hoxby (Eds), *College choices: The economics of where to go, when to go and how to pay for it* (pp. 63-100). Chicago: University of Chicago Press.

Heller, D. & Marin, P. (Eds). (2002). *Who should we help? The negative social consequences of merit scholarships.* Cambridge, MA: The Civil Rights Project, Harvard University.

No Child Left Behind Act of 2001, Pub. L. No. 107-110, 115 Stat. 1425 (2002).

St. John, E.P., & Hu, S. (2006). The impact of guarantees of financial aid on college enrollment: An evaluation of the Washington State Achievers Program. In E.P. St. John (Ed.), *Readings on equal education: Vol. 21. Public policy and equal educational opportunity: School reforms, postsecondary encouragement, and state policies on postsecondary education* (pp. 211-256). New York: AMS Press, Inc.

Venegas, K. (2006). Internet inequalities: Financial aid, the internet, and low-income students. *American Behavioral Scientist.* Tierney, W.G., Venegas, K., De La Roda, M.L., Issue Editors, Financial aid and access to college: The public policy challenges. 49(12): 1652-1669. Thousand Oaks, CA: Sage Publications.

Part I

Reframing

CHAPTER 1

THE CULTURAL ECOLOGY OF FINANCIAL AID DECISION MAKING

William G. Tierney and Kristan Venegas

Relatively little attention has been paid to the kinds of fiscal information that students and parents receive before, during, and after the financial aid application process. Despite the growing literature on financial aid and college access, there is still much that remains unknown about the financial aid decision making process from the perspective of students and their families. Past research on financial aid has been able to shed light on the outcomes of student decision making, but rarely does the research present a clear picture of the processes of those decisions. In large part, researchers have yet to understand how students and their families figure out how to navigate various financial aid options. There is also a lack of modeling attempts to explain, rather than simply describe, the financial aid process as it is experienced by students and their families. As we elaborate below, the constructs and models that exist usefully explain the decision making process from a theoretical perspective, but the frameworks are less well equipped to identify the ways in which the financial aid process "works" for those who experience it.

1

Copyright ©2007 AMS Press, Inc. All rights reserved.

Typically, the financial aid application process has been folded into a discussion of college admission, enrollment patterns, and, in some cases, persistence. This practice has resulted in a body of work that does not fully explore the effects of the financial aid process as a separate and meaningful part of decision making about college attendance. Our suggestion here is that a clearer understanding of how financial aid is interpreted by those who use it has the potential of improving services to those most in need of financial support. Simply stated, better knowledge of the ways that students and parents find out about, apply for, and accept financial aid packages is one way to bolster that understanding.

When parents are considering whether to take out a loan for their student's education, does it make a difference in the decision if they have not taken out loans in the past? How does the accuracy of perceptions of cost and repayment influence the decision making process? The answers to such questions are frequently based more on cultural constructs of cognitive processes than on rational decisions and information or lockstep stage-dictated events and experiences. Yet within the existing research on financial aid, college consumers are assumed to behave along similar lines regardless of who they are. The evolving actions and perceptions of key stakeholders cannot be fully accounted for if contextual situations are overlooked.

For example, a preponderance of research has examined populations who attend elite institutions and large state systems. What is missing from this research is a detailed evaluation of how admission processes and financial aid assistance mechanisms enable or discourage students to attend particular institutions. It is possible, in this case, that like the "cooling out" function of community colleges (Clark, 1960), there too is a "cooling out" function based on access to financial aid. From the perspective of the federal and state governments, the contradictory acts of stating that a college education is important and cutting funding for college attendance and raising tuition send mixed messages to potential applicants that have not been fully explored. Finally, from the perspective of pre-college practitioners, that is, the high schools and early intervention programs that prepare students for college-going and the organizations that support college-going, there is a dearth of information that focuses on the ways in which the financial aid process is communicated and supported within these environments. How do these messages impact students' and parents' sense of opportunity, and how do they manifest themselves in the college choice process?

The paper has two parts. First, models that have guided previous research in the area of college choice and financial aid, particularly those works that emphasize the process between the individual and his or her decision making processes, are reviewed. Studies that have examined relationships between college-going and financial aid, as well as studies that have attempted to make predictions and analyze those predictions about the relationships between financial aid and college are considered. We then discuss areas that require further attention and posit a new approach, what we call the "cultural ecology" of financial aid decision making. Our assumptions in this paper are that financial aid for college is positive and accurate information about college is positive. Financial aid for college is helpful to the students who use it, and to society, which benefits from those who have a college degree. We also assume that the student is the primary college decision maker, supported by parents, peers, and others.

Financial Aid Research in Theory and Practice

A recent paper on the problems of theory in qualitative work on college access outlines five theoretical approaches (St. John, 2006). The author positions these theoretical approaches as derived from economic theory, social attainment theory, theories of social and cultural capital, and theories related to educational preparation. These perspectives deserve further attention in future research, but to analyze all of them sufficiently is beyond the scope of this text. What we focus on here are two theoretical approaches: rational choice (economically derived) and college choice (based in social and cultural capital approaches) that have garnered a great deal of attention; we leave for future analysis studies pertaining to attainment research and the like.

The use of rational choice and college choice theories in the study of financial aid has been helpful in shedding light on a student's understanding of financial aid as an important part of the college-going process. However, these constructs have been limited in their descriptions of the processes of financial aid acquisition. Just as little attention has been given to students' and parents' knowledge of the financial aid process, even less attention has been paid to high schools, college preparation programs, and institutional agents of these processes. In the following chapter we first define rational choice theory and college choice theory, and then turn to a discussion of the theories in relation to financial aid.

Defining Rational Choice

Rational choice theories are built on the notion that when given adequate and accurate information on a particular topic, decision makers will reach similar decisions, based on similar evidence with the expectation of similar outcomes. This idea is part of a theory of human capital investment in which individuals make decisions about their lives to increase their capabilities in the work force based on the interrelationships of income, educational attainment, consumption, and returns on investment (Becker, 1964; Schulz, 1961). The assumption at work is that there is value to the individual and the economy during and after college. Even while in college, an individual begins to contribute to economic consumption in new and increased ways. Individuals have increased access to additional resources and utilize these resources throughout college and after graduation.

In the case of financial aid, students and their families would review their family finances, think about the costs and benefits of college attendance, find out what kind of financing is available for college, and then make a decision about where, when, and how to attend college. They would also begin the planning process early in the student's educational career while continuing to follow market trends in higher education and to adjust their preparation accordingly. Economists have posited equations based on rational choice to frame investigations of the role of student aid packages in college choice (Avery & Hoxby, 2003; Long, 2003). Considering these equations is a useful way to understand how rational choice functions. Basic assumptions about what it means to choose a college and use financial aid are also highlighted.

Assume that Manuel is academically prepared to attend a four-year college, that he has taken numerous advanced placement classes, and that his SAT scores are 1400. He also comes from a low-income family. One assumption of rational choice theorists in relation to Manuel's scenario is that because he has a very high college aptitude he will attend a four-year college; his choice is not whether to attend college but where to attend. A second assumption is that Manuel will make a choice as a "rational" chooser, irrespective of his financial situation; he will choose his most desired institution regardless of any constraints. A third assumption is that he will then select his optimal choice and only then begin to make arrangements to seek the most affordable means of paying tuition.

However, the fact that Manuel is a low-income student suggests that he may have limited resources to pay for college. His parents may not have gone to college, they may not have a bank account, and they may not like the idea of Manuel living away from home. Manuel also lives in a low-income neighborhood and attends a high school with few college preparatory resources. His friends are likely either to go to the local community college or to get a job. Manuel is limited in his abilities to make the same kinds of decisions compared to a student who is not low-income and/or whose parents have different assumptions regarding education and have different educational backgrounds. Manuel may be able to select a college that makes the most sense for him based on his academic preparation and aspirations, but there is no clear accounting for how he will be able to pay for the costs of college attendance.

Rational Choice and Research on College-Going and Financial Aid

Rational choice models have been implemented in studies of college-going from at least three different perspectives: student demand, persistence and enrollment, and student aspiration. A number of studies have implemented a rational choice model based on the notion of "student demand" for higher education, positioning decisions about college financing as an integral element of the college-going decision (Heller, 1999; Kane, 1995; McPherson & Schapiro, 1991; St. John, 1994; St. John & Noell, 1989). This concept derives from demand theory which asserts that the desired quantity of a product, good, or service is balanced by the income of the buyer, the costs of other desired and needed items, and the actual price of the product, service, or good (Leslie & Brinkman, 1987). These studies emphasize the relative effect of tuition pricing and financial aid awards as they relate to enrollment.

Rational choice theory has also framed studies of college persistence by asserting that the amount of financial aid received by pre-college students affects decisions about enrollment and persistence (McPherson, Schapiro, & Winston, 1993; Massy, 1996; McPherson & Schapiro, 1998).

Models that consider students' enrollment and persistence patterns acknowledge that college and financial aid decisions are based on tangible and intangible factors that extend beyond academic concerns. For example, the use of the nexus model, which emphasizes a student-institution-fit perspective with an economic viewpoint, broadens an understanding of the relationship between a student and his or her institutional choices (Paulsen & St. John, 2002). This theory was devised as a "means of looking across the sequence of student choices, focusing on how factors that affect earlier choices could also influence subsequent choices" (p. 191). The financial nexus theory focuses on students who perceive low tuition and costs of living as an important part of their college decisions; they carry these attitudes throughout their college careers and, perhaps, beyond. Theorists suggest that this model can be used to understand how students make choices, to provide a framework to make cross-group comparisons, and to identify situated contexts that affect the nature of college choice. Through the process of designing this theoretical model, persistence decisions among varying student populations were conducted and found to support the notion that indeed, students' previous decisions about college guided their future choices (Paulsen & St. John, 1997; St. John, Paulsen, & Starkey, 1996).

Students' individual aspirations and perceptions have also been studied through a rational lens (King, A.F., 2001; King, J.E., 1999; Choy, 2001). J.E. King's study of financial aid and decision making found that students' decisions regarding college and financial aid are impacted by a number of different people. However, some of the influential decision makers are considered marginal consumers, alluding to the notion that although they give their opinions on a student's pathway to college, they most often are not equipped with the college or financial aid knowledge needed to make an informed decision. Although the argument is made that the most informed influencers should be school guidance counselors and college financial aid officers, the data do not share whether these practitioners are in fact "rationally informed" or whether they had as much influence on decision making as other "rationally uninformed" parents, friends, or mentors might have had.

Another meta-analysis of 22 studies on college choice suggests that there is a clear lack of assessment of the knowledge that students and their mentors possess, even though these individuals are consistently noted as the key players in the decision making game (Terenzini, Cabrera, & Bernal, 2001). As such, the theoretical model of rational choice, in which one individual can be a rational economic actor who makes decisions about financial aid and college-going based on informed and active evaluations of available options conflicts with less certain and more fluid possibilities that exist in the realm of financial aid decision making.

Methodological Approaches and Rational Choice Theory

Most of the studies that utilize rational choice theory have been quantitative and span the aforementioned areas of research—student demand, persistence and enrollment, and student aspirations or perceptions. Investigations of these concepts that use rational choice theory have considered the opinions or experiences of large groups of people and/or synthesize the results of a number of studies. Logistic regression models have been used to analyze national data sets. In the case of the various meta-analyses of financial aid studies, standardization has been a typical method of evaluation.

For example, Grodsky and Jones (2004) investigated students' and parents' knowledge of college costs using data from the 1999 National Household Education Survey. Using particular branches of the questionnaire, the researchers operationalized such concepts as race/ethnicity and social class as independent variables. The dependent variables included two models. The first set of models emphasized parents' abilities to provide an estimate of tuition. The second set of models evaluated the difference between the real costs of college and parents' estimates of college costs (without any financial aid taken into account). Through a process that included logistic regression, followed by an evaluation of OLS models and the equality of conditional variance, the researchers found a relationship between parents' understanding of tuition costs and social class.

Another methodological approach that was implemented in rational choice based studies is standardization. Standardization is a process of taking similar variables from studies that investigate the same problem and creating some baseline "meta-variables" that can be analyzed alongside one another to form overarching findings. Standardization efforts are an important part of the meta-analysis process because authors are better able to make the case for synthesized conclusions. Leslie and Brinkman's (1987) study, which included 25 empirical works on student demand, also were able to be standardized. In this case, Leslie and Brinkman attempted to standardize the conversion of changes in tuition, the changes in college costs over time and in relation to the consumer price index, and the enrollment changes in the traditionally aged college-going cohort. After aligning these variables, the authors were able to assert a negative relationship between the costs of college and enrollment indicating that students were less likely to enroll in college if they perceived college costs to be too high.

Critiquing Rational Choice

While studies have used versions of this theory to investigate issues related to college choice and financial aid, rationality in and of itself does not explain what it means to make choices about student aid, regardless of whether those choices are located at the level of the individual or through an evaluation of student enrollment behaviors (St. John & Elliot, 1994). When one views college and financial aid decision making as more of an economic choice, it can become less of a socially complex choice. Admittedly, a rational choice means more than the assumption that everyone would make the same "logical" decision based on the same set of inputs. What is not indicated in either equation, however, is a determination of the effort and risk of college, which though not monetary, also afford a great cost (Young & Reyes, 1987).

Further, Fitzgerald (2003) posits that a hidden curriculum of college and financial aid knowledge is necessary to choose the right college and to secure the right kind of aid package. He claims that this secret knowledge disables marginal consumers from making rational decisions. Others agree with this assertion, and state "the capability for rationality is limited due to the fact that a person cannot usually access and accurately process all of the information germane to a particular situation" (Rassmussen, 2003, p. 9). Even if information on financial aid were available to all students, it is not reasonable to assume that all students absorb or utilize information in the same complete way. Research on "average" versus "marginal" consumers of college show that even the "average" consumer has much less information on the real costs of college than we usually anticipate he or she does (McPherson & Schapiro, 1988; Morgan, 2002).

Defining College Choice

College choice is an overarching term that encompasses various theories that highlight the individual and group processes related to the decision to participate in higher education. College choice research primarily emerged from sociological and economic disciplines. Blau and Duncan (1967) were among the first to propose a college choice process that considered the effects of student academic ability, socioeconomic status, and occupational aspirations. Later modifications and additions to the model included the impact of peers, school personnel and environment, and mentors (Sewell & Armer, 1966; Sewell, Haller, & Portes, 1969; Sewell & Hauser, 1975; 1980). Although researchers continue to utilize the experiences of individual students and their families as a main focus of their work, they have painted the role of school context and other sociocultural effects with broad brushstrokes (Farkas, 1996).

College choice theories also have emerged from student development theory, which relies on two main tenets: (1) individuals make decisions as part of an individual developmental process, and (2) individuals are empowered to make these decisions while weighing a variety of different influences. Erikson (1968), for example, provides five stages of development to outline the process that individuals traverse throughout their lifetimes. College choice theories use a similar "building block" schema. Perhaps the most popular of the college choice models used in the study of financial aid is that of Hossler, Braxton, and Coopersmith (1989). They created the model in an effort to create a college choice theory that:

> can enhance the accumulated knowledge on student college choice...lead to more effective policy decisions...allows students to benefit from an improved understanding college choice... (to) make college more accessible to students... (p. 283).

College choice models, like the one posited by Hossler, Braxton, and Coopersmith, emphasize the information-processing and decision making stages prior to college-going. The authors suggest that a pre-college student moves through five stages during the college choice process:

1. Deciding to pursue postsecondary education;
2. Selecting and engaging in appropriate academic preparation;

3. Preparing for and taking college entrance examinations, such as the SAT or the ACT;
4. Choosing and applying to particular colleges or universities; and,
5. Gaining acceptance, making financial aid and other enrollment arrangements.

The college choice model identifies and separates the different stages of the college selection experience. The identification of five separate points of decision making is located during the "pre-college phase" concluding with the final college selection. The experiences that occur during each phase result in a final college-going decision.

College Choice and Research on College-Going and Financial Aid

Like the college choice model, the rational choice model also relies on the perceptions and experiences of the individual but hypothesizes that the series of decisions that students and their families make about college are based on a specific and reasonable set of pre-existing individual factors. In the college choice model, a framework for understanding the selection process is outlined without regard to the particular "pre-existing conditions" that might be present for students. Recent versions of the college choice model have begun to identify non-academic inputs as part of the college selection process (MacGowan, 2002), though for the most part, these frameworks emphasize an intent to pursue postsecondary education and the academic preparation necessary to achieve that goal. The next section of this paper discusses the ways in which college choice theory has been used to study financial aid.

For example, during the awareness stage, individuals begin to develop an opinion about college-going. How this awareness blooms is not certain, although some research suggests that the decision to attend college begins by the ninth grade (Bonous-Hammouth & Allen, 2005). How these decisions come about and what combination of influences impact the college dream remains unclear (Alexander & Cook, 1979; Kao & Tienda, 1998). Parents, school counselors, mentors, and the media can be instrumental (Millett & MacKenzie, 1996; Levine & Nidiffer, 1996). Embedded within these decisions, of course, is the dilemma of how to pay for college. Little research exists that delineates the priority that paying for college is given in deciding whether to go to college. While some studies have considered the ability to pay from a financial perspective (St. John, 2001; Cabrera, Castaneda, Nora, & Hengstler, 1992), few have provided a detailed account of how students' perceived ability to pay for college impacts the end decision to attend (Levine & Nidiffer, 1996; Macy, 2000). We also do not have an accurate understanding of those students who decide against attending college due to financial reasons (Orfield, 1992; McDonough, 1997). Hybrid models of the college choice theory that have been used to consider financial aid have also termed this part of the college-going and financial aid process as the "awareness" stage (MacGowan, 2002).

Research on the ways in which students select college suggests that these decisions are mediated by students' immediate environments, including their participation in extracurricular activities, such as college preparation programs (Stanton-Salazar, 2002; Bonous-Hammouth & Allen, 2005; Macy, 2000). Again there are a number of external influences that play into this stage and determine student opportunities to obtain proper preparation, including the availability of college guidance and advanced placement level courses (McDonough, 1997; Corwin, Venegas, Oliverez, & Colyar, 2004). Few studies of financial aid have actually grappled with this stage of the college-going process. In most of these studies, the sample population includes students who are matriculating or have recently completed college. As such, the data that are reported may be missing key parts of the academic preparation or financial aid process insofar as participants may not be able to recollect every detail or experience as it happened (MacGowan, 2002; Haro, Rodriguez, & Gonzalez, 1994; Macy, 2000).

For students who will rely on financial aid for college, the interaction and preparation stage may be one of the first instances in which they realize financial support will be necessary, and one of the first instances in which they actively seek funding in the form of applying for standardized testing fee waivers (King, 1999). Testing is an area that deserves additional attention, especially in light of the fact that many states are beginning to track students into special programs that guarantee financial aid, based on their performance in grades and state-level testing (St. John, Musoba, Simmon, Chung, Schmidt, & Peng, 2002), or give free aid in the form of a scholarship for students with particularly high scores (Venegas, 2005).

Some models of college choice consider college selection to be a "sub-process" stage in which three key events must take place (MacGowan, 2002). The first event is the development of a final group of colleges to which the student will apply for admission. The second event is the act of applying to colleges, which includes the actual completion and submission of the applications. The third stage of this subprocess stage is deciding. There is a great deal of waiting in this stage; the student has applied for admission and waits to see what colleges will offer acceptance. After hearing from the colleges, the student must decide which college to attend, or whether he or she even will attend college. Although financial aid is not mentioned here, our own research has shown that concerns about financial aid usually reach a point of action during this stage of the college-planning process. Technically speaking, this is the time period during which students begin to apply for financial aid. Failure to apply for financial aid during these months of waiting to hear back from colleges can result in no aid offer from the state and/or federal government (Tierney, Corwin, & Colyar, 2005).

The final stages of college choice models are the first moments when financial aid is explicitly mentioned (Hossler, Schmidt, & Vesper, 1999; MacGowan, 2002; Hossler, Braxton & Coopersmith, 1989). Financial aid decision making, as it relates to college-going, appears to be placed so late in the college choice stage because theorists have traditionally linked the financial aid choice to institutional choice (McPherson, Schapiro, & Winston, 1993; Massy, 1996; Kahlenberg, 2004). The arguments made at this stage however, are quite similar to the ones made within rational choice theory. Aid decisions are based on tangible and intangible factors, including student-fit with an institution (St. John & Starkey, 1995, St. John et. al, 1996; Cabrera, Nora, & Casteneda, 1993).

Methodological Approaches and College Choice Theory

Studies using college choice theory as a theoretical underpinning have called on quantitative and qualitative research methods. Since college choice theory can be conceptualized as a total process or as individual steps, researchers who work from this perspective have studied the college-going process in a number of ways. Flint's (1992) study of early awareness of college financial aid used causal modeling techniques to estimate various influences on the college choice process. His model drew on Hossler, Braxton, and Coopersmith's (1989) work, as well as others, and used three types of variables. The first type included background variables, such as family background, gender, race and ethnicity, family income, and parental educational levels. College savings and financial aid awareness variables included the kinds and number of savings plans that students and parents had and the potential number of siblings who might also attend or currently attended college. The third set of variables comprised college search variables such as the degree of knowledge about specific college admission requirements, income differences between families and degree aspirations. The mediating variables of financial aid awareness might be best placed within this block of variables. Analysis of these variables revealed that awareness does appear to influence choice, and that not all types of financial aid are equal in affecting choice. The study concludes with a suggestion that a deeper consideration of the role of awareness and prevention of myths about financial aid are crucial.

Paulsen and St. John's (2002) study of the nexus between college choice and persistence also begins with college choice theory. Although the authors lean towards a "financial nexus" approach, the model still highlights the importance of the sequence of student choices in relation to financial aid. Using this model to explore persistence across four income groups of students, the researchers create five types of variables. A first set of variables relate to student background. A second set of dichotomous variables measure perceptions and expectations. The third set of variables relates to college experiences. The fourth set involves student aspirations. The fifth and final set of variables includes grants, loans, and work-study in their actual amounts. Drawing data from the 1987 National Postsecondary Student Aid Survey (NSAS 87), the researchers perform a series of logistic regression analyses. Their findings show that there are differences among social classes in choice, knowledge, and persistence with a negative relationship between this construct and low-income status.

Beth Macy (2000) has worked with what she termed "the poor" and financial aid, and has built upon the research of Levine and Nidiffer (1996), another well-known qualitative study of financial aid recipients. Macy's work is driven by two complimentary streams of influence: her own personal experience as a federal Pell grant recipient, and the support of the College Board, which seeks to document the power of student assistance (p. 1). Macy has interviewed 20 college graduates who had benefited from the use of the federal Pell grant program. She then identifies six factors that influenced the success of her study participants:

(1) an early awareness of higher education and financial aid;
(2) the ability to break from family patterns;
(3) the importance of peers;
(4) the critical role of mentors and college outreach;
(5) the desire for personal growth and enhanced self-esteem; and,
(6) the importance of early college success and goal setting (p. 6).

Although Macy's work, like Levine and Nidiffer's, illuminates the general findings regarding low-income students' financial aid pathways, a broader view that includes a wider range of Pell grant recipients or considers effects over time might create a stronger picture of the process of acquiring aid.

Critiquing College Choice
Like rational choice theory, college choice models have worked when studying college-going because they attempt to consider the importance of weighing the costs and benefits of attending college. For financial aid researchers to build upon this approach, more emphasis on the financial aid related triggering events is important. Since these events begin at any stage of the model, so should consideration of the role of financial aid decision making on college-going. Until now, what these models have not been able to do is to elucidate how these decisions are made, and what specific individual factors affect the financial aid decision making process. Instead, we are left with a series of predictions and implications for better aid practice and policy.

Using an analysis of equity and college attendance, Gladieux's (2004) study has found that a rich low-achieving student is more likely than a poor high-achieving student to attend a four-year college or university. Haro et al. (1994) have found that students' misperceptions about the actual costs of college resulted in the need for low-income students to take on part-time jobs to supplement their financial aid and in some cases extended their time to degree completion, both prior to and after enrolling in college courses. The studies that have been framed using the theoretical approaches discussed here have been effective in portraying a picture of the financial aid decision making landscape, but have been unable to clearly illuminate or interpret what those pictures mean. What is missing is a closer understanding of the financial aid decision making process in and of itself, separate from the college admission process. The instrumental knowledge that is needed to navigate the college acceptance process is different than the content knowledge that is needed to complete the financial aid process.

The Cultural Ecology of Financial Aid Decision Making

Financing college is a process that begins prior to the start of high school, and it continues to be affected by contexts that reside beyond the schoolhouse doors (Villalpando & Solorzano, 2005). By acknowledging that financial aid acquisition is its own meaningful and complicated process and is part and parcel of the college admission experience, researchers have begun to identify ways in which students and their families perceive financial aid (Tomás Rivera Policy Institute, 2004; Perna, 2004; Flint, 1992). Some information exists about the post-financial aid application and packaging stages; however, a gap still exists in the research in regard to how students and their families construct their ideas and actions about the financial aid and application process. A rational theorist might consider consumer processes as inputs of financial aid decisions, and a college choice proponent might locate these perceptions as decisions that lead to actions in stages four and five. Most research on the stages before the financial aid packages pertains to statistical gatherings of attitudes, and emphasizes the behaviors and beliefs of parents rather than of the students themselves (Flint, 1992; Choy, 2001). Accordingly, we offer here a model that emphasizes a cultural approach to understanding the financial aid process and financial aid decision making. Our intent is to suggest the scaffolding of a framework that will enable researchers to understand how people interpret and make decisions about financial aid.

Defining Cultural Choice

Although the use of culture is a relatively new approach for the study of how people make decisions about financial aid, culture has been employed as a framework for studying various facets of college life. Jun (2002) and Colyar (2002), for example, worked from a cultural framework when they investigated college-going decisions of low-income urban youth. Moffatt (1989) conducted an ethnography of under-graduates, Rhoads (1994) studied gay college students, and Holland and Eisenhart (1990) looked at women in college. All of these authors utilize the concept of culture in their analyses. Clark (1972) has utilized a cultural framework in the study of a college "saga"; Becher and Trowler have employed a similar perspective in the study of academic life (2001). Tierney (1988b) also has worked from a cultural perspective when he looked at leadership and faculty life. Thus, a cultural framework has been of use in multiple projects and has proven to be helpful in understanding how individuals and groups perceive and construct their environments.

We define culture as an interpretative approach to understanding the environments in which people live and work. To be sure, we accept the social world as a given, but, following Geertz (1973; 1983) and others (Tierney, 1988a; 1989; Giroux, 1987; Giroux & McLaren, 1986), the focus turns to how individuals interpret that social world and give meaning to their lives and decisions. Even though a social world exists "out there" and is not simply a mental construct of an individual, the possibility also exists that people's perceptions will influence the social world. Thus, the language, symbols, and perceptions of individuals are of particular importance when one wishes to understand how people make sense of and interpret a particular topic such as financial aid.

We have employed the phrase "cultural ecology" to denote that the focus is less on internal mechanisms within an organization and more on the broader environment. That is, a study of the faculty role in governance may well work from a cultural framework and much of the study will emphasize internal processes of communication. Financial aid decision making, however, crosses multiple contextual boundaries. Students and families not only work within a school or college, but also have to come to terms with loan agencies, banks, and state and federal governments, to name but a few such external agents. Thus, a cultural focus on this particular topic is more ecological than a topic such as faculty governance insofar as the environment plays a critical role.

The reviews of rational choice and college choice theory in this paper suggest that while each approach has merit, neither approach explores the processes of financial aid decision making from the ground up. Rational choice theorists make assumptions about what rational consumers know about financial aid. College choice theorists treat financial aid decision making as part of the college-going process and overlook the potential impact of financial aid on college enrollment, especially for low-income students. And yet, the college-going and financial aid process involves the interactions of students, parents, high school guidance and college counselors, college-level financial aid counselors, mentors, and peers, among others (Tierney & Hagedorn, 2002). Hence, an exploration of the perceptions and behaviors of students is useful in order to come to terms with how students and their families make sense of financial aid.

A cultural approach operates from the assumption that student perceptions and behaviors of financial aid have four primary sites that demand investigation. First, perceptions get constructed at educational sites (Olson & Rosenfeld, 1984), where most information about college is supposedly communicated. We employ the term "educational environment" rather than "school environment" to under-score that postsecondary institutions also influence how students perceive financial aid. Second, families also are an important part of the college-going experience (Choy, 2001; Levine & Nidiffer, 1996). Peers, mentors, and out-of-class opportunities also play a role in how individuals construct their perceptions of financial aid. Finally, the social environment of the neighborhood and community also needs to be considered when constructing a framework for understanding how students think about financial aid.

Thus, studying financial aid decision making from a broad-based cultural approach allows for the inclusion of multiple forces that impact students simultaneously throughout the decision making process. These forces can be conceptualized as represented in Figure 2. Although these impacts are overlapping, it is clear that their effects deserve individual attention.

Figure 1: A Cultural Approach for the Study of Financial Aid Decision Making

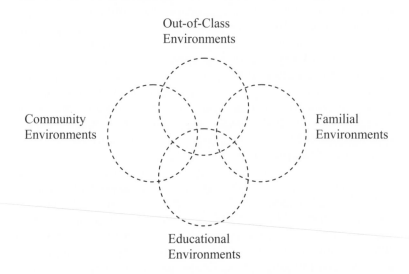

Out-of-Class
Environments

Community
Environments

Familial
Environments

Educational
Environments

Educational Environments.   Recent research on access to college information points towards the role of the education institution in college-going (MacGowan, 2002; Tornatzy, Cutler, & Lee, 2002; Valenzuela, 1999). When using a cultural model for trying to come to terms with how people make financial aid decisions, a basic unit of analysis in most cases is the school. The definition of high school employed here is an expanded one that includes student and teacher interaction, counselor and student communication, and the like. We are suggesting that research on financial aid decision making needs to consider the educational environments of students, and the ways in which information about financial aid is provided, received, and interpreted.

Even in the case of two students with the same income, a student who attends a high school or college with a rigorous campaign for aid awareness may well be at an advantage when compared to a student in an institution that does not. The first student has more chances to be informed about financial aid processes. What is unknown is how those messages are received and interpreted. Similarly, there are also variations by state that may affect financial aid awareness. Students in Indiana, for example, who participate in the 21st Century Scholars program (St. John et al., 2002), may be much better informed about state aid options than federal aid options. As a result, a student may be more likely to stay in state for college than to explore other options for college, or be less likely to apply for supplemental scholarships. Thus, the ecology of the educational environment comes into play as a crucial factor.

Out-of-Class Environments. Although a few qualitative studies have considered the role of these important "others" in the lives of students with regard to financial aid (Levine & Nidiffer, 1996; Macy, 2000), it is clear that peers and mentors have the potential to shape student access to financial aid from the data gathering stage through the decision making stage. Past theoretical constructs frequently have overlooked these actors in the process of financial aid decision making. The out-of-class setting includes extracurricular activities such as sports, college preparation programs, financial aid workshops, and other school site-based events. Externally funded outreach programs, which are supposed to be main bridges between high schools and colleges, will be of particular interest. Little is known about the information dissemination processes of financial aid in such programs, although many claim to provide financial aid service to their clients (Tierney & Venegas, 2004). In-school and out-of-school peers presumably have some kind of an impact on the financial aid decision making of their peers. From past findings on the role of peers in college-going, research has shown that peers play a significant role in preparing for the technical aspects of college-going (Gibson, Gándara, & Koyama, 2004).

Familial Environments. While family background is important, past conceptualizations of students and family need to be extended to include the active roles that they play in financial aid decision making. Understanding parental educational attainment is, of course, central to gauging a family's experience with college-going and financial aid. However, knowing that a parent has attended college is only one marker for predicting parents' "college knowledge," or increased involvement in their child's college-going. Some parents perceive a college education as essential for their child and others do not. Some think it is important for a son to attend college and not so important for a daughter.

As with all cultural investigations, the point is not to decide whether people's interpretations are "good" or "bad" but instead to be able to interpret them as they do. Once one understands how people make sense of their world the possibility exists to develop ways that will enable individuals to change it. As Bronfenbrenner (1979) delineates in his conceptualization of the individual within an ecological environment of influence, individuals (in this case, students and their families) can exert agency based on the following personal practices:

(1) inhibiting or inviting relationships with peers and others;
(2) reactions to and explorations of one's own social environments;
(3) how individuals engage and persist through increasingly complex activities; and
(4) how individuals view their agency in relation to their perceived environment.

A deeper investigation of student and parent agency and what it means in terms of financial aid acquisition can illuminate the issues that students and their families experience in direct and clear ways. Since the study of families and financial aid has been primarily from a perspective of tuition cost and benefit analysis (Grodsky & Jones, 2004), a closer understanding of the ways in which students and their families learn about financial aid and engage in financial aid activities is important. Other areas of student and family life that impact financial aid decision making, such as the existence of college savings plans and the use of banking institutions, also deserve attention.

Community Environments. People's views on college-going are also influenced by their perceptions of the multiple communities they inhabit. Even communities where a preponderance of individuals has not attended college will have differences in the manner in which they construct their ideas about the importance of college. Race, ethnicity, religion, and bonds of kinship all impact differentially on a child's perception of college. Our point here is not that any category is simplistically determinative — Jews value education more than Protestants, for example — but that economic class is also not determinative. Or rather, the community in which one lives helps frame how individuals interpret financial aid. Yet, simply because someone is poor does not mean that he or she will perceive financial aid in a similar manner to someone else who is poor. We need fine-grained analyses that provide local interpretations to overarching issues such as financial aid.

Using the Cultural Choice Model

When one employs the framework suggested here and calls upon an ethnographic approach to gather data, it is possible to compare the ways in which financial aid information is distributed at one institution versus another in a localized manner that is generally not possible through surveys. There are two benefits to such an approach. First, fine-grained analyses enable researchers to gain a sense of how individuals construct their ideas about how to pay for college in ways that are not likely to be captured through other methodologies. Second, such data can play a role in verifying, confirming, or refuting large-scale studies and point out new areas for investigation and analysis. This schema enables researchers to begin to connect the dots on the "who," "what," "why," and "how" of the financial aid process for a student population as they exist in a particular schooling environment. Through the use of these methods, the ability to shed light on questions such as the following become possible:

1. What are the problems that (a) secondary schools, (b) students and families, and (c) postsecondary institutions encounter that hinder financial aid acquisition?
2. What are the kinds of information, communication, and activities that need to take place between schools and postsecondary organizations and/or local agencies?
3. What kinds of discussions need to occur with students and their parents about financial aid?
4. What is the most effective environment for discussions about financial aid?
5. What needs to change within the school so that discussions about access to financial aid are clear, systematic, and thorough?

Past studies of financial aid have considered the problem of aid from a variety of perspectives, but have generally not been able to come to terms with answering these kinds of questions.

Perhaps the greatest import of a cultural approach is the creation of a lens to view the problems and opportunities that arise during the year-to-year and day-to-day process of financial aid acquisition for pre-college students. Why do some students persist through the financial aid process, while others opt out? There is a need to know how and why students and their families make the decisions that they make with regard to financial aid and college-going, particularly in the case of low-income students and students of color who are the fastest growing populations of college-age students, and yet the least likely to attend college.

References

Alexander, K.L., & Cook, M.A. (1979). The motivational relevance of education outcomes are uncertain. *Journal of Labor Economics, 11*(1), 48-83.

Avery, C., & Hoxby, C.M. (2003). *Do and should financial aid packages affect students' college choices?* NBER Working Paper #9482. National Bureau of Economic Research. Cambridge, MA.

Becher, T. & Trowler, P. (2001). *Academic tribes and territories: Intellectual enquiry and the cultures of discipline.* Berkshire, United Kingdom: Open University Press.

Becker, G. (1964). *Human capital: A theoretical and empirical analysis with special reference to education.* New York: National Bureau of Economic Research.

Blau, P.M., & Duncan, O.D. (1967). *The American occupational structure.* New York: Wiley.

Bonous-Hammouth, M., & Allen, W. (2005). A dream deferred: The critical factor of timing in college preparation and outreach. In W.G. Tierney, J.A. Colyar, and Z.B. Corwin (Eds.) *Preparing for college: Nine elements of effective outreach.* Albany, NY: State University of New York Press.

Bronfenbrenner, U. (1979). *The ecology of human development: Experiments by nature and design.* Cambridge, MA: Harvard University Press.

Cabrera, A.F., Castaneda, A., Nora, A., & Hengstler, D. (1992). The convergence between two theories of college persistence. *Review of Higher Education 13*(3): 303-336.

Cabrera, A.F., Nora, A., & Castaneda, M.B. (1993). College persistence: Structural equations modeling test of an integrated model of student retention. *Journal of Higher Education 64* (2): 123-139.

Choy, S.P. (2001). Students whose parents did not go to college. Findings from *The Condition of Education 2001. National Center for Education Statistics.* U.S. Department of Education: Office of Educational Research and Improvement, Washington, DC. NCES 2001-126.

Clark, B. (1972). The organizational saga in higher education. *Administrative Science Quarterly, 17*(2), 178-184.

Clark, B. (1960). The cooling out function in higher education. *American Journal of Sociology, 65,* 569-576.

Colyar, J. (2002). *Understanding student stories: A narrative ethnography of minority student experiences in the first year of college.* Los Angeles, CA: University of Southern California.

Corwin, Z.B., Venegas, K.M., Oliverez, P.M., & Colyar, J.E. (July 2004). School counsel: How appropriate guidance affects college going. *Urban Education 39(*4), 442- 457.

Erikson, E. (1968). *Identity, crisis and youth.* New York: Norton.

Farkas, G. (1996). Human capital or cultural capital? Ethnicity and poverty groups in an urban school district. New York, NY: Aldine de Gruyter.

Fitzgerald, B.K. (November/December 2003). The opportunity for a college education: Real promise or hollow rhetoric? *About Campus,* 3-10.

Flint, T. (1992). Early awareness of college financial aid: Does it expand choice? *Review of Higher Education, 16*(3), 309-327.

Geertz, C. (1973). *The interpretation of cultures.* New York: Basic Books.

Geertz, C. (1983). *Local knowledge.* New York: Basic Books.

Gibson, M., Gándara, P., & Koyama, J. (2004). *School connections: US Mexican youth, peers, and school achievement.* New York: Teachers College Press.

Giroux, H.A. (1987). Authority, intellectuals, and the politics of practical learning. *Teachers College Record, 88*(1), 22-40.

Giroux, H.A., & McLaren, P. (1986). Teacher education and the politics of engagement: The case for democratic schooling. *Harvard Educational Review, 56*(3), 213-238.

Gladieux, L.F. (2004). Low income student and the affordability of higher education. In R.D. Kahlenberg (Ed.). *America's untapped resource: Low income students in higher education.* New York: The Century Foundation Press.

Grodsky, E., & Jones, M. (2004). *Real and imagined barriers to college entry: Perceptions of cost.* Paper presented at the annual meeting for the American Sociological Association. San Francisco, CA.

Haro, R.P., Rodríguez, Jr., G., & González, Jr., J. (1994). *Latino persistence in higher education.* San Francisco: Latino Issues Forum.

Heller, D.E. (1999). The effects of tuition and state financial aid on public college enrollment. *Review of Higher Education, 23*(1): 65-89.

Holland, D., & Eisenhart, M.A. (1990). *Educated in romance: Women, achievement and college culture.* Chicago: University of Chicago Press.

Hossler, D., Braxton, J., & Coopersmith, G. (1989). Understanding the study of college choice. In J. Stuart (Ed.). *Higher education: Handbook of theory and research. Vol. V:* 231-288.

Hossler, D., Schmidt, N., & Vesper, N. (1999). *Going to college: How social, economic, and educational factors influence decisions students make.* Baltimore: Johns Hopkins University Press.

Jun, A. (2002). *From here to university: Access, mobility, and resilience among Latino youth.* New York: Routledge Press.

Kahlenberg, R.D. (Ed.) (2004). *America's untapped resource: Low income students in higher education.* New York: The Century Foundation Press.

Kane, T. (1995). *Rising public college tuition and college entry: How well do public subsidies promote access to college?* (NBER Working Paper Series No. 5164). Cambridge, MA: National Bureau of Economic Research.

Kao, G., & Tienda, M. (1998). Educational aspirations of minority youth. *American Journal of Education, (106),* 349-384.

King, A.F. (2001). Fiscal inequalities and direct student aid policies: The impact of institutional choice on lower income students. *Peabody Journal of Education, 76*(1), 136-49.

King, J.E. (1999). *Money matters: The impact of race/ethnicity and gender on how students pay for college.* Washington, DC: American Council on Education.

Leslie, L.L., & Brinkman, P.T. (1987). Student price response in higher education: The student demand studies. *The Journal of Higher Education, 58*(2), 181-204.

Levine, A., & Nidiffer, J. (1996). *Beating the odds: How the poor get to college.* San Francisco: Jossey-Bass.

Long, B.T. (2003). How have college decisions changed over time? An application of the conditional logistic choice model. *Journal of Econometrics (121)*1-2, 271-296.

MacGowan, B.R. (2002). *A student-centered model of college choice: Opportunity structures for college-bound Black students.* Alexandria, VA: Multicultural Institute for Advanced Thinking in Admission and Practice. Macy, B. (2000). *From rusty wire fences to wrought-iron gates: How the poor succeed in getting to—and through—college.* Washington, DC: The College Board.

Massy, W. (Ed.) (1996). *Resource allocation in higher education.* Ann Arbor, MI: University of Michigan Press.

McDonough, P.M. (1997). *Choosing colleges: How social class and schools structure opportunity.* Albany, NY: State University of New York.

McPherson, M.S., & Schapiro, M.O. (1998). *The student aid game: Meeting the need and rewarding talent in American higher education.* Princeton, NJ: Princeton University Press.

McPherson, M.S., & Schapiro, M.O. (1991). Does student aid effect college enrollment. New evidence on a persistent controversy. *American Economic Review, 81*(1): 309-318.

McPherson, M.S., Schapiro, M.O., & Winston, G.C. (1993). *Paying the piper: Productivity, incentives, and financing in U.S. higher education.* Ann Arbor, MI: University of Michigan Press.

Millett, C.M., & McKenzie, S. (November, 1996). *An exploratory student of college purchase options: How financial aid widens minorities' choices.* Paper presented at the Annual meeting of the Association for the Study of Higher Education.

Moffatt, M. (1989). *Coming of age in New Jersey: College and American culture.* New York, NY: Rutgers University Press.

Morgan, S.L. (2002). Modeling preparatory commitment and non-repeatable decisions: Information-processing, preference formation and educational attainment. *Rationality and Society 14*: 387-429.

Olson, L. and Rosenfeld, R.A. (1984). Parents and the process of gaining access to student financial aid. *Journal of Higher Education 55*(44): 455-480.

Orfield, G. (1992). Money, equity, and college access. *Harvard Educational Review, 62*(3), 337-372.

Paulsen, M.B., & St. John, E.P. (March/April 2002). Social class and college costs: Examining the financial nexus between college choice and persistence. *Journal of Higher Education, 73*(2), 189-236.

Paulsen, M.B., & St. John E.P. (1997). The financial nexus between college choice and persistence. In R. Voorhees. (Ed.) *Researching student financial aid: New Directions for Institutional Research 95.* San Francisco, CA: Jossey-Bass.

Perna, L.W. (2004). *Impact of student aid program design, operations, and marketing on the formation of family college-going plans and resulting college-going behaviors of potential students.* Boston, MA: The Education Resources Institute, Inc. (TERI).

Rassmussen, C.J. (2003). *"To go or not to go": How the perceived costs and benefits of higher education influence college decision making for low-income students.* Paper presented at the Annual Meeting of the Association for the Study of Higher Education. Portland, OR.

Rhoads, R. (1994). *Coming out in college: The struggle for queer identity.* Westport, CT: Greenwood Publishing Group.

Schulz, T.W. (1961). Investment in human capital. *American Economic Review, 51*(1), 1-17.

Sewell, W.H., & Armer, J.M. (1966). Neighborhood context and college plans. *American Sociological Review, 31*(2), 159-168.

Sewell, W.H, Haller, A.O. & Portes, A. (1969). The educational and early occupational attainment process. *American Sociological Review 34*(1), 82-92.

Sewell, W.H., & Hauser, R. (1980). The Wisconsin longitudinal study of social and psychological factors in aspirations and achievements. In A. Kerckhoff (Ed.) *Research in the sociology of education and socialization.* Greenwich, CT: JAI Press.

Sewell, W.H., & Hauser, R. (1975). *Education, occupation and earnings: Achievement in early career.* New York: Academic Press.

St. John, E.P. (2006). Contending with financial inequality: Rethinking the contributions of qualitative research to the policy discourse on college access. *American Behavioral Scientist, 49*(12), 1604-1619.

St. John, E.P. (2001). The impact of aid packages on educational choices: High tuition/high loan and educational opportunity. *Journal of Student Financial Aid, 31*(2), 35-54.

St. John, E.P. (1994). *Prices, productivity, and investment: Assessing financial strategies in higher education.* ASHE-ERIC Higher Education Report Number 3. Washington, DC: George Washington University.

St. John, E.P., & Elliot, R.J. (1994). Reframing policy research: A critical examination of research on federal student aid programs. In J.C. Smart (Ed.). *Higher education: Handbook of theory and research, Vol. X,* 126-180. New York: Agathon Press.

St. John, E.P., Musoba, G.D., Simmons, A., Chung, C.G., Schmit, J., & Peng, C.Y.P. (2002). *Meeting the access challenge: An examination of Indiana's Twenty-First Century Scholars Programs.* Paper presented at the Association for the Study of Higher Education Annual Meeting. Sacramento, CA.

St. John, E.P., & Noell, J. (1989). The effects of student financial aid on access to higher education: An analysis of progress with special consideration of minority enrollment. *Research in Higher Education, 30,* 563-582.

St. John, E.P., Paulsen, M.B., & Starkey, J.B. (1996). The nexus between college choice and persistence. *Research in Higher Education, 37,* 175-220.

St. John, E.P., & Starkey, J.B. (1995). An alternative to net price: Assessing the influence of prices and subsidies on within-year persistence. *Journal of Higher Education, 66*(2), 156-186.

Stanton-Salazar, R.D. (2002). *Manufacturing hope and despair: The school and kin support networks of U.S.-Mexican youth.* New York: Teachers College Press.

Terenzini, P.T., Cabrera, A.F., & Bernal, E.M. (2001). *Swimming against the tide: The poor in American higher education.* College Board Report No. 2001-1: New York, NY.

Tierney, W.G. (1989). Symbolism and presidential perceptions of leadership. *Review of Higher Education, 12*(2), 153-166.

Tierney, W.G. (1988a). Organizational culture in higher education: Defining the essentials. *Journal of Higher Education, 59*(1), 2-21.

Tierney, W.G. (1988b). *The web of leadership: The presidency in higher education.* Greenwich, CT: JAI Press.

Tierney, W.G., Corwin, Z.B, & Colyar, J.E. (Eds.). (2005). *Preparing for college: Nine elements of effective outreach.* Albany, NY: State University of New York Press.

Tierney, W.G. & Hagedorn, L.S. (Eds.) (2002). *Increasing access to college: Extending possibilities for all students.* Albany, NY: State University of New York Press.

Tierney, W.G., & Venegas, K.M. (2004). Addressing financial aid in college preparation programs. The Lumina Foundation for Education working paper series. Center for Higher Education Policy Analysis, Los Angeles, CA.

Tomás Rivera Policy Institute. (2004). *Caught in the financial aid information divide: A national survey of Latino perspectives on financial aid.* University of Southern California, Los Angeles, CA. Retrieved August 30, 2004 from www.trpi.org.

Tornatzy, L.G., Cutler, R., & Lee, J. (2002). *College knowledge—What Latino parents need to know and why they don't know it.* Tomás Rivera Policy Institute Policy Report. University of Southern California, Los Angeles, CA.

Valenzuela, A. (1999). *Subtractive schooling: U.S-Mexican youth and the politics of caring.* New York: State University of New York Press.

Venegas, K.M. (2005). *Aid and Admission: Narratives of pre-college, low-income urban Latina high school students.* Los Angeles, CA: University of Southern California.

Villalpando, O., & Solórzano, D.G. (2005). The role of culture in college preparation programs: A review of the literature. In W.G. Tierney, J.A. Colyar, and Z.B. Corwin (Eds.) *Preparing for college: Nine elements of effective outreach.* Albany: State University of New York Press.

Young, M.E., & Reyes, P. (1987). Conceptualizing enrollment behavior: The effect of student financial aid. *Journal of student financial aid, 17*(3), 41-49.

CHAPTER 2

SEEING MORE OF THE EDUCATIONAL INEQUITIES AROUND US: VISIONS TOWARD STRENGTHENING THE RELATIONSHIPS BETWEEN HIGHER EDUCATION AND SOCIETY

Penny A. Pasque

During our regular trips to the Cornell Ornithology lab, my friend said to me that knowing more about birds enables people to see more of what is around us every day. We operate from what we know — the red breasted robin flies north in the springtime — but often we fail to consider the numerous varieties of birds, migration patterns, and environmental support structures and barriers that are enacted every day. Education is also a pervasive entity that surrounds us, much like the familiar bird, and many people consider issues of educational equity and social justice from the point of reference that is known and familiar. We, higher education leaders and policy makers, need to know more about the intricacies of the multiple relationships between higher education and society and how the accompanying assumptions and implications of perspectives, policies, and procedures affect farther than any one person may see directly.

37

Copyright ©2007 AMS Press, Inc. All rights reserved.

The every day relationships between higher education and society are changing in the twenty-first century. Specifically, we see changes taking place in terms of who pays for college, who gains access to college, and the universities' role in the global marketplace. For example, there have been decreases in public support for higher education (KRC Consulting, 2002; Porter, 2002) and in state funding for public colleges and universities (Brandl & Holdsworth, 2003; Cage, 1991; Hansen, 2004), at a time when state and federal policies have linked higher education to the market in order to create jobs and increase economic viability (Jafee, 2000; Slaughter & Rhoades, 1996).

Lee and Clery (2004) point out that "recent state budget cutbacks, along with the declining *share* of state funding devoted to higher education, suggest that state colleges and universities have reason to be concerned about the reliability of government support" (p. 34). It has also been projected that higher education state budget allocations will continue to decrease throughout the next decade (Jones, 2002). These changes put pressure on college and university leaders for economic survival and on state legislators to create policies that increase the number of high school graduates, improve college access and promote graduation from college in order to increase states' "education capital" and states' economic development.

In addition to this financial retrenchment and political mandate, disparities regarding who has access to college remains. For example, Carnevale and Fry (2001) found that in 1997, nearly 80 percent of high school graduates from high-income families went directly into higher education, while only 50 percent of high school graduates from low-income families went on to higher education. In the same year they found that 46 percent of college-age White high school graduates were enrolled in college, whereas only 39 percent of African American and 36 percent of Latina/o high school graduates were enrolled in college. However, these statistics speak nothing of the high school graduation rates for students of the same populations, where, in 2000, 77 percent of African Americans ages 18 to 24 completed high school and only 59.6 percent of Latina/os completed high school (American Council on Education [ACE], 2002). In light of these statistics, approximately 39 percent of 77 percent of all 18 to 24 year old African Americans and 36 percent of 59.6 percent of all 18 to 24 year old Latina/os were enrolled in postsecondary education;[1] a much smaller proportion than any one statistic reveals alone.

U.S. statistics reported by the Pathways to College Network (2004) are even more compelling. They state that by their late 20's more than one-third of Whites have at least a bachelor's degree but only eighteen percent of African Americans and ten percent of Latina/os have attained degrees. These statistics will dramatically change over the next 15 years when one to two million *additional* young adults will be seeking access to higher education and a large proportion of the potential students in this group will be from low-income families, and be students of color (Carnevale & Fry, 2001), albeit access to which institutions of postsecondary education is not always fully addressed and may continue to add to current inequities (Brint & Karabel, 1989; Hurtado & Wathington, 2001).

The support structures and barriers that influence access to higher education continue to shift and this has led contemporary theorists, practitioners and legislators to attempt to understand higher education's current role in contemporary society. A number of national initiatives and dialogues have been held across the country in order to gather leaders together to discuss the future of the relationship between higher education and society (American Association of Colleges and Universities [AACU], 2002; AACU, 2006; ACE, 2006; Campus Compact & AACU, 2006; National Forum on Higher Education for the Public Good, 2002; W.K. Kellogg Foundation, 2002). Higher education leaders who engage in this ongoing dialogue about higher education's responsibilities to society come to the conversation with competing visions, paradigms, and worldviews. These leaders (legislators, university presidents, national association leaders, faculty, and administrators) often talk about higher education's responsibility to serve society in extremely different ways and may — intentionally or unintentionally — labor against each other (Pasque & Rex, under review). In addition, leaders often talk about "society," the "public," or "communities" as abstractions, rather than provide specific inclusive or exclusive definitions. Kezar (2004) urges that if legislators, policy makers, and the public are unclear about why higher education is important to society, then other public policy priorities may gain support at the expense of higher education.

Uncovering various visions of higher education's relationships to society is paramount during this time of dramatic change in higher education. If a more thorough understanding of the perspectives that surround us is not offered, then White male cognitive processing models of the academy communicated in academic discourse genres may continue to perpetuate the current ideas of higher education's relationship with society without consideration of alternative perspectives (Pasque, 2007). Stated another way, there is a danger of paying attention only to the red breasted robin and not to the plethora of birds and environmental factors that surround us.

In addition, each leader's perspective has different sets of ideas, assumptions, and implications for the perpetuation or interruption of current paradigms in research and policy about equal educational opportunity for the public good. By understanding more about various worldviews of higher education's relationship with society, and the tensions created between these views, we are able to see more of the perspectives that surround us and make more informed choices about how to work toward systemic and equitable change. In essence, it becomes imperative to view multiple frames — and tensions between these frames — simultaneously in order to pull forward the strong points of one or more ideas or to strengthen arguments for effective policy and action. In addition, by viewing the same policy or action through multiple frames, we may consider whether or not we are truly enacting equitable and just policies and actions for all people in our society or just for the few that we can see around us on the day we choose to open our eyes.

Specifically, this study illuminates various leaders' competing visions, paradigms, and worldviews of higher education's relationship with society as found in the literature in order to increase our understanding of the perspectives that surround us. In addition, my hope is that this information will help to increase communication between leaders, influence policy decisions, and inform us so *we* may create equitable, ideosyncratic, and systemic change in the field of education. I explore research articles, theoretical writing, and speeches of higher education leaders, present a typology of the conceptualizations of higher education's relationships with society, and share a critical analysis in order to move toward increased awareness and understanding among and between higher education leaders as we make change and address contemporary educational policies and paradigms. Through a more nuanced under-standing of what is and is not included in higher education leaders' perspectives, this analysis helps to elucidate some of what is currently being addressed and ignored in the leaders' perspectives.

The Approach

In the *Archeology of Knowledge*, Foucault (1976) describes that whoever holds the power regarding what counts as knowledge, also has power over policy, systems, access to education, etc. In the field of higher education, it is university presidents, legislators, faculty, administrators, and national association researchers who hold knowledge around higher education's multiple relationships with society and are the leaders in the field. Further, people often accept what leaders say as truth and allow them to be spokespeople for such truth (Johnstone, 2002). This chapter concentrates on higher education leaders, who may or may not consider themselves gatekeepers for the field, but who do hold knowledge about higher education's multiple relationships with society.

In order to explore the contemporary literature, the following orienting questions were asked: What are the different contemporary conceptualizations of higher education's relationship with society that have been developed by higher education leaders? What are the benefits, and supporting evidence for these benefits, of higher education for society (or for individuals that may then benefit society) that are associated with the various conceptualizations? And, importantly, what are the implications of the relationships between conceptualizations?

For this study, I reviewed 187 contemporary (1980-2005) articles, books, and speeches that mention higher education's relationships with society in higher education, business, economics, K-12 education, policy, political science, psychology, and sociology. A theoretical sampling process (Strauss & Corbin, 1999) was used where sources were gathered from an extensive and systematic search of library databases, relevant websites, course syllabi, conversations with colleagues immersed in the topic, and select references from relevant articles (Hart, 1998). Themes were inductively compared across articles (Strauss & Corbin, 1999). As a tool for analysis, I created a table that changed over the course of the collection of articles to reflect the themes that emerged from various sources and the typology presented here emerged from this table. In order to delimit the research, I concentrated on articles that talked about higher education as a (or "for the") public good, common good, or the public benefits of higher education. This analysis specifically excludes perspectives that view higher education as only a private benefit; a public benefit solely as a by-product of a private, individual benefit (Friedman & Friedman, 1980; See Bloom, Hartley & Rosovsky, 2006).

A Typology of Contemporary Conceptualizations

There are four conceptualizations of higher education's relationships with society that emerged directly from the literature review: *The Private Good, The Public Good, Public and Private Goods as Balanced,* and *Public and Private Goods as Interconnected/Advocacy.* In this section, I share each conceptualization, offer a few examples that represent each conceptualization, and share the benefits and evidence that support the conceptualizations.

The Private Good
        The Relationships between Higher Education and Society.   The literature that explores higher education's relationships with society through investing in the private individual is extensive. The primary authors who hold a *The Private Good* conceptualization include economists, policy scholars, legislators, and government agencies (Bartik, 2004; Becker, 1964/1993; Brandl & Weber, 1995; Gottlieb & Fogarty, 2003; Small Business Association, 2004; Weiss, 2004; Weissbourd & Berry, 2004a, 2004b). These higher education and business leaders' vision is that educating the private individual will contribute to the public good through an increase in economic growth, thereby defining the public good as local, state, and national economic vitality. Their primary argument is to sustain resources such as continued government subsidization of colleges and universities, so that individuals may participate in higher education, which will, in turn, influence the public good. This is reminiscent of a traditional input-output model where there is an emphasis on educating individual people (input) and then these individuals work to increase the national, state, and local economies (output). In this sense, it is different from the Friedman and Friedman (1980) perspective as the benefits to

society are public and private, albeit delivered from private goods. In addition, economic rationalists believe that the national economy will suffer if higher education does not privatize research to protect its own interests (Brown & Schubert, 2000; Currie & Newson, 1998). In this conceptualization, higher education is the "engine of growth" for the economy (Becker & Lewis, 1993) and there is a substantial dialogue among and between constituencies who hold this perspective, often directed at policy makers as the primary audience.

Supportive Evidence.   One example of the benefits and evidence to support these benefits from *The Private Good* conceptualization is from Gottlieb and Fogarty (2003). Gottlieb and Fogarty state that a number of economists are concerned with the theoretical aspects of human capital and provide empirical evidence that local or national benefits of higher education exceed individual benefits. Human capital is defined as individual earnings, state and individual rates of return on investment, and national and local economic growth (Becker, 1964/1993; Blinder & Weiss, 1976; Gottlieb & Fogarty, 2003; Weiss, 1995). Specifically, Gottlieb & Fogarty found that educational level is one of the strongest predictors of economic welfare for a city. This idea justifies higher education as a value to market economies and as a societal good. Gottlieb and Fogarty use 1980 and 2000 US Census data and found that among 267 metropolitan areas in the US, "an educated workforce is a significant determinant of subsequent per capita income growth" (p. 331). They found that educational attainment (defined as the percentage of the population with at least 4 years of college) was a significant predictor of per capita income growth for local cities at a 4 percent increase ($p < .001$) over 20 years. The authors controlled for any increase in labor force participation, specialization in manufacturing, size of the city, and region of the country. Gottlieb and Fogerty reason that this information should encourage national legislators to financially support individuals to attend colleges and universities in order to support the national, public good.

In addition, Day & Newburger (2002) of the U.S. Census Bureau found a significant increase in earnings with education level. The average annual wage for high school dropouts is $18,900, for individuals with a high school degree is $25,900, and for individuals with a college degree is $45,400. Further, the National Center for Education Statistics (Decker, 1997) found that postsecondary education training may increase an individual's weekly earnings up to $140 more than a person who has not received education beyond high school. Finally, DesJardins (2003) concludes from his study about the economic benefits of higher education that public subsidization of public higher education is a "win-win proposition" (p. 196) for the State of Minnesota.

The Public Good

The Relationships between Higher Education and Society. The higher education leaders who talk about the relationship between higher education and society from The Public Good perspective are usually university presidents and key spokespeople for national higher education associations who state a vision for the future of an institution or the system of higher education (Cantor, 2003; Campus Compact, 2004; Guarasci & Cornwell, 1997; Rosenstone, 2003). These scholars believe that higher education's primary role is to educate students to participate in a diverse society and this will contribute to society. Further, principles of democratic education and exemplar pedagogy simultaneously help educators develop students for effective civic participation in a pluralistic society.

For example, Guarasci and Cornwell (1997) state that higher education has a responsibility to society to encourage citizenship through civic education, to prepare students for a diverse democracy and to participate in the public good. They argue that institutions of higher education must do more than reform the curriculum to further democratic aims and call for system-wide revisions to hierarchical organizational strategies and compartmentalized ways of knowing and being. It is not enough to educate for the public good, but higher education institutions must also operate as a public good. One way Guarasci suggests that Wagner College (where Guarasci serves as president) enact this vision is through creating service-learning programs and living learning programs which not only provide education for students to participate in society, but also connect academic and student affairs throughout the institution. Collaboration between faculty and staff will help the institution model a diverse democracy for the benefit of society.

A second example of this perspective is from Cantor (2003; 2007) who talks about the significant relationship between higher education and society and addresses higher education's responsibility to create diverse learning environments. As the Chancellor of the University of Illinois in 2003, Cantor challenges university community members to consider "higher education for the public good" throughout the institution. She provides financial and institutional support to programs and departments that have goals and objectives consistent with this vision of the public good. Cantor announces funding for a new center for democracy and an expansion of the intergroup dialogue program through the creation of an intergroup dialogue living-learning program for undergraduates. Cantor connects these initiatives with the university's responsibility to the local community and the state.

> For this country to move together peacefully, it will not suffice to integrate the boot camps and not the military academies, the juror boxes and not the judiciary, the emergency room and not the operating theater, the factory and not the boardroom, the classroom and not the professorate, the voting booth

and not the Congress. Real integration can not [sic] happen until Americans of all colors learn with and from each other in the best classrooms of this land and thereby position themselves for leadership. (p. 4)

Cantor focuses on the education of students through civic engagement for the public good. The individual benefits of *The Private Good* conceptualization are not included in her message.

A final example of *The Public Good* perspective is from Rosenstone (2003), political science professor and dean of the college of liberal arts at the University of Minnesota who addresses the private good, but specifically argues against it. He contends that higher education administrators do not need to communicate the economic benefits of universities, but should educate legislators, business, and civic leaders to recognize the importance of research and how the dissemination of knowledge serves the greater public good. He furthers that universities need to rededicate themselves to their core principles, realize that no university can do it all, (i.e., they should determine disciplinary specialization/s), educate policy makers and the public about the idea of the university as a public good, and enhance research creativity.

The concept of social capital is mentioned in many of *The Public Good* conceptualizations, as defined by Putnam. Putnam (1995) states,

By analogy with notions of physical capital and human capital — tools and training that enhance individual productivity — social capital refers to features of social organization such as networks, norms, and social trust that facilitate coordination and cooperation for mutual benefit (p. 67).

The decline of social capital is a theme of Putnam's work (1995; 2001), yet there can be interventions to increase social capital. Factors in the decline of social capital centrally include television, which is seen as having a profound privatizing impact that undercuts social capital in a society (Putnam, 1995). Further, it is Putnam who devised a social capital index utilizing national data sets including such factors as community organizational life, engagement in public affairs, volunteerism, informal sociability, and level of social trust in a state's population. An increase in these social capital factors will enhance the public good, similar to Cantor and Guarasci's argument for an increase in civic engagement. Principles of Putnam's social capital are found in the education and movement initiatives that Rosenstone and other leaders describe.

Supportive Evidence.   There are a number of qualitative, quantitative, and mixed methods studies that support educating students to participate in society for the public good (Kerrigan, 2005; Markus, Howard, & King, 1993; Maxwell, Traxler-Ballew, & Dimopoulos, 2004; Perry & Katula, 2001; Rowley & Hurtado, 2003). One highly cited study considers student participation through service-learning (Astin et al, 2000). Astin et al. conducted a mixed-methods longitudinal study that included 22,236 undergraduates throughout the United States. The quantitative impact of service-learning was assessed on eleven different dependent measures and controlled for institutional and student characteristics. Participation in service-learning showed significant positive effects on all eleven outcome measures: academic performance, values, self-efficacy, leadership, choice of a service career, and plans to participate in service after college. The qualitative aspect of the study involved in-depth case studies of service-learning on three different campuses. The qualitative findings suggest that service-learning is effective as it facilitates an increased sense of personal efficacy, awareness of the world, awareness of one's personal values, and engagement in the classroom. Astin et al. also found that both faculty and students "develop a heightened sense of civic responsibility and personal effectiveness through participation in service-learning courses" (p. 5). Together, the quantitative and qualitative findings suggest "providing students with an opportunity to process the service experience with each other is a powerful component of both community service and service-learning" (p. 3). The study also found that undergraduate participation in service-learning increases civic engagement after college.

A second example of evidence for a public good perspective of higher education is from Gurin, Dey, Hurtado, and Gurin (2002). This example considers student participation in a diverse democracy during and after the time students are in college and was used as evidence for the defense in the *Grutter vs. Bollinger* (2003) and *Gratz vs. Bollinger* (2003) U.S. Supreme Court cases about affirmative action. The authors identify patterns of educational benefits on the single institution level and across institutions. The researchers utilized two longitudinal databases. The institutional database included 1,129 White students, 187 African American students, and 266 Asian American students. The national database (Cooperative Institutional Research Program) included 10,465 White students, 216 African American students, 496 Asian American students, and 206 Latino/a students. Students were surveyed their first year, and again four years later. The study controlled for ethnic/racial composition of the high school and precollege neighborhood, gender, high school GPA, SAT, parents' educational attainment as a measure of the student's socioeconomic background (SES), and institutional features.

Gurin et al. (2002) use structural diversity (the number of people from diverse groups), informal interactional diversity (the frequency and quality of intergroup interaction), and classroom diversity (learning about and gaining experience with diverse people) as factors in this study. Specifically, the authors examined the relationship between these different types of diversity and four dependent variables (intellectual engagement, academic skills, citizenship engagement, and racial/cultural engagement). Multiple regression analyses determined that in the national study, informal interactional diversity and classroom diversity "explained between 1.5 percent and 12.6 percent of the variance in the different educational outcomes for the four [racial] groups. In the Gurin study, the three diversity experiences explained between 1.9 percent and 13.8 percent of the variance across the educational outcomes of the three [racial] groups" (p. 358). Outcomes were significant (p < .05 or less) for each racial group. The findings show that the "actual experiences students have with diversity consistently and meaningfully affect important learning and democracy outcomes of a college education" (p. 358). Based on the results, the authors argue for more structural, classroom, and interactional diversity on college campuses.

Public and Private Goods: A Balance
    The Relationships between Higher Education and Society. The scholars in this Public and Private Goods: A Balance (or Balanced) section acknowledges both the public good and private good benefits to society, as previously defined. The authors are typically policy analysts or researchers at national higher education associations (Baum & Payea, 2004; Boulus, 2003, Callan & Finney, 2002; Institute for Higher Education Policy, 1998; IHEP, 2005; Wagner, 2004). Scholars with this view write about a "both/and" model where higher education is both a public and a private good. The authors do not, however, address interconnections between the public good and the private good; the two aspects may influence one another, yet each entity is described as separate from the other. This public and private goods argument is most often used to expand the benefits of higher education beyond solely the private good, and argue for continued support or assessment of higher education.

Figure 1: *The Array of Higher Education Benefits.*

	Public		Private
Economic	• Increased Tax Revenues • Greater Productivity • Increased Consumption • Increased Workforce Flexibility • Decreased Reliance on Government Financial Support		• Higher Salaries and Benefits • Employment • Higher Savings Levels • Improved Working Conditions • Personal / Professional Mobility
Social	• Reduced Crime Rates • Increased Charitable Giving/Community Service • Increased Quality of Civic Life • Social Cohesion / Appreciation of Diversity • Improved Ability to Adapt to and Use Technology		• Improved Health / Life Expectancy • Improved Quality of Life for Offspring • Better Consumer Decision Making • Increased Personal Status • More Hobbies, Leisure Activities

The Institute for Higher Education Policy (1998) in *Reaping the Benefits: Defining the Public and Private Value of Going to College.*

The Institute for Higher Education Policy's (IHEP, 1998) *Array of Benefits* best represents this conceptualization and it is cited often by leaders in the field of higher education (see Figure 1). The *Array of Benefits* is a figure that adds the "economic" and "social" benefits as oppositional categories to the "private" and "public" oppositional categories. This illustration validates the frequently discussed perspective of the "private/ economic" benefits of higher education such as higher salaries, benefits and savings. It also furthers our understanding of the role of higher education in society by including "public/economic," "private/social," and "public/social" benefits. IHEP describes these four categories as mutually exclusive, but the authors briefly mention that a private, economic benefit could spill over onto the public, economic benefit category. Supportive evidence for this perspective is cited by the IHEP within each category.

The IHEP recommends a more formal system for measuring and reporting the benefits of higher education in order to increase public support for higher education across the nation. This system could ensure that legislators, parents, and all stakeholders are informed about the benefits of attending college. It also could help policy makers and higher education administrators shift the way society invests in higher education, from a private/economic to a public/social good, as the private/economic good is garnering too much attention. They purport that such a national report will increase understanding of the benefits of higher education and help further dialogue about the issue.

Finally, some authors in this conceptualization, such as Callan and Finney (2002), address the idea of "capital," but in terms of "educational capital." Educational capital (also cited as academic capital) in these contexts is defined as both private goods (including human capital) and public goods (including social capital) yielded by higher education. The combination of human capital and social capital addressed in these conceptualizations is found in the increasingly cited

American sociologist James Coleman's (1988) use of "social capital." Coleman's theory of social capital is grounded in a structural-functionalist theoretical frame. Coleman attempts to merge sociology and economics using "the economists' principle of rational action for use in the analysis of social systems proper, including but not limited to economic systems, and to do so without discarding social organization in the process" (Coleman, 1988). Here, social capital is defined by its function including the social structures and actions of people within the structure. This theory is utilized in numerous research studies and helps scholars identify a number of factors related to educational outcomes (for a literature review of 443 journal articles on social capital from 1986-2001, see Dika & Singh, 2002).

Public and Private Goods: An Interconnected/Advocacy Conceptualization

The Relationships between Higher Education and Society. The scholars who perceive the relationship between higher education and society as Interconnected each have two similarities. First, the authors state that there is mutual interdependence between the public and private good; the location where one ends and the other begins is blurred. Second, the authors each passionately describe a crisis in higher education where action from leaders is needed to shift the focus of the higher education from a capitalistic, market-driven emphasis to one that better serves the public good. The scholars who conceptualize the relationship between higher education and society — where the public and private good interconnect — are primarily tenured faculty from the social sciences (Giroux & Giroux, 2004; Kezar, 2005; Larabee, 1997; Parker, 2003; Pitkin & Shumer, 1982; Rhoades & Slaughter, 2004).

In this *Interconnected* conceptualization, higher education's role in a democracy needs to acknowledge the public and private realms as well as privilege the inter-connections between them. The authors view this interconnection as the crux of a crisis in the academy where change in leaders' perspectives about, and behaviors regarding, the academy is needed. Political capital and making change to actualize a true and inclusive democracy is central. The authors believe it is particularly important for leaders within colleges and universities to initiate this change. In *Balanced* perspective, one may consider each factor that contributes to the relationship between higher education and society as mutually exclusive, whereas in this perspective, the intersections of various aspects within and outside of the academy render isolation of factors virtually impossible.

Most scholars with the *Interconnected* perspective identify people with a economic neoliberal view — who support the marketization of higher education — as a problem and believe there is a lack of leadership and governance within the academy. The authors fear that if there is not a change in how stakeholders perceive and act upon higher education's relationship with society, then higher education will be increasingly perceived as a private good, or a commodity. The authors often identify solutions as increased access to education, multicultural education, and civic engagement for a diverse democracy, and a change in leadership.

Supportive Evidence. For clarity, I have divided this conceptualization into three categories, based on the primary focus of the authors. For example, Parker (2003) and Pitkin and Shumer (1982) connect the notion of civic engagement and multicultural education with a diverse democracy as a way to focus on the intersections between the public and private good. Larabee (1997), Rhoades and Slaughter (2004), and Kezar (2005) focus on higher education as a marketplace and the political nature of the intersection of the public and private good. The Girouxs (2004) connect all of these issues together as they address this blurred vision of the relationship between higher education and society. However, there are definite overlaps in these subcategories, which is indicative of this conceptualization's resistance to finite boundaries.

Civic Engagement and Multicultural Education as the Intersection of the Public and Private

Parker (2003) addresses the relationship between higher education and society through his conceptualization of idiocy vs. citizenship where the idiot is the "private, separate, self-centered" (p. 2) person and the citizen is the public actor. Parker actually breaks down this dichotomy through democratic citizenship education where "an understanding of both *pluribus* (the many) and *unum* (the one), and an understanding that the two are, in fact, interdependent" (p. 1). Parker believes that institutions of higher education have not fully grasped the connection between these two, as mirrored in the perceived dichotomy between public and private good, and in the separation between multicultural and citizenship education for participation in a diverse democracy. Parker furthers that higher education can promote the interconnection of the *pluribus* and *unum* through multicultural education, which he links to democratic citizens, which leads to a culturally, racially, and politically diverse society (also see Torres, 1998). These various aspects progress from one another and are also inextricably linked. The higher education–society relationship includes responsibility to the public, private, and its intersections, where unity arises *from* diversity, as opposed to creating a dichotomy. In this manner, Parker believes that higher education needs to fulfill its responsibility to educate students for the private good and the public good of society.

Pitkin and Shumer (1982) connect the public and private good, but from a perspective of radical criticism where they specifically address issues of privilege and oppression. The authors state that the "crucial function" of civic engagement in and out of higher education is to connect the private good with that of the public good. Their call is in "revolutionizing" the power of our democracy by "transforming people from consumers, victims, and exploiters into responsible citizens, extending their horizons and deepening their understanding, engaging their capacities, their suppressed anger and need in the cause of justice" (p. 48). Pitkin and Shumer further that "The idea of democracy is the cutting edge of radical criticism, the best inspiration for change toward a more humane world, the revolutionary idea of our time. The basic idea is simple: people can and should govern themselves" (p. 43). The authors are clear that the crucial function of political engagement is to connect the personal, individual good with the public good.

The Marketplace and the Political Nature of the Intersection of Public and Private

A number of authors discuss the rise in the commercialization of research in recent years and the potential for additional collaboration between higher education and industry. Yet, in this conceptualization, the authors argue that this is not in the interest of the public good (Bok, 2003; Kerr, 1963/2001; Kezar, 2005; Slaughter & Rhoades, 1996).

Professor of K-12 education, Labaree (1997), discusses the narrow pursuit of private advantage at the expense of the public. He states, "by constructing a system of education so heavily around the goal of promoting individual social mobility, we have placed public education in service to private interests" (p. 261). Labaree's perspective of the current state of higher education is often mirrored through state budget allocations, as more of the cost for college is moving away from the state and being placed on to the individual family. Labaree argues that the push and pull between the public and private good results in a no-win situation. Labaree argues for attention to be paid to all that is "fundamentally political" (p. 16) or the intersections of both the public and private good. Here, the interconnection of public and private *is* the political capital arena, which he believes to be central to the education discussion.

Higher education scholars, Rhoades and Slaughter (2004), have witnessed the shift in the U.S. from an industrial to a knowledge- and information-based economy. The authors state that this shift, coupled with a decrease in state funding, has served as a catalyst for an increase in the generation of income from institutions' teaching, research, and service areas. There may be a transformation in the economy and in a "blurring of the boundaries" (p. 38) between profit and non-profit. This transformation comes from an increase in "neo-liberal and neo-conservative politics and policies that shift government investment in higher education to emphasize education's economic role and cost efficiency" (p. 38), which, in turn, has led to administrators' need to increase market capitalism on campus in order to survive. The authors believe faculty has been too complacent in the face of these changes. They argue that in this political environment, colleges and universities need to be more public and provide alternatives to academic capitalism in this changing economy. Higher education needs to provide access to postsecondary institutions, prepare citizens for a diverse democracy, and address social problems and issues.

Rhoades and Slaughter (2004) include specific recommendations for change including increasing access to higher education and preparing citizens to engage in a democracy. They also argue for faculty, national associations, and faculty unions to "reprioritize the democratic and educational functions of the academy" to include "more public discussion and more public accountability" (p. 57). Rhoades and Slaughter urge faculty, associations, and unions to examine who benefits from the current system and to advocate for the inclusion of people who have been historically excluded. The authors argue for a "'re-publicizing' of U.S. colleges and universities" (p. 57).

Higher education scholar Kezar (2005) established that "the [economic] neoliberal philosophy was one of the main forces driving the move away from the traditional charter between higher education and society, a tradition built on a communitarian philosophy of the public good" (p. 454). Economic neoliberals are defined as people who believe in a free-market economy, which includes institutions of higher education. Kezar's analysis shows the myriad ways higher education for the public good has been reconceptualized as privatized public institutions through economic neoliberal philosophy. Kezar argues that if the shift of higher education from public/social good to a private/economic good is not interrupted by leaders in the academy, then "even if we want to alter the social charter [between higher education and society], it may not be possible to revitalize lost areas of the public good" (p. 26).

The Political, the Marketplace, and Educating for a Diverse Democracy

Henry Giroux, professor of secondary education, and Susan Searls Giroux, teacher of English and education, share their concern that higher education is under attack by economic neoliberals in their book, *Take Back Higher Education: Race, Youth, and the Crisis of Democracy in the Post-Civil Rights Era* (2004). The authors view public education as being redefined as a private good in order to further stratify the White upper/upper-middle class and the poor/working class who are predominantly people of color. The "take back" argument centers on the belief that higher education administrators and faculty members are passively enabling corporations to take over colleges and universities. Giroux and Giroux (2004) state that strengthening the relationship between higher education and society requires "rejecting the model of the separation between the public and the private domains and recognizing instead their mutual dependence" (p. 40). The lines between the historically separated entities are blurred and a university that acts as a public good must recognize that the false dichotomy of public and private has historically perpetuated racism and classism; a university might "open up a space for more than just a democracy" (p. 213). In this conceptualization, the public and the private are both critical to the success of the democracy. The authors state that the current, significant concentration on market values stratifies the "haves" and the "have-nots" thereby decreasing the value of higher education as a public good. This argument is echoed by a number of other scholars (Bowen & Bok, 1998; Brint & Karabel, 1989; Green & Trent, 2005; Hagedorn & Tierney, 2002; Larabee, 1997).

The Girouxs address how to revitalize the relationship between higher education and society through the creation of a *"paideia"* (p. 37), or a "prodigious political educational process," in order to develop the skills and abilities that an educated citizenry, participants in a diverse democracy, requires. In this conceptualization, and similar to Pitkin and Shumer (1982), neither privileged nor oppressed people are excluded from access to higher education or participation in a democracy. In this vision of higher education, race and civic education cannot be extracted from the context of the U.S.'s multiracial and multiethnic society. This also means educating the entire public through multicultural education.

Finally, the authors in this interconnected conceptualization refer to political theory and state how important race, ethnicity, gender, and socioeconomic status are to the relationship between higher education and society. The inclusion of all things political is reflective of the notions of social capital, as defined by French sociologist, Pierre Bourdieu (1986) whose definition of social capital connects three sources of capital (economic, cultural, and social) in order to create an aggregate of resources linked to a network of relationships. Social capital, in this context, can be converted into economic capital. Bourdieu defines social capital as grounded in theories of symbolic power and social reproduction where social capital is a tool of reproduction for the privileged. This is quite distinct from Coleman's (1988; 1992) use of social capital described earlier.

A Critical Analysis of the Relationships Among Conceptualizations

What are the relationships — or lack thereof — between these various conceptualizations of higher education's relationship with society? And, more importantly, what are the implications of these relationships? In this section I share four visions that further the conversation about the relationships between higher education and society by sharing general observations and implications about the connections between conceptualizations.

A More Comprehensive Vision of the Benefits of Higher Education for Society

The first general observation is that numerous scholars cite the *Array of Benefits* IHEP (1998) typology when talking about the benefits of higher education as it is clear and easy to understand. The *Array of Benefits* represents only three of the four conceptualizations that emerged from this review. For example, the *Private* conceptualization is found within the private/individual and private/social quadrants; the *Public* is found within the public/social quadrant; and the *Balanced* conceptualization is completely represented. The *Inter-connected/Advocacy* conceptualization is not currently represented in the model. If the model was more reflective of all four conceptualizations, then it could be utilized to advance relationships between leaders from all four different conceptualizations, and not remain limited to describing only three conceptualizations.

Figure 2: *The Benefits of Higher Education for Society.*

	Public	Private
Economic	• Increased Tax Revenues • Greater Productivity • Increased Consumption • Increased Workforce Flexibility • Decreased Reliance on Government Financial Support	• Higher Salaries and Benefits • Employment • Higher Savings Levels • Improved Working Conditions • Personal / Professional Mobility
Social	• Reduced Crime Rates • Increased Charitable Giving / Community Service • Increased Quality of Civic Life • Social Cohesion / Appreciation of Diversity • Improved Ability to Adapt to and Use Technology	• Improved Health / Life Expectancy • Improved Quality of Life for Offspring • Better Consumer Decision Making • Increased Personal Status • More Hobbies, Leisure Activities

Adapted by Penny A. Pasque from the Institute for Higher Education Policy (1998) in *Reaping the Benefits: Defining the Public and Private Value of Going to College.*

I have adapted the *Array of Benefits* model in an attempt to include all four conceptualizations (see Figure 2). The *Benefits of Higher Education for Society* model consists of dotted lines, and a fading of color from the center (dark) to the edges (light) in order to portray the interconnections between quadrants. Also, in a similar fashion to the Johary Window[2] (Luft, 1970), the different quadrants expand and contract to reflect various relationships between the quadrants (see Figures 3 & 4). In this model, the quadrants may take different shapes in order to reflect higher education's changing relationship with society at a particular point in time, or to represent the different conceptualizations of leaders. For example, in the *Interconnected* conceptualization, the authors argue that the private/economic quadrant has recently been expanding, therefore the private/economic quadrant is larger, and the color is darker (see Figure 3). Yet, as previously described, the scholars prefer a larger public/social quadrant where the public/social quadrant is larger and darker (see Figure 4). This adapted model visually represents the relationship and fluidity between the quadrants.

If the *Interconnected/Advocacy* is not represented within a model of higher education benefits and the model remains limited to three conceptualizations, then the current model might further miscommunication among scholars with different conceptualizations and from different fields and disciplines. A comprehensive model that is both clear and easy, such as the adapted *Benefits of Higher Education for Society* model could expand the dialogue with scholars and with leaders outside of higher education in order to increase under-standing of the benefits of higher education to legislators, business leaders, and the public. This revised model has the potential to further the current literature and to help garner legislative and public support for higher education. In addition, if scholars continue to cite the *Array of Benefits* model without fully exploring the fluidity between the categories, then it will continue to limit conceptualizations of higher education's relationships with society to the exclusion of an important perspective.

Figure 3: *The Current Benefits of Higher Education for Society*

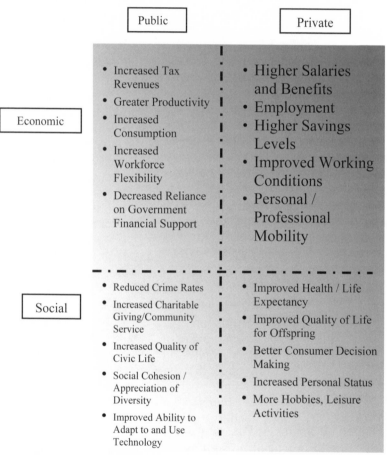

Adapted by Penny A. Pasque from the Institute for Higher Education Policy (1998) in *Reaping the Benefits Defining the Public and Private Value of Going to College.*

Figure 4: *The Envisioned Benefits of Higher Education for Society: An Interconnected Conceptualization.*

	Public	Private
Economic	• Increased Tax Revenues • Greater Productivity • Increased Consumption • Increased Workforce Flexibility • Decreased Reliance on Government Financial Support	• Higher Salaries and Benefits • Employment • Higher Savings Levels • Improved Working Conditions • Personal / Professional Mobility
Social	• Reduced Crime Rates • Increased Charitable Giving / Community Service • Increased Quality of Civic Life • Social Cohesion / Appreciation of Diversity • Improved Ability to Adapt to and Use Technology	• Improved Health / Life Expectancy • Improved Quality of Life for Offspring • Better Consumer Decision Making • Increased Personal Status • More Hobbies, Leisure Activities

Adapted by Penny A. Pasque from the Institute for Higher Education Policy (1998) in *Reaping the Benefits: Defining the Public and Private Value of Going to College.*

A Conflict of Visions of the Relationships Between Higher Education and Society

The second observation is that if scholars continue to disagree among themselves about the definition and benefits of higher education for society, let alone the evidence and strategies for change in the system, then how can the system of higher education advance theory-to-practice through policy and campus initiatives toward change? Public policy scholar and historian, Sowell, helps to illuminate this point. In *A Conflict of Visions: Ideological Origins of Political Struggles*, Sowell (2002) describes his sense of the public and private good, and in his conjecture the private good becomes the "constrained vision" and the public good becomes the "unconstrained vision" of society. In the constrained vision, individual benefits might persuade a person to act in hir[3] own self-interest or for "inner needs" which s/he "would not do for the good of his fellow man" (p. 22). Sowell believes that the way to combat the self-centeredness of benefiting the private, or individual good, is through intervention with trade-offs, which assists in balancing the public benefits to society. Sowell's unconstrained vision is one where people are "capable of creating social benefits" (p. 23) without the need for the intervention of trade-offs.[4] Here, members of society follow through on a solution such as civic engagement because it is the right thing to do for the good of society. More specifically, in addition to juxtaposing the constrained and the unconstrained visions of community members, Sowell positions the public good perspective in opposition to private good. He does not formulate a continuum because,

> In one sense [a continuum would] be more appropriate to refer to less constrained visions and more constrained visions instead of the dichotomy used here. However, the dichotomy is not only more convenient but also captures an important

distinction... Every vision, by definition, leaves something out — indeed, leaves *most* things out. The dichotomy between constrained and unconstrained visions is based on whether or not inherent limitations of man are among the key elements included in each vision. The dichotomy is justified in yet another sense. These different ways of conceiving man and the world lead not merely to *different* conclusions but to sharply divergent, often diametrically opposed, conclusions on issues ranging from justice to war, There are not merely differences of visions but conflicts of visions. (p. 33)

In Sowell's dichotomy, if one views higher education as a public good, then the conceptualization will negate any vision of higher education as a private good, therefore the person will view higher education only as an unconstrained (or uncontested) vision and never as a constrained (or contested) vision. Sowell's vision includes no way for people with contested values to come to understand one another or reach a set of solutions or next steps in order to make change. It follows that those who perceive higher education as a public good are diametrically opposed to those who perceive higher education as a private good that could lead to public goods. The benefits and recommendations for change in order to increase higher education's role in serving the public in these two perceptions will not overlap.

Sowell's argument is supported by the Marwell & Ames (1981) free riding experiment about investment in the private vs. public good. Free riding "refers to the absence of contribution towards the provision of a public good by an individual, even though he or she will not be excluded from benefiting from that good" (p. 296). The authors found that participants voluntarily contributed 40 percent to 60 percent of their resources to the public good despite the experiments attempts to maximize self-interest. However, the authors also found that economic graduate students only contributed an average of 20 percent of their resources to the public good. The economic students were more likely to free ride than any other group of students. There is a cyclical nature to this perspective, where a student learns about self-interest economic models, and then perpetuates them. Frank (2005) argues that economists should be taught about self-interest models and the public good, where students receive exposure to contested and uncontested notions of the public good in order to break this cycle of self-interest for economic students, and so they may view the public good as more than simply the contested vision.

Sowell's vision can be seen in the dichotomy between those who believe there is a crisis in higher education, such as Giroux and Giroux, and the *Private Good* authors such as Gottlieb and Fogarty. For example, we can see this dichotomy by positioning Larabee's political "no-win" argument next to DesJardins's economic "win-win" argument. If Sowell's vision is true, then the primary implication is that the *Private Good* and the *Interconnected* are diametrically opposed and will never come to an understanding, only tradeoffs. This will stifle progress toward strengthening the relationships between higher education and society, where neither conceptualization will advance. Implications for scholars are that they will not be able to see or communicate from "the other" vision, and they will keep communicating from their own perspective without others fully comprehending, or without listening to other perspectives. This implies that students and the public will hear competing propaganda about higher education from both visions, yet may not always be able to decipher meaning if it is shared from "the other" perspective. This could hinder an increase in awareness and understanding among leaders and slow down initiatives for change including public and legislative support for public colleges and universities.

However, as mentioned, the four conceptualizations that emerged from the literature are not mutually exclusive.

Therefore, the potential for advancing the conversation between constituencies about the benefits of higher education may not be as bleak as Sowell envisions. For example, similar to a pendulum, the extremes help push the national conversation further than before, in one direction or another. This may help the national dialogue move further to the *Private Good* or further to the *Interconnected* side of the vision. We (higher education leaders) need the extremes to push the conversation beyond the status quo. Yet, it is often the less radical perspectives (i.e., the *Public* and the *Balanced*) that receive the support needed for implementation, as they are not as extreme and may not appear as threatening as the other perspectives. In this manner, each conceptualization adds to the theory and practice of higher education for the public good and helps to increase awareness about various perspectives and benefits of the relationships between higher education and society.

Higher education researcher Powell and sociologist Clemens (1998) also believe that the public good will always be "unsettled and contested and is part of the unsettled and contested nature of politics itself" (p. 4); that the argument will never come to a conclusion. It is through conflict, dissention, and discussion that ideas are furthered. Yet, St. John, Kline, & Asker (2001) assert that arguments about higher education increasing human capital, economic development, and affecting equity issues, enable liberal interests (i.e., affirmative action and educational equity for social justice) and conservative interests (i.e., economic development) to come together. This perspective also resists Sowell's notion of contested visions.

Visions of Capital Further Miscommunication
A third observation is that some conceptualizations are reminiscent of each other, yet the principles of the conceptualization are different, such as with the *Public* and the *Interconnected* concepts of the relationships between higher education and society. Leaders might think that they

are supporting one another, or that they agree with one another based on a similarity in language, yet might actually labor against one another. For example, a number of scholars from each conceptualization mention "capital," yet each define it with extremely different theoretical underpinnings.

The *Private Good* conceptualization addresses "human capital" as a primary component in the relationship between higher education and society. Human capital is highly connected to individual wage rates, state and individual rates of return on investment, and national and local economic growth (Becker, 1964/1993; Blinder & Weiss, 1976; Gottlieb & Fogarty, 2003; Weiss, 1995). This is distinctly different from how the other three conceptualizations utilize "social capital." The *Public Good* conceptualization addresses social capital as imperative to serving the public good and the scholars often cite Putman (1995; 2001) for a definition. Putnam (1995; 2001) defines social capital as the value of social networks. The *Balanced* and the *Interconnected* conceptualizations, however, address the importance of human and social capital. The *Balanced* concept addresses both forms of capital as quantifiable, as is found in Coleman's (1988) definition of social capital that is utilized to determine a quantitative relationship between social capital and educational outcomes. The *Interconnected* conceptualization addresses social capital from Bourdieu's (1986) perspective, where social networks facilitate access to social capital. Bourdieu's construction of social capital also includes issues of political capital and systemic oppression. Further, Hagedorn and Tierney (2002) and Giroux and Giroux (2004) specifically name Bourdieu and extend Bourdieu's definition to include issues of cultural capital (also see Tierney, 2003).

If the relationship between conceptualizations and the notion of "capital" remains unexplored as related to the relationships between higher education and society, then this ambiguity could add to a further disconnect between conceptualizations and miscommunication between scholars.

Scholars might assume they mean the same thing when they use "social capital," yet the words often have vastly different definitions. Lack of mutual understanding has important consequences when trying to work with legislators, the public, or with colleagues at the same institution, when attempting to garner support for policies to increase access to higher education.

Inclusive and Exclusive Visions of "The Public"

A final observation is that each scholar assumes that there is a "public" in U.S. society (B. Baez, personal communication, November 8, 2004). I found no authors that address the relationship between higher education and the pubic that argued that the "public" does not exist. In addition, who is included and excluded in the public, as subject, is different for each author. For example, in the *Private Good* conceptualization, a number of scholars talk about the public as an abstraction — without defining who is included or excluded in their concepts of the public or society. There are very few mentions of class, gender, and race. By failing to define the public, there is an assumption that the public, as subject, follows the dominant paradigm and includes people who have traditionally been considered in the "public" such as able-bodied, White, Christian, heterosexual men and those who assimilated to U.S. culture (Bell, 1997). The *Public Good* conceptualization includes every participant in the diverse democracy as the public, including U.S. citizens and community members who are not U.S. citizens. This definition is loose and open-ended. Some of the *Balanced* scholars define the public as diverse and inclusive (Baum & Payea, 2004; IHEP, 1998; Wagner, 2004) and some do not (Boulus, 2003; Callan & Finney, 2002; Public Sector Consultants, 2003). The *Interconnected/ Advocacy* scholars each include the diverse public in their definition and specifically name the underrepresented and disenfranchised as people to include in definitions of the public.

If the public, as subject, is not defined as we try to strengthen the relationships between higher education and society, then there is an assumption about who the "public" includes and excludes and, by default, the definition will include only people with dominant social identities. This could lead to miscommunication and misinterpretation between conceptualizations if the definition of the public is left to the readers' interpretation. Furthermore, if the subject/public is intentionally defined as inclusive, it enables scholars in each conceptualization to address the pervasive historic inequities in order to strengthen the relationship between higher education and *all* of society. Lack of attention to intersectionality — the intersections of class, race, ethnicity, gender, sexual orientation, ability, etc. — creates serious limitations in college contexts (Chesler, Peet, & Sevig, 2003; Myers et al., 1991; Sevig et al., 2000). If the public is not defined as inclusive, then people historically excluded from that public will not be included as the future of higher education is envisioned, nor will they reap the benefits identified in any of these conceptualizations.

Conclusion

By understanding more about various worldviews of higher education's relationships with society, I believe that we are able to see more of what is around us; the *Private, Public, Balanced,* and *Interconnected/Advocacy* frames. Each frame operates with a different set of assumptions and implications for the perpetuation or interruption of the current cycles of power and privilege. Numerous other scholars have talked about the importance of using different frames to understand further what is around us. For example, Bolman and Deal (1997) contend that considering organizations from a structural, human resource, political, *and* symbolic frame help us make sense of organizations and make educated choices in innumerable situations. Hardiman and Jackson (1997) argue that people simultaneously hold various social identities (race and ethnicity, gender, sexual orientation, religion, physical/psychological/developmental disability, class, and age) and that the ability to see the horizontal and vertical relationships between target and agent identities helps us to acknowledge and break the cycle of oppression.

Each of the four frames offered in this chapter proposes a different set of ideas about how to make change for the public good — where the public is inclusive of all people in the U.S., or not. While I certainly have my own particular preferences for the perspectives presented, in this chapter I argue that knowing more about multiple frames expands our awareness of the varying perspectives held by higher education leaders. Acknowledging multiple existing frames also helps us explore the tensions between perspectives in order to make educated choices and break the cycle of what is currently not working in the system of education.

By way of example, Brint and Karabel (1989) describe the caste system that has been created through our universities, community colleges, and trade schools. They map out for us the disparity between the "dreams" of American youth to go to college, and the diversions that take place within the hierarchy of the system. Specifically, if a student attends a two-year institution, or even a four-year lower tiered university, they have little chance of gaining access to a research university or Ivy League institution. Furthermore, even when students utilize community colleges as a stepping-stone to four-year institutions, there are still disparities in the type of education they will receive during their college career. In addition, gaps in rates of college enrollment have grown for African Americans and Latina/os as compared to Whites. The gap between African American and White continuation rates has been widening since 1999 (Mortenson, 2006) and the gap between Latina/o and White rates is even wider than that of African Americans and whites.[5] These quantitative differences are further exploited by the qualitative disparities between the various colleges and universities (Larabee, 1997; Galston, 2001). Access is not equitable and all institutions are not created equal. "Education serves as a sorting mechanism" (Galston, 2001, p. 225) and increasing the number of graduates does not automatically remove the systemic degradation that is inherent in the academy.

The *Private, Public, Balanced,* and *Interconnected* perspectives each have a very different approach toward acknowledging and addressing issues of inequity as outlined by Brint and Karabel and Mortensen.[6] Brandl and Weber (1995) argue that the answer lies in competition and community and suggest that state funding for higher education be shifted primarily to individuals themselves, where competition drives student choice and dollars to colleges and universities. By viewing this same policy suggestion through multiple frames, we may see if we *really are* enacting equitable education policy for all people, or just for the few "robins" that we see around us. Scholars from various other frames have argued against competition and the privatization of higher education as they believe it continues to stratify the privileged and the oppressed (Blumenfeld & Raymond, 2000; Bowen & Bok, 1998; Giroux & Giroux, 2004; Green & Trent, 2005; Hagedorn & Tierney, 2002; Larabee, 1997). Engaging different frames helps us pull forward different aspects of particular frames in order to provide an unfamiliar or new lens that may be more useful when considering issues.[7] It also enables us to move away from dominant cognitive processing models communicated in academic discourse genres in order to acknowledge existing, and create additional, equitable processes (Pasque, 2007).

The nature of higher education is changing in terms of who pays for college, who gains access to college, and the role of college and universities in the marketplace. Higher education leaders who engage in this ongoing dialogue and enact policy come to the conversation with competing visions, paradigms, and worldviews. Multiple frames help us interrogate the assumptions and implications of varying perspectives. In this sense, it may increase our multiple understandings of the various issues and bolster our argument as we address educational inequities. In addition, reducing the abstraction of "the public" enables us to intentionally address the intersectionality of various identities, identify support structures, and alter barriers to an equitable education as we try to change the relationship between higher education and society that we see, know, and experience every day.

Notes

[1] These statistics do not include information about Native American or Asian American students. In addition, they do not break down the statistics within racial and ethnic groups that uncover further disparity within and between student populations.

[2] Joe Luft and Harry Ingham (Luft, 1970) created The Johary Window to describe self-disclosure. The four quadrants, or sections of a window separated by a pane, are: open, hidden, blind, and unknown. The open quadrant is information that a person knows about him/herself, and other people know about that person. The hidden quadrant is what a person knows about him/herself, yet does not reveal to others. The blind quadrant is information known to others and not to him/herself. The unknown quadrant is information not known to the person him/herself or to others.

[3] "His/her" is currently being referred to as "hir" in the field of student affairs and beyond. Hir is inclusive of males, females, and transgendered persons.

[4] Tradeoffs are one of the foundational principles of economic theory (Buchanan & Tullock, 1962).

[5] Again, these statistics do not address the disparities between all groups of people of color, or break down the statistics within racial and ethnic groups that can uncover further disparity between student populations.

[6] Mortensen, Brint, and Karabel also approach research, scholarship and practice from particular perspectives.

[7] These adapted figures and a version of this chapter have been shared and discussed with Jamie Merisotis from the Institute for Higher Education Policy.

References

American Association of Colleges and Universities. (2006). *Liberal Education and America's Promise.* Retrieved on March 8, 2006 from www.aacu.org/advocacy.

American Association of Colleges and Universities. (2002). *Greater expectations: A new vision for learning as a nation goes to college.* Washington, DC: Author.

American Council on Education. (2002). *Minorities in higher education, 2001-2002. Nineteenth annual status report.* Washington, DC: Author.

Astin, A.W., Vogelgesang, L.J., Ikeda, E.K., & Yee, J.A. (2000). *How service learning affects students.* Los Angeles, CA: Higher Education Research Institute.

Bartik, T.J. (2004). *Increasing the economic development benefits of higher education in Michigan* (No. 04-106). Kalamazoo, MI: Upjohn Institute.

Baum, S., & Payea, K. (2004). *Education pays 2004: The benefits of education for individuals and society.* New York: College Board.

Becker, G.S. (1964/1993). *Human capital: A theoretical and empirical analysis with special reference to education* (3rd ed.). Chicago: University of Chicago Press.

Becker, W.E., & Lewis, D.R. (1993). *Higher education and economic growth.* Boston: Kluwer Academic Publishers.

Bell, L.A. (1997). Theoretical foundations for social justice education. In B. Adams, L.A. Bell & P. Griffin (Eds.), *Teaching for diversity and social justice*. New York: Routledge.

Blinder, A.S., & Weiss, Y. (1976). Human capital and labor supply: A synthesis. *The Journal of Political Economy, 84*(3), 449-472.

Bloom, D., Hartley, M., & Rosovsky, H. (2006). Beyond private gain: The public benefits of higher education. In P.G. Altbach & J. Forrest (Eds.), *International Handbook of Higher Education*. Dordrecht: Springer Press.

Blumenfeld, W.J., & Raymond, D. (2000). Prejudice and discrimination. In M. Adams, W.J. Blumenfeld, R. Castañeda, H.W. Hackman, M.L. Peters, & X. Zúñiga (Eds.), *Readings for diversity and social justice*. New York: Routledge.

Bok, D. (2003). *Universities in the marketplace: The commercialization of higher education*. Princeton, NJ: Princeton University Press.

Bolman, T.E., & Deal, L.G. (1997). *Reframing organizations: Artistry, choice and leadership* (2nd ed.). San Francisco: Jossey-Bass.

Boulus, M.A. (2003). *Challenges and implications: Declining state support of Michigan public higher education*. Lansing: Presidents Council State Universities of Michigan.

Bourdieu, P. (1986). The forms of capital. In J. Richardson (Ed.), *Handbook of theory and research for the sociology of education* (pp. 241-258). Westport, CT: Greenwood Press.

Bowen, W.G., & Bok, D. (1998). *The shape of the river: Long term consequences of considering race in college and university admissions*. Princeton, NJ: Princeton University Press.

Brandl, J., & Holdsworth, J.M. (2003). On measuring what universities do: A reprise. In D.R. Lewis & J. Hearn (Eds.), *The public research university: Serving the public good in new times*. New York: University Press of America.

Brandl, J., & Weber, V. (1995). *An agenda for reform: Competition, community, concentration.* Minneapolis, MN: Office of the Governor.

Brint, S., & Karabel, J. (1989). *The diverted dream: Community colleges and the promise of educational opportunity in America, 1900-1985.* New York: Oxford University Press.

Brown, R., & Schubert, J.D. (2000). *Knowledge and power in higher education: A reader.* New York: Teachers College Press.

Buchanan, J.M., & Tullock, G. (1962). *The calculus of consent: Logical foundations of constitutional democracy.* Ann Arbor: The University of Michigan Press.

Cage, M.C. (1991, June 26). Thirty states cut higher-education budgets by an average of 3.9% in fiscal 90-91. *The Chronicle of Higher Education,* pp. A1-2.

Callan, P.M., & Finney, J.E. (2002, July/August). Assessing educational capital: An imperative for policy. *Change, 34*(4), 25-31.

Campus Compact. (2004). *National coalition.* Retrieved November 12, 2004 from www.campuscompact.org.

Campus Compact & American Association of Colleges and Universities. (2006). *Center for liberal education and civic engagement initiatives.* Retrieved March 8, 2006 from http://www.compact.org/clece/detail.php?id=4.

Cantor, N. (2003). *Celebration of diversity: A call for action keynote address.* Retrieved December 2, 2003, from http://www.oc.uiuc.edu/chancellor/cantor11_19.htm.

Cantor, N. (2007). *The Emerging Challenges to Higher Education.* Remarks presented at the Center for the Study of Higher and Postsecondary Education 50th Anniversary Inaugural Event, Ann Arbor, MI.

Carnevale, A.P., & Fry, R.A. (2001). *Economics, demography, and the future of higher education policy.* New York: National Governors' Association.

Chesler, M., Peet., M., & Sevig, T. (2003). Blinded by whiteness: The development of white students' racial awareness. In E. Bonilla-Silva & E. Doane (Eds.), *White out: The continuing significance of racism* (pp. 215-230). New York: Routledge.

Coleman, J. (1992). Some points on choice in education. *Sociology of Education, 65*(4), 260-262.

Coleman, J. (1988). Social capital in the creation of human capital. *American Journal of Sociology, 94*(Issue Supplement), S95-S120.

Currie, J., & Newson, J. (1998). *Universities and globalization: Critical perspectives.* Thousand Oaks, CA: Sage.

Day, J.C., & Newburger, E.C. (2002). *The big payoff: Educational attainment and synthetic estimates of work life.* Washington DC: US Department of Commerce, Economics, and Statistics Administration, US Census Bureau.

Decker, P.T. (1997). *Findings from Education and Economy: An Indicators Report.* Washington, DC: National Center for Education Statistics.

DesJardins, S.L. (2003). The monetary returns to instruction. In D.R. Lewis & J. Hearn (Eds.), *The public research university: Serving the public good in new times.* New York: University Press of America.

Dika, S.L., & Singh, K. (2002). Applications of social capital in educational literature: A critical synthesis. *Review of Educational Research, 72*(1), 31-60.

Foucault, M. (1976). *The archaeology of knowledge.* New York: Harper & Row.

Frank, R.H. (2005, February 17). If firmly believed, the theory that self-interest is the sole motivator appears to be self-fulfilling. *The New York Times,* p. C2.

Friedman, M., & Friedman, R. (1980). *Free to choose: A personal statement.* New York: Harcourt Brace Jovanovich.

Galston, W.A. (2001). Political knowledge, political engagement, and civic education. *Annual Review of Political Science, 4*, 217-234.

Giroux, H.A., & Giroux, S.S. (2004). *Take back higher education: Race, youth, and the crisis of democracy in the post-civil rights era.* New York: Palgrave Macmillan.

Gottlieb, P.D., & Fogarty, M. (2003). Educational attainment and metropolitan growth. *Economic Development Quarterly, 17*(4), 325-336.

Gratz vs. Bollinger, 123 S. Ct. 2411 (2003).

Green, D.O., & Trent, W. (2005). The public good and a racially diverse democracy. In A.J. Kezar, T.C. Chambers, & J. Burkhardt (Eds.), *Higher education for the public good: Emerging voices from a national movement.* San Francisco: Jossey-Bass.

Grutter vs. Bollinger, 123 S. Ct. 2325 (2003).

Guarasci, R., & Cornwell, G.H. (1997). *Democratic education in an age of difference: Redefining citizenship in higher education.* San Francisco: Jossey-Bass.

Gurin, P., Dey, E.L., Hurtado, S., & Gurin, G. (2002). Diversity and higher education: Theory and impact on educational outcomes. *Harvard Educational Review, 72*(3), 330-366.

Hagedorn, L.S., & Tierney, W.G. (2002). Cultural capital and the struggle for educational equity. In W.G. Tierney & L.S. Hagedorn (Eds.), *Increasing access to college: Extending possibilities for all students.* Albany: State University of New York Press.

Hansen, H. (2004, March 15). Granholm, Cherry announce commission on higher education and economic growth. Retrieved April 9, 2004 from www.michigan.gov /printerFriendly/0,1687,7-168--88248--,00.html.

Hardiman, R., & Jackson, B. (1997). Conceptual foundations for social justice courses. In B. Adams, L.A. Bell & P. Griffin (Ed.), *Teaching for diversity and social justice.* New York: Routledge.

Hart, C. (1998). *Doing a literature review: Releasing the social science research imagination.* Thousand Oaks, CA: Sage.

Hurtado, S., & Wathington, H. (2001). Reframing access and opportunity: Problematic state and federal higher education policy in the 1990s. In D.E. Heller (Ed.), *The states and public higher education policy: Affordability, access and accountability.* Baltimore: Johns Hopkins University Press.

Institute for Higher Education Policy (IHEP). (2005). *The investment payoff: A 50-state analysis of the public and private benefits of higher education.* Washington, DC: Author.

Institute for Higher Education Policy (IHEP). (1998). *Reaping the benefits: Defining the public and private value of going to college.* Washington, DC: Author.

Jafee, A.B. (2000). The U.S. patent system in transition: Policy innovation and the innovation process. *Research Policy,* 29(4-5), 5331-5557.

Johnstone, B. (2002). *Discourse analysis.* Malden, MA: Blackwell Publishers.

Jones, D. (2002). *Policy alert: State shortfalls projected throughout the decade.* Washington DC: The National Center for Public Policy and Higher Education.

Kerrigan, S. (2005). College graduates' perspectives on the effect of capstone service-learning courses. In M. Martinez, P.A. Pasque, & N. Bowman (Eds.), *Multidisciplinary perspectives on Higher Education for the Public Good.* Ann Arbor, MI: National Forum on Higher Education for the Public Good.

Kezar, A. (2004). Obtaining integrity? Reviewing and examining the charter between higher education and society. *The Review of Higher Education, 27*(4), 429-460.

Kezar, A.J. (2005). Challenges for higher education in serving the public good. In A.J. Kezar, A.C. Chambers, & J. Burkhardt, (Eds.), *Higher education for the public good:*

Emerging voices from a national movement. San Francisco: Jossey-Bass.

KRC Research and Consulting. (2002, October). *National summit: Higher education's role in serving the public good.* Ann Arbor, MI: Author.

Labaree, D.F. (1997). *How to succeed in school without really learning.* New Haven, CT: Yale University Press.

Lee, J., & Clery, S. (2004). Key trends in higher education. *American Academic, 1*(1), 21-36.

Luft, J., (1970). *Group processes: An introduction to group dynamics* (2nd ed.). Palo Alto, CA: National Press Books.

Markus, G.B., Howard, J.P.F., & King, D.C. (1993). Integrating community service and classroom instruction enhances learning: Results from an experiment. *Educational Evaluation and Policy Analysis, 15*(4), 410-419.

Marwell, G., & Ames, R.E. (1981). Economists free ride, does anyone else?: Experiments on the provision of public goods, IV. *Journal of Public Economics, 15*(3), 16.

Maxwell, K.E., Traxler-Ballew, A., & Dimpoulos, F. (2004). Intergroup dialogue and the Michigan community scholars program: A partnership for meaningful engagement. In J. Galura, P.A. Pasque, D. Schoem, & J. Howard (Eds.), *Engaging the Whole of Service-Learning, Diversity and Learning Communities.* Ann Arbor, MI: OCSL Press.

Mortenson, T. (2006, March 29). Retrieved on April 6, 2006 on http://postsecondaryopportunity.blogspot.com.

Myers, L., Speight, S., Highlen, P., Cox, C., Reynolds, A., Adams, E., & Hanley, T. (1991). Identity development and world view. *Journal of Counseling and Development, 70*, 54-63.

National Forum on Higher Education for the Public Good. (2002). *National Leadership Dialogue Series.* Retrieved March 8, 2006 http://www.thenationalforum.org /projects_nlds.shtml.

Parker, W. (2003). *Teaching democracy: Unity and diversity in public life.* New York: Teacher's College Press.

Pasque, P.A. (2007). Toward strengthening the relationships between higher education and society: A qualitative analysis of the discourse among higher education leaders. (Doctoral dissertation, University of Michigan, Ann Arbor, 2007). *Dissertation Abstracts International.*

Pasque, P.A. & Rex, L.A., (under review). Leaders' perspectives on higher education for the public good.

Pathways to College Network. (2004). *A shared agenda: A leadership challenge to improve college access and success.* Washington, DC: Author.

Perry, J.L., & Katula, M.C. (2001). Does service affect citizenship? *Administration & Society, 33*(3), 330-365.

Pitkin, H.F. & Shumer, S.M. (1982). On participation. *Democracy, 2,* 43-54.

Porter, K. (2002). *The value of a college degree* (Report No. CHE-RR-93-00-0036).Washington, DC: ERIC Clearinghouse on Higher Education. (ERIC Document Reproduction Service No. ED470038).

Powell, W.W., & Clemens, E.S. (1998). *Private action and the public good.* New Haven, CT: Yale University Press.

Public Sector Consultants, Inc. (2003). *Michigan's higher education system: A guide for state policy makers.* Lansing: Author.

Putnam, R.D. (2001). *Bowling alone: The collapse and revival of American community.* New York: Simon & Schuster.

Putnam, R.D. (1995). Bowling alone: America's declining social capital. *Journal of Democracy, 6*(1), 65-77.

Rhoades, G., & Slaughter, S. (2004). Academic capitalism in the new economy: challenges and choices. *American Academic, 1*(1), 37-59.

Rosenstone, S.J. (2003). The idea of a university. In D.R. Lewis & J. Hearn (Eds.), *The public research university: Serving the public good in new times.* New York: University Press of America.

Rowley, L.L., & Hurtado, S. (2003). Non-monetary benefits of undergraduate education. In D.R. L.J. Hearn (Ed.), *The public research university: Serving the public good in new times*. New York: University Press of America.

St. John, E.P., Kline, K.A., & Asker, E.H. (2001). The call for public accountability: Rethinking the linkages to student outcomes. In D.E. Heller (Ed.), *The states and public higher education policy: Affordability, access and accountability*. Baltimore: Johns Hopkins University Press.

Sevig, T., Highlen, P., & Adams, E. (2000). Development and validation of the self-identity inventory (SII): A multicultural identity development instrument. *Cultural Diversity and Ethnicity Minority Psychology, 6*(2), 168-182.

Slaughter S., & Rhoades, G. (1996). The emergence of a competitiveness research and development policy coalition and the commercialization of academic science and technology. *Science, Technology and Human Values, 21*(3), 303-339.

Small Business Association. (2004). *21st century jobs*. Retrieved November 27, 2004 from http://www.sba.gov/.

Sowell, T. (2002). *A conflict of visions: Ideological origins of political struggles*. New York: Basic Books.

Strauss, A., & Corbin, J. (1999). *Basics of qualitative research: Techniques and procedures for developing grounded theory* (3rd ed.). Thousand Oaks, CA: Sage.

Tierney, W.G. (2003). Remembrance of things past: Trust and the obligations of the intellectual. *The Review of Higher Education, 27*(1), 1-15.

Torres, C.A. (1998). *Democracy, education, and multiculturalism*. New York: Rowman & Littlefield.

Wagner, P. (2004). Higher education in an era of globalization: What is at stake? In F.K. Odlin, & P.T. Manicas (Eds.), *Globalization and higher education*. Honolulu: University of Hawai'i Press.

Weiss, A. (1995). Human capital vs. signaling explanations of wages. *The Journal of Economic Perspectives,* 9(4), 133-154.

Weiss, J.D. (2004). *Public schools and economic development: What the research shows.* Cincinnati, OH: KnowledgeWorks Foundation.

Weissbourd, R., & Berry, C. (2004a). *The changing dynamics of urban America.* Chicago: CEOs for Cities an Alliance for a New Urban Agenda.

Weissbourd, R., & Berry, C. (2004b). *Grads and fads: The dynamics of human capital location.* Washington, DC: Brookings Institute Press.

W.K. Kellogg Foundation. (2002). Leadership for civil society: A first in a series of dialogues. Battle Creek: Author.

CHAPTER 3

STUDENTS' VOICES AND GRADUATE SCHOOL CHOICES: THE ROLE OF FINANCES IN THE LIVES OF LOW-INCOME, HIGH-ACHIEVING STUDENTS OF COLOR

Edward P. St. John

Questions related to financial access to undergraduate and graduate education for high-achieving students of color is a topic of national interest (Bowen & Bok, 1998; St. John, 2003). With the changes now underway in affirmative action, the issue of financial barriers to graduate education merit consideration as part of the discourse about graduate admissions and financial support of graduate students. If undergraduate students from low-income families face financial difficulties paying for college and accrue debt in process, they could view the prospect of paying for graduate school immediately after college as cost prohibitive. On the other hand, if undergraduate students know they will have financial support for graduate study, then they should be more likely to plan for this option.

The Gates Millennium Scholars (GMS) Program was designed to create new pathways through college and, for students in selected fields, through graduate school for talented low-income students from diverse racial/ethnic backgrounds. Early research on the GMS program indicates that it has increased opportunities to enroll and persist in

85

Copyright ©2007 AMS Press, Inc. All rights reserved.

selective colleges (Allen, Bonous-Hammarth, & Suh, 2004; Lee & Cleary, 2004; St. John & Chung, 2004a). When undergraduates receiving GMS awards graduate from college, they also have funding available for graduate school if they choose to enroll in one of the high demand fields supported by the program. In the near future, the number of graduate students with GMS awards should climb. The small size of the initial graduate student sample (Lodato Nichols, Zimowski, Lodato, & Ghadialy, 2004) limited our capacity to examine the impact of GMS on graduate student choices using the initial survey data. However, it was possible to provide some initial insights into the role of finances in the choices made by graduate students by examining interviews. Yet the impact of GMS on graduate education will probably be more substantial in the future, given the large number of current and future GMS recipients who will be making decisions about graduate school, with an anticipated 20 cohorts of students receiving awards. Therefore it is important to consider the logical basis for assessing the impact of GMS on decisions about graduate education.

The problem addressed in this chapter is that the topic of equal opportunity in graduate education is under theorized, especially with respect to the role of financial aid. One potential area of theory that could apply to this problem is economic theory on human capital (Becker, 1964). There is research evidence that students respond to financial aid, including loans, in their decisions to enroll in graduate school (Andrieu & St. John, 1993; Wieler, 1994). While this line of inquiry captures the financial aspects of the problem, it also includes an understanding of the diversity questions that are so important in studies of educational attainment among minority students (Allen et al., 2004). This chapter uses the student-choice construct (St. John, Asker, & Hu, 2001) as a basis for speculating about the potential role of financial aid in increasing educational opportunity, then uses focus group interviews with students receiving aid through

GMS to determine if the voices add to the understanding of the role of finances in creating and expanding educational opportunity.

Background

While the educational choices of undergraduate and high school students have been extensively studied, especially with respect to the role of finances (Heller, 1997; St. John et al., 2001), this topic has not been as extensively studied for graduate students. When considering the role of finances in the choices about graduate school by high achieving students of color, it is just as important to consider the role of background, as it is for their high school and college peers. This study adapts the student-choice construct to provide a conceptual lens for examining the choices students make about colleges.

The student-choice construct (St. John, Asker & Hu, 2001) argues that students make their educational choices in situated contexts of the lived experiences. This approach involves examining how student background, exposure to work, and experience of education programs (i.e., curriculum and services) and policies (i.e., student aid) influence the formation of aspirations and choices over time, from the perspective of graduate students. This construct identifies a sequence of potential choices, from decisions about K-12 school through graduate education, differing from a more commonly known model of college choice (e.g., Hossler, Schmidt & Vesper, 1999) that focuses only on college en-rollment.

The logic of the student-choice construct has been used to retheorize a number of complicated problems related to student outcomes. While college choice models for prices, student aid, and net prices, these intermediate variables are influenced by policy on public finance. The balanced access model evolved from the student-choice construct (St. John, 2003), providing a basis for studying the effects of school reforms and public finance polices on access to higher education (St. John, 2006). The student-choice construct also provided a logical basis for thinking through these linkages. The sequential logic of this construct has also been used in research that examines the nexus between college choices and persistence (Paulsen & St. John, 1997, 2002; St. John, Paulsen, & Starkey, 1996), a line of inquiry that has helped illuminate the role of habitus in continuity of choice patterns (Berger, 2000).

The student-choice construct also provides a logical basis to begin the process of retheorizing the role of finances in the college choice process. As background, I examine the features of the GMS program that relate to educational choices about graduate education, then consider how this type exploratory inquiry is informed by prior research using the student-choice construct.

Features of the GMS Program

The GMS program was initiated in 2000 with a one billion dollar commitment from the Bill & Melinda Gates Foundation to provide new opportunities for a generation of low-income minority students to pioneer new pathways in American society. In 2000, GMS funded about 1,000 freshmen, a larger number of continuing undergraduate students, and a smaller number of graduate students (about 200). In 2001, an additional 1,000 freshman received awards and additional 1,000 students will receive awards each year for the next 18 years. The focus group interviews included students in the 2000 and 2001 cohorts and included graduate students as well as undergraduates.

In addition to providing student aid for meritorious, low-income minority undergraduates, GMS provides financial incentives for these undergraduates to go on for advanced study in fields in which they are underrepresented. A key feature of the program includes a commitment to support GMS students through graduate education if they choose one of four priority fields: education, engineering, library and information science, and science, including computer science. Rather than starting by funding freshmen, GMS filled the entire pipeline in the first year of the program, funding first-year students, continuing undergraduates, and graduate students in the designated fields.

Financial aid is only part of the GMS story. The program also provides leadership programs that informed students about tactics for completing undergraduate educations, introduced future opportunities for leadership in education and other fields, and gave them opportunities for interaction with each other. Many GMS students faced major transitions after receiving their awards. They no longer found it necessary to work extensive hours to fund their education and they had the opportunity to engage in their learning environments in new ways (St. John, 2006). Students entering GMS as first-time undergraduates entered college with new and expansive opportunities to learn, to engage in student and civic activities, and to socialize. They had the opportunity to build cultural capital—the resources for learning—that would not have been possible without this funding.

The Gates Foundation also funded both an evaluation study that generated extensive focus group interviews and a longitudinal tracking study that will follow GMS recipients and non-funded applicants through their college years and beyond. Initial comparisons of freshman students in the 2000 and 2001 cohorts reveal that GMS students are much more engaged in college than their peers who did not receive funding (Allen et al., 2004; Hurtado, Nelson Laird & Perorazio, 2004; Sedlacek & Sheu, 2004). The analyses of the focus group conversations reveal how GMS enabled recipients to become more involved and gives evidence of the impact of this involvement.

Finding Perspective for this Inquiry
The student-choice construct assumes that students make educational choices in the situation contexts of their lived lives; life circumstances influence aspirations for and

choices about education; prior educational choices shape and influence current choices; and public and institutional policies, including financial policies, influence educational outcomes through a sequence of choices. The construct posits a sequence of choices and policy linkages and there is growing empirical evidence that education and public policies can influence these outcomes:

- Preparation for college is influenced by family background, the schools attended, the family stability (employment and transience), and educational programs and systems. Education reforms influence educational programs and systems (Musoba, 2004; St. John, 2006), but does not have a direct linkage to family contexts and parental employment.
- Formation of postsecondary educational aspirations is based on early educational experiences, family contexts, and exposure to work and educational environments. Comprehensive postsecondary encouragement programs (provide academic support, encourage parents, and make commitments to provide financial support) influence aspirations, preparation, and college choices (Musoba, 2004; St. John & Hu, 2006; St. John, Musoba, Simmons, Chung, Schmidt, & Peng, 2004).
- Choices to enroll in college are influenced by family, preparation, aspirations, and finances. Controlling for other factors, financial aid has a substantial influence on enrollment, especially by low-income students (Heller, 1997; St. John, 2003).
- College choices, including decisions to enroll in four year colleges, are influenced by these predecessor events as well as financial aid. State education policies are associated with the flow of students between public and private colleges, but not enrollment rates (St. John, 2006). There is substantial prior evidence that financial aid improved opportunity to

enroll in four-year and private colleges, a general finding supported by research on GMS (St. John & Chung, 2004a).

- Major choices are influenced by prior experiences, aspirations, and choices. There is recent evidence that debt burden negatively influences decisions by high achieving minority students to enter science and math majors (St. John & Chung, 2004b).

- Persistence decisions are also influenced by current and prior educational experiences, but can be influenced by student financial aid, especially for low-income students (St. John & Chung, 2004a). In addition, there is substantial evidence that the financial considerations in the college choice process have a sustained influence on decisions about continuous enrollment (Paulsen & St. John, 2002; St. John, Paulsen & Carter, 2005; St. John, Paulsen & Starkey, 199).

Thus the role of finances, encouragement, and education polices are relatively well established in quantitative research on college preparation, enrollment, and persistence for undergraduate opportunities for low-income students. In the theorizing about the student-choice construct, it has been argued that there is a similar sequence of situated choices about graduate education (St. John, Asker & Hu, 2001), but this line of inquiry has not been developed. This inquiry takes an initial step toward the illuminations of such a sequence by examining focus group interviews with undergraduate and graduate students in the GMS program.

If there is evidence that GMS influences students' decisions about graduate education and expanding opportunity, then it is important to untangle the extent to which this effect is attributable to the additional financial resources or to the additional leadership opportunities offered by the GMS program. By using the student-choice construct as a guide, it was possible to illuminate some of the ways GMS enables more students to pioneer new pathways. As the nation retreated from the commitment to equalizing opportunity, the Gates Foundation provided the opportunity for a generation of minority students to explore new educational pathways.   This study was designed to provide a window on those diverse pathways.

Research Approach

The focus group transcripts provided a window on the lived experiences of GMS students.   From reviewing the transcripts it became abundantly apparent that the topics discussed in the focus groups could help to contextualize the analyses of the impact of GMS presented in subsequent chapters. Below I provide an overview of the methods used for the focus groups and the interpretative approach used in this analysis.

The Focus Groups
McKenzie Group conducted a comprehensive evaluation of the GMS program.   They conducted surveys and interviews with students and collected data from other diverse sources.   Their report provided information for the Gates Foundation on the operations of the program. It also provided an overview of the methods used in the focus groups and summarized the findings from the focus groups, but did not provide comments from the transcripts. Therefore it seemed appropriate to examine these transcripts more closely.
Focus groups of GMS recipients were conducted in Chantilly (VA), Los Angeles (CA), San Jose (CA), and Washington (DC). Students from the 2000 and 2001 recipient cohorts were interviewed, including freshmen, continuing undergraduates, and graduate students.   Students were invited from traditional public and private colleges as well as minority serving colleges (e.g., historically black colleges and universities [HBCUs], tribal/tribally controlled

colleges). A total of 113 students attended the four focus group meetings. Multiethnic groups and single group focus sessions were conducted.

The focus group interviewers asked similar questions about the ways students heard about the program, their college experiences, and about the GMS leadership training. While not all students responded to all of the questions, a similar set of questions was asked in each of the sessions. The focus group sessions were recorded and transcribed. A small number of the students in each of the focus group sessions were already in graduate school, or were considering graduate education

Conversations in focus groups often functioned as a catalyst for exploring topics in depth, a phenomenon that was evident in these transcripts. Indeed, students in the focus groups explored themes that emerged in the training sessions, as well as responded to points other students raised. Thus, in addition to providing a consistent set of questions and responses, the transcripts provided insight into the conversations among GMS recipients about issues of common interest.

Interpretive Approach

Higher education researchers use an array of interpretive methods in qualitative research. Creswell (1998) suggests that researchers use grounded theory, an approach that involves seeing what themes emerge. In a prima facie sense, I used this approach. Indeed, this chapter explores a set of issues that differ fundamentally from the questions I had when I began to review the transcripts. Initially I had hoped to learn more about the academic preparation and college applications. However, what emerged were images of the situated contexts in which students made their educational choices. The focus group leaders had not explored college choice or academic preparation, so I misunderstood their intent when I started reviewing the transcripts. However, the transcripts proved to be of great value.

My concern about grounded theory is that I realize that all of us interpret through the logical frames we hold (St. John & Elliott, 1994). While we should strive for neutrality in both quantitative and qualitative analyses, we also interpret through understandings we bring to our research. Our hypotheses, hunches, and questions are informed by our experience, just as students' educational choices are informed by, or situated in, their prior experiences.

Thus, my interpretations of the focus group interviews are best understood in terms of the theoretical constructs I have tried to develop over time. I am interested in student choice and have developed an alternative way of viewing this phenomenon. When I reviewed the transcripts, themes related to the situated contexts of students' lives emerged, possibly because of my commitments to building an understanding of the ways individuals make choices (e.g., St. John & Ridenour, 2001, 2002) and my commitment to social justice (St. John, 2003). Thus, while grounded theory is an aspect of the process I used, my interpretive perspective explains the patterns that were visible to me.

Focus on Graduate Education

While the focus of this analysis of the focus group interviews is on graduate education, the analysis starts with an overview of the entire focus group population. This was an important step because an aim of the program when it was created was to fill the education pipeline of scholars, giving awards to first-time undergraduates who received the awards before or during their freshman year, continuing undergraduates who received awards while they were in college, and students who applied for the program as graduate students. A previous paper focused on how student learned about the GMS program (St. John, 2006). This chapter explicitly examines the ways students' spoke of their graduate education choices. It focuses on the voices of graduate students, but also considers undergraduate students' speculations about graduate school.

Graduate Education Choices

Graduate students, like undergraduates, make choices within a stream of life events. The prior chapters illustrate the pervasive role of situated contexts on educational choices for undergraduates. Therefore, it is reasonable that prior choices will influence current and future choices for graduate students. For students who are graduating from college and making decisions about whether to go on to graduate school, their prior educational choices and experience are likely to influence their choices. So it is logical to expect that undergraduates in the 2000 and 2001 cohorts will make choices within the streams of their life experiences, in their own situated life circumstances. It is also apparent that students with GMS awards will have had different experiences in college than their peers who did not receive awards because they will have had more time for engaging in campus activities (Hurtado et al., 2004). It is reasonable to expect that these experiences will influence their eventual choices about graduate education. Based on what has been learned about undergraduates, it is possible to speculate, or hypothesize, about the ways GMS awards could influence the graduate choice sequence outlined below.

As part of the discussion of the choice sequence below, a review of the focus group interviews is integrated with a conceptualization of the choice sequence for graduate students. While the conceptualization process began before I reviewed the transcripts from the focus group, after reviewing these transcripts it became clear that there was qualitative information related to the choice sequence for graduate students. In the discussion of each part of the choice sequence for graduate students, I suggest a conceptual approach from an understanding of the literature, then integrate information gleaned from the review of the focus group transcripts.

Aspiring to Attend Graduate School

Being a GMS recipient will influence more students to aspire to attend graduate school (hypothesis 1). Knowing they will have financial support for graduate school should influence at least some GMS recipients to raise their aspirations from completing college to completing graduate school. Logically, it would be appropriate to examine the influence of GMS, student background, college type, major, achievement in college, and engagement in academic and cultural activities in college on whether students aspire to go on to graduate school. It should be possible to complete this type of analyses with existing databases on undergraduates. These analyses would provide information about whether GMS influenced the predisposition to attend graduate school.

The review of focus group transcripts confirms that GMS expands aspirations for graduate education. Entering college knowing that they would have funding for graduate education, albeit in only selected fields, provided the opportunity to dream, to expand visions of the possible. One of the undergraduates in the focus groups put it this way:

> *It's humbling, in a way. It's intimidating, but it really is—wow, I can do that, too, because I'm one of them, where I'm supposed to be. And in that sense, that transition from a master's to a doctorate, I now know a couple of names to call, like depending on the university.*

Another student's comments echoed this impact of aspirations: "*This is one of the hugest ways the GMS Program has impacted education, in that after finishing my undergrad, having felt like I finally learned how to do really well in college, I can move directly into graduate school instead of, you know, worrying about finances.*"

These comments were a few of the many that illuminated the increased sense of the hope resulting from GMS support. It is entirely possible that GMS recipients would have higher aspirations as a result of receiving this long-term support. However, it is just as likely that the funding will influence subsequent choices.

Enrolling in Graduate School

The promise of GMS awards for graduate school will increase the chances that undergraduate GMS recipients will attend graduate school. With data from the planned follow-up study of the 2000 continuing students—and eventually with follow-up studies of the two freshman cohorts—it should be possible to examine whether the GMS awards influenced the decision to enroll in graduate school after college. GMS provides financial support for graduate education in selected fields, but not in the high demand fields of law, medicine, and business. The clear intent is to provide opportunities in fields in which people of color are underrepresented. However, high-earning professional fields also provide financial incentives for student choice, so the monetary effects of GMS on the decision to enroll would be mitigated somewhat by the higher earnings of some of these other fields.

To untangle the impact of GMS on whether students enroll, it would be necessary to consider the effects of GMS, student background, college type, major, achievement in college, and engagement in academic and cultural activities, cumulative debt, and financial and academic reasons for choosing a graduate school. It is also possible to examine the effects of accumulated debt on whether students enroll.

The transcripts revealed that some currently enrolled students had extended their education because of the support. There were comments from education graduate students that the GMS Program made it possible for them to get into teaching more quickly, and possibly made it possible to enter the field at all. Preparing to become a teacher requires that students spend time in classrooms, which means they have less time to work. One credential student commented:

Well, I'm student teaching right now, and so that's like, you know, five days a week, all day. And, you know, I don't get a chance to work. But with Gates Millennium I don't have to worry as much about that, and plus I can still pay my rent, you know, and other expenses. So it's helping me tremendously outside of academia.

Another education graduate student commented:

I was just going to take a semester off [after finishing the masters program] *but they sent me a check. So I applied to sign up for a whole bunch more classes to finish up my credential just because I had all this money in my pocket.*

If the GMS Program is having this sort of early impact on the education choices of a small number of students, we should expect even more substantial effects over time. However, for students making the transition between undergraduate school and graduate school, the decisions to seek GMS funding were intertwined with their decisions about field of study.

The Choice of Graduate Field

The prospect of receiving GMS awards increases the number of undergraduate GMS recipients who select graduate programs in science/math, engineering, education, and library/information sciences (hypothesis 3). In addition to encouraging GMS awardees to aspire to go to graduate school, it provides support for graduate education only if students enroll in specific fields. Therefore, when data is available on the 2000 cohort, it is important to examine the impact of GMS on the types of graduate programs students chose. This analysis would use a model similar to the major choice analysis conducted using GMS surveys (St. John & Chung, 2004b). It would be appropriate to examine the effects of GMS, student background, college type, major, academic achievement, engagement, cumulative debt, and financial and academic reasons for choosing a graduate school. It could be limited to students who entered graduate school or include all students in the graduate populations, if enrollment in graduate school in other fields was included as an outcome variable in the multinomial model.

The focus group transcripts provided insight into the ways GMS provided incentives to rethink plans for graduate education, especially in fields like education. The GMS Program constrains the fields for graduate study. For students interested in those areas or who were uncertain about fields, this support provided a clear and obvious incentive. However, students who were not as interested in these fields raised questions about the constraints. One of the students expressed this tension as follows:

> *There are only six different fields that are going to be paid for. And unless I say, oh, I'm going to get my teaching degree, they're not going to pay for graduate school, which irks me because they're saying, to everyone, you have to be a leader. And a filmmaker like has ultimate message and it gets to everyone, whoever sees it. And like I just feel like that it's kind of—I think they're being a little narrow about it.*

There were many comments expressing concern about the restrictions on graduate fields. For example:

> *You can't even do medicine, med school. So that really upsets me because, I mean, if we're going to be the leaders of the future, we have to be able to make decisions in politics. We have to be able to be good doctors. But the scholarship is restricted—like to you can't be in the politics side. You can't be a lawmaker. You can't have like international things.*

Cleary the prospect of future funding was weighing on the minds of undergraduate students. The quote from education students (above) illustrated that for students who are into the selected fields, the funding expanded opportunity. However, as the comments by the two students above illustrate, students whose interests had not settled on related majors, the restrictions on graduate field gave them food for thought.

The process of making choices about fields and responding to the incentives in GMS is highly compatible with the ways cultural capital is formed in middle-income families. Parents encourage their children to choose graduate education in fields that are a family priority and then scrape together funding to help out. This process of cultural reproduction is especially important in middle-class fields—such as education and library science—that do not necessary pay enough to pay off large sums of debt (see Chapter 9). Therefore GMS functions as a targeted form of cultural capital acquisition, much as social class reproduces cultural capital within middle-class families. However, in this case the GMS Program provides the resources and encouragement for the accrual of cultural capital for advanced learning.

Choice of Graduate Institution

Receiving GMS awards will enable more students to attend graduate schools at private universities. While there is a long tradition of research on college choice, research on the type of institutions graduate students choose to attend has been limited. Given the great disparity in costs of attending graduate programs at public and private universities, a study that examined this choice outcome could have implications for public policy. It might also be of interest to the Gates Foundation and universities with graduate programs, given the renewed interest in expanding graduate education in some states.

It is logical to view the choice of graduate school as a function of GMS, student background, college type, major, achievement in college, engagement in academic and cultural activities, cumulative debt, and financial and academic reasons. There are at least two approaches to the analysis. One would have a dichotomous outcome, comparing the choice of private colleges to public colleges for students who enrolled. The other would use a multinomial model to compare enrollment in public colleges and enrollment in private colleges to not enrolling in graduate school.

From the focus group interviews it was apparent that undergraduates were aware that their possible choices of institutions had been expanded because of GMS. One student explained:

> *And Stanford is like $40,000. That's like bare minimum, like living on nothing. And minimum a doctoral program in my field is, four years, maybe. So that's like 40 times four, which a little too much for me to be thinking on my own. So, and I guess being a Gates Scholar, it really does leave you more open, like I could still think about doctoral programs if I could get an assistantship.*

While there were not many examples of this type of institution-specific thinking evident in the focus group interviews, the comments illustrate how the GMS Program could influence educational choices. Through exposure at the GMS meetings or even through paying attention to options mentioned by professors in courses, many students will learn they can gain access to elite programs because the resources are committed through GMS.

Persistence in Graduate School

Receiving a GMS award in graduate school will improve persistence in graduate school and degree attainment. When the follow-up data is available, it should be possible to conduct a comprehensive analysis of persistence by graduate students. Such a study could examine the impact of background, achievement, college choice variables, amount of debt and scholarships, undergraduate major, program area, level of aspiration (masters vs. doctorate), reasons for choosing graduate school, engagement in graduate school, and achievement in graduate school on continuous enrollment. It will be necessary to wait for such a study because of the limited size of the current sample. Hopefully the follow-up studies will have a sufficient number of students to conduct such a comprehensive analysis. This type of analysis of persistence by minority graduate students could have a great deal of informative value for universities and policymakers interested in graduate education.

There was evidence from the focus group interviews that GMS helped graduate students stick with it. The following was one of many examples: *"For me, it made a big difference knowing I was going to get the finance because . . . I had just finished the credential and I just finished my masters, and knowing that GMS would even pay for the doctoral program encouraged me, you know, to go and apply. And actually, the conference was very empowering. . ."*

Many people make education choices incrementally; as they gain experience and high initial successes, they begin to dream. This is how new pathways are created. Rather than reproducing what is possible, GMS appears to be helping students discover new possibility and to create new pathways.

Retheorizing Graduate Student Choices

This review of focus group interviews has illustrated that a pipeline of high achieving, low-income students has entered college and will eventually be facing choices about graduate school. GMS students are not limited to choosing the four preferred fields, but their will only receive financial support for graduate education if they go on in one of those fields. Based on the review of the ways graduate students spoke of graduate school, the following hypotheses were generated:

- Being a GMS recipient will influence more students to aspire to attend graduate school (hypothesis 1).
- The promise of GMS awards for graduate school will increase the chances that undergraduate GMS recipients will attend graduate school (hypothesis 2).
- The prospect of receiving GMS awards increases the number of undergraduate GMS recipients who select graduate programs in science/math, engineering, education, and library/information sciences (hypothesis 3).
- Receiving GMS awards will enable more students to attend graduate schools at private universities (hypothesis 4).
- Receiving a GMS award in graduate school will improve persistence in graduate school and degree attainment (hypothesis 5).

The focus group interviews provided compelling evidence related to each of these hypotheses. In their own voices students described how their choices in these areas were influence by receiving GMS awards. The National Organization on Research at the University of Chicago (NORC) follow-up surveys of GMS now provide data on GMS students and comparisons students that can be used to examine these outcomes using quantitative data. In addition, given the aims of the program and initial evidence of success, there is reason to posit an additional hypothesis: As students gain success with attainment of graduate degrees in their fields, many will go on and have successful careers, becoming leaders in their communities and their professional fields. As the GMS program continues, it will be important to consider these long term effects as well.

This study of graduate students in GMS raises questions about the role of student financial assistance for graduate students. The early evidence from GMS is that choices about graduate study are influenced by the availability of funding. This illuminates a challenge for faculty in graduate programs who are concerned about attracting high achieving, low-income students of color into their graduate programs. Constructing packages that ensure financial support is an important step, as is communicating this aid availability to prospective students. Since eligibility for most federal and state student grants programs ceases before students enter graduate school, it is critical that faculty consider financial support as part of the graduate admissions process.

Notes

[1] Prepared for the "Making Access Real: Building capacity in higher education," American Educational Research Association, Montreal, CN, April 2005. The focus groups interviews examined in this paper were conducted by McKenzie and Associates (now part of American Institutes of Research) and funded by the Bill & Melinda Gates Foundation. The support provided to the Bill & Melinda Gates Foundation for this research in gratefully acknowledged. The interpretations presented in this paper are the author's and do not reflect policies or positions of the foundation.

References

Allen, W.R., Bonous-Hammarth, M., & Suh, S.A. (2004). Who goes to college? High school context, academic preparation, the college choice process, and college attendance. In E.P. St. John, *Students: Studies of the Gates Millennium Scholars Program* (pp. 71-114). New York: AMS Press, Inc.

Andrieu, S.C., & St. John, E.P. (1993). The influence of prices on graduate student persistence. *Research in Higher Education, 34*(4), 325-359.

Becker, G.S. (1964). *Human capital: A theoretical and empirical analysis with special reference to education.* New York: Columbia University Press.

Berger, J.B. (2000). Optimizing capital, social reproduction, and undergraduate persistence: A sociological perspective. In J.M. Braxton (Ed.), *Reworking the student departure puzzle* (pp. 95-124). Nashville, TN: Vanderbilt University Press.

Bowen, W.G., & Bok, D. (1998). *The shape of the river: Long-term consequences of considering race in college and university admissions.* Princeton, NJ: Princeton University Press.

Creswell, J. (1998). *Qualitative Inquiry and Research Design; Choosing Among Five Traditions.* Thousand Oaks, CA: Sage Publications.

Heller, D.E. (1997). Student price response in higher education: An update to Leslie and Brinkman. *The Journal of Higher Education, 68*(6), 624-659.

Hossler, D., Schmit, J., & Vesper, N. (1999). *Going to college: How social, economic, and educational factors influence the decisions students make.* Baltimore: Johns Hopkins University Press.

Hurtado, S., Nelson Laird, T.F., & Perorarzio, T.E. (2004). The transition to college for low-income students: The impact of the GMS Program. In E.P. St. John (Ed.), *Readings on equal education: Vol. 20. Improving access and college success for diverse students: Studies of the Gates Millennium Scholars Program* (pp. 155-182). New York: AMS Press, Inc.

Lee, J.B., & Clery, S.B. (2004). How do college choice and persistence for GMS recipients compare to minority students who received Pell? In E.P. St. John (Ed.), *Readings on equal education: Vol. 20. Improving access and college success for diverse students: Studies of the Gates Millennium Scholars Program* (pp. 201-218). New York: AMS Press, Inc.

Lodato Nichols, B.L., Zimowski, M., Lodato, R.M., & Ghadialy, R. (2004). The survey of diverse students. In E.P. St. John (Ed.), *Readings on equal education: Vol. 20. Improving access and college success for diverse students: Studies of the Gates Millennium Scholars Program* (pp. 23-44). New York: AMS Press, Inc.

Musoba, G.D. (2004). Postsecondary encouragement for diverse students: A reexamination of the Twenty-first Century Scholars Program. In E.P. St. John (Ed.), *Readings on equal education: Vol. 19. Public policy and college access: Investigating the federal and state roles in equalizing postsecondary opportunity* (pp. 153-180). New York: AMS Press, Inc.

Paulsen, M.B., & St. John, E.P. (2002). Social class and college costs: Examining the financial nexus between college choice and persistence. *The Journal of Higher Education, 73*(3), 189-236.

St. John, E.P. (2006). *Education and the public interest: School reform, public finance, and access to higher education.* Netherlands: Springer.

St. John, E.P. (2003). *Refinancing the college dream: Access, equal opportunity, and justice for taxpayers.* Baltimore: Johns Hopkins University Press.

St. John, E.P., Asker, E.H., & Hu, S. (2001). College choice and student persistence behavior: The role of financial policies. In M.B. Paulsen & J.C. Smart (Eds.) *The finance of higher education: Theory, research, policy & practice* (pp. 419-436). New York: Agathon Press.

St. John, E.P., & Chung, C.G. (2004a). The Impact of GMS on financial access: Analyses of the 2000 cohort. In E.P. St. John (Ed.), *Readings on equal education: Vol. 20. Improving access and college success for diverse students:*

Studies of the Gates Millennium Scholars Program (pp. 115-153). New York: AMS Press, Inc.

St. John, E.P., & Chung, C.G. (2004b). Student aid and major choice: A study of high-achieving students of color. In E.P. St. John (Ed.), *Readings on equal education: Vol. 20. Improving access and college success for diverse students: Studies of the Gates Millennium Scholars Program* (pp. 217-248). New York: AMS Press, Inc.

St. John, E.P., & Elliot, R.J. (1994). Reframing policy research. In J.C. Smart (Ed.), *Higher Education: Handbook of theory and research.* New York: Agathon.

St. John, E.P., & Hu, S. (2006). The impact of guarantees of financial aid on college enrollment: An evaluation of the Washington State Achievers Program. In E.P. St. John (Ed.), *Readings on equal education: Vol. 21. Public policy and equal educational opportunity: School reforms, postsecondary encouragement, and state policies on postsecondary education* (pp. 211-256). New York: AMS Press, Inc.

St. John, E.P., Musoba, G.D., Simmons, A.B., Chung, C.G., Schmit, J., & Peng, C.J. (2004). Meeting the access challenge: An examination of Indiana's Twenty-first Century Scholars Program. *Research in Higher Education, 45*(8), 829-873.

St. John, E.P., Paulsen, M.B., & Carter, D.F. (2005). Diversity, college costs, and postsecondary opportunity: An examination of the college choice-persistence nexus for African Americans and Whites. *The Journal of Higher Education, 76*(5), 545-569.

St. John, E.P., Paulsen, M.B., &. Starkey, J.B. (1996). The nexus between college choice and persistence. *Research in Higher Education, 37*(2), 175-220.

St. John, E.P., & Ridenour, C.S. (2002). School leadership in a market setting: The influence of private scholarships on education leadership in urban schools. *Leadership and Policy in Schools, 1*(4), 317-344.

St. John, E.P., & Ridenour, C.S. (2001). School leadership in a market setting: The influence of private scholarships on educational leadership in urban schools. *Policy Research Report,* No. 01-08. Bloomington, IN: Indiana Education Policy Center.

Sedlacek, W.E., & Sheu, H.B. (2004). Correlates of leadership activities of Gates Millennium Scholars. In E.P. St. John (Ed.), *Readings on equal education: Vol. 20. Improving access and college success for diverse students: Studies of the Gates Millennium Scholars Program* (pp. 249-264). New York: AMS Press, Inc.

Weiler, W.C. (1994). Expectations, undergraduate debt and the decision to attend graduate school: a simultaneous model of student choice. *Economics of Education Review, 13,* 29-41.

Part II

Building Understanding

CHAPTER 4

IMPROVING EDUCATIONAL OPPORTUNITIES FOR COLLEGE STUDENTS WHO WORK

Laura W. Perna, Michelle Asha Cooper, and Chunyan Li

College students who cannot pay the price of attendance from some combination of personal financial resources and grants typically have three options: do not attend college, borrow money using public and private loans, and/or work. Data show that increasing shares of students are utilizing both loans and work to pay for college-related expenses (Baum, 2005). Much attention has focused on growth in borrowing (e.g., Baum, 2005; Perna, 2001), as well as potential consequences of borrowing for various aspects of students' educational experiences including persistence and degree completion (DesJardins, Ahlburg, & McCall, 2002; St. John, 2003) and graduate school enrollment (Ehrenberg, 1991; Fox, 1992; Choy & Carroll, 2000; Perna, 2004; Weiler, 1991).

Less attention has focused on the consequences of working, even though most students work some number of hours while they are enrolled, regardless of the type of institution they attend (Choy & Berker, 2003; King & Bannon, 2002; McMillion, 2005; National Postsecondary Student Aid Study [NPSAS]:04). The percentage of full-time college students who are employed has increased steadily over the past three decades, rising from 36 percent in 1973 to 48 percent in 2003 (Fox, Connolly & Snyder as cited

109

Copyright ©2007 AMS Press, Inc. All rights reserved.

in Baum, 2005). The share of full-time college students who work at least 20 hours each week has also been growing, rising from 17 percent in 1973 to 30 percent in 2003 (Fox et al. as cited in Baum, 2005).

College students may realize several benefits from employment, including earning the financial resources that are necessary to pay college-related expenses and/or the costs of life-style choices, and acquiring career-related knowledge and experiences.   However, because time is limited, spending time working necessarily reduces the amount of time available for educational activities (Baum, 2005; Pascarella & Terenzini, 2005; Stinebrickner & Stinebrickner, 2004). Therefore, employment likely reduces the quality of educational experiences for at least some portion of students.

Purpose of the Chapter

The prevalence of working and the restrictions that working places on students' time for educational activities raises the following question for campus officials: What can institutions do to improve the educational experiences of students who work? To address this overarching question, the paper first examines the following subquestions: What is the nature of student employment? Why do students work? What are the consequences of working for students' educational experiences?

The chapter concludes by suggesting four strategies that institutions may adopt to promote the educational success of undergraduates who work. In short, institutions should: (1) determine the characteristics and consequences of employment for students at their own institution; (2) reduce students' financial need to work by controlling the costs of attendance, maximizing the availability of need-based grants, and encouraging students to borrow responsibly; (3) improve the quality of students' employment experiences by expanding on-campus employment opportunities and supporting increases in Federal Work-study funding; and (4) adapt the delivery of education to better meet the needs of working students.

This paper addresses the research questions through a review of prior research and descriptive analyses of data from the (NPSAS:04). Sponsored by the U.S. Department of Education, the NPSAS is a cross-sectional survey that describes the ways that students and their families pay the price of attending college. When appropriate weights are applied, the data are representative of undergraduates attending four-year, two-year, and less-than-two year colleges and universities nationwide. The analyses of the NPSAS:04 data describe the prevalence of employment among undergraduates, the characteristics of undergraduates who work, and the relationship between working and various educational outcomes. Although alternative explanations for the observed relationships are not controlled, the data provide insights into the phenomenon of college students who work.

What Is the Nature of Student Employment?

Before determining how to respond, campus officials must first understand the characteristics of student employment. This section uses data from NPSAS:04 to describe the prevalence of student employment, the demographic characteristics of working students, and the type of employment in which students engage.

Prevalence of Student Employment
    The majority of undergraduates now work while enrolled. Table 1 shows that, in 2003-04, about 75 percent of dependent undergraduates and 80 percent of independent under-graduates worked while attending college. Working dependent undergraduates averaged 24 hours of work per week while enrolled, while working independent undergraduates averaged 34.5 hours per week (NPSAS:04).

Table 1. Percentage of undergraduates who worked, and average number of hours worked, by dependency status and institutional type: 2003-04

Dependency status	Total	Public 4-year	Private 4-year	Public 2-year	Private for-profit
Percentage who worked while enrolled					
Dependent	75.2	72.7	71.2	81.5	67.7
Independent	80.0	80.4	84.0	79.2	79.6
Average number of hours worked*					
Dependent	24.1	22.3	20.0	27.7	27.2
Independent	34.5	32.0	35.4	34.9	36.5

Notes: Analyses are weighted by WTA00 study weight
*Average hours worked does not include students who worked no hours
Source: Analyses of NPSAS: 2004 Undergraduate Students.

The frequency and amount of working do not vary by the type of institution attended among independent under-graduates but do vary among dependent undergraduates. Working is relatively more common among dependent undergraduates at public two-year institutions, where 81.5

percent of 2003-04 dependent undergraduates worked while enrolled, and relatively less common at public four-year institutions, private four-year institutions, and private for-profit institutions, where 73 percent, 71 percent, and 68 percent, respectively, of dependent undergraduates worked while enrolled (Table 1). Working dependent under-graduates who attended public two-year colleges and private for-profit colleges averaged a higher number of hours of employment per week (28 hours and 27 hours, respectively) than their counterparts who attended public four-year institutions (22 hours) and private four-year institutions (20 hours, NPSAS:04).

Demographic Profile of Students Who Work
Although the differences are generally not substantial, the likelihood of working while enrolled appears to vary based on students' race/ethnicity, family income, parents' educational attainment, enrollment pattern, and place of residence, but not based on students' gender. Table 2a shows that a smaller percentage of Asians than of Whites, Blacks, and Hispanics worked while enrolled among both dependent undergraduates (67% versus 77%, 73%, and 74%) and independent undergraduates (73% versus 80%, 81%, and 82%). When they do work, Asians also average fewer hours of work per week than Whites, Blacks, and Hispanics. Table 2a shows that working dependent Asian undergraduates averaged 22.1 hours of work per week, while Whites averaged 23.7, Blacks averaged 25.1, and Hispanics aver-aged 26.1. Among working independent undergraduates, the average number of hours worked per week ranged from 32.3 for Asians, to 34.4 for Whites, 35.0 for Blacks, and 34.5 for Hispanics (Table 2a).

Table 2a. Characteristics of undergraduates who work by dependency status: 2003-04

Characteristic	Percentage Who Work		Average Number of Hours Worked/Week	
	Dependent	Independent	Dependent	Independent
Total	75.2	80.0	24.1	34.5
Sex				
Male	73.4	82.1	24.6	35.5
Female	76.9	78.8	23.6	33.8
Race/ethnicity				
White	76.6	80.1	23.7	34.4
Black/African American	72.6	80.9	25.1	35.0
Hispanic/ Latino	74.2	82.4	26.1	34.5
Asian/Other Pacific Islander	66.8	72.5	22.1	32.3

The relationship between working and sociodemographic characteristics varies based on students' financial dependency status. Working while enrolled is slightly less common among dependent undergraduates with family incomes of $100,000 or more than among dependent undergraduates with lower incomes. In contrast, the share of independent undergraduates who work is smaller among those with the lowest incomes than among those with higher incomes. While parental educational attainment is unrelated to the likelihood of working while enrolled among independent undergraduates, working while enrolled is less common among dependent undergraduates whose parents have not completed high school (69%) or have completed advanced degrees (71%) than among undergraduates whose parents have completed a high school diploma (79%) or some college (79%).

Table 2b. Characteristics of undergraduates who work by dependency status: 2003-04

	Percentage Who work		Average Number of Hours Worked/Week	
	Dependent	Independent	Dependent	Independent
Income				
Less than $30,000 (dependent)	74.6	--	25.4	--
$30,000 - $59,999 (dependent)	78.5	--	24.5	--
$60,000 - $99,999 (dependent)	76.5	--	23.7	--
$100,000 or more (dependent)	69.6	--	22.4	--
Less than $10,000 (independent)	--	71.8	--	30.0
$10,000 - $19,999 (independent)	--	81.3	--	32.9
$20,000 - $29,999 (independent)	--	82.4	--	35.6
$30,000 - $49,999 (independent)	--	83.4	--	36.0
$50,000 or more (independent)	--	82.5	--	37.3
Parent's highest education				
Did not complete high school	69.7	77.7	27.1	35.2
High school	78.5	79.7	25.5	35.4
Some college	79.4	81.3	25.2	34.0
Bachelor's degree	73.5	79.7	23.4	34.0
Advanced degree	71.1	81.2	21.6	33.1

Both enrollment status and place of campus residence are related to students' employment status, especially among dependent students. Smaller shares of both dependent and independent undergraduates who are enrolled mostly full-time rather than mostly part-time work while enrolled. Table 2c shows that 73 percent of dependent undergraduates who are enrolled mostly full-time work while enrolled compared with 82 percent of dependent undergraduates who are enrolled mostly part-time. Living on-campus is associated with lower rates of working, and, among those who work,

Table 2c. Characteristics of undergraduates who work by dependency status: 2003-04

	Percentage Who Work		Average Number of Hours Worked/Week	
	Dependent	Independent	Dependent	Independent
Enrollment pattern				
Mostly full-time (FT)	73.1	75.2	22.2	32.0
Mostly part-time (PT)	82.2	83.6	29.9	36.1
FT & PT equally	80.2	77.0	27.2	33.3
Residence				
On campus	64.8	77.4	19.3	29.7
Off campus	78.6	79.9	25.2	34.9
Living with parents	79.7	81.5	25.9	31.9

Note: Analyses weighted by WTA00
Source: Analyses of NPSAS:2004 Undergraduate Students.

fewer hours worked per week. Table 2c shows that only 65 percent of dependent undergraduates who live on campus work while enrolled, compared with 79 percent of dependent undergraduates who live off campus and 80 percent of dependent undergraduates who live with their parents. Table 2c shows that the average number of hours worked per week among working dependent undergraduates is 19.3 for those who live on campus, compared with 25.2 for those who live off campus and 25.9 for those who live with their parents.

Type of Employment

Work-study employment is substantially less common than non-work-study employment among both dependent and independent undergraduates. Table 3 shows that, in 2003-04, only 7 percent of working dependent under-graduates and 2 percent of working independent under-graduates held only work-study jobs, 8 percent of working dependent undergraduates and 3 percent of working independent undergraduates held both work-study and non-work-study jobs, and 85 percent of working dependent undergraduates and 95 percent of working independent undergraduates held only non-work-study jobs.

Work-study employment is relatively more common among dependent undergraduates who attend private four-year colleges and universities than among undergraduates who attend other types of institutions. In 2003-04, 43 percent of dependent undergraduates who attended private four-year institutions and who worked held work-study jobs, compared with 14 percent of working dependent under-graduates who attended public four-year institutions, 6 percent of working dependent students who attend private for-profit institutions, and 5 percent of working dependent undergraduates who attended public two-year institutions (Table 3).

Table 3. Distribution of undergraduates by type of job, institutional type, and dependency status: 2003-04

| | Type of job | | |
	Regular job only	Work-study/ assistantship only	Both
Dependent students			
Total	85.2	7.0	7.8
Public 4-year	86.3	6.5	7.2
Private 4-year	57.4	21.9	20.7
Public 2-year	95.5	1.6	2.9
Private for-profit	93.9	2.4	3.7
Independent students			
Total	95.0	2.1	2.8
Public 4-year	93.1	3.1	3.8
Private 4-year	92.9	2.8	4.3
Public 2-year	95.7	1.9	2.4
Private for-profit	97.9	0.9	1.3

Note: Analyses are weighted by WTA00 study weight
Source: Analyses of NPSAS: 2004 Undergraduate Students.

    In terms of location of employment, the majority (91%) of 2003-04 working dependent undergraduates worked off-campus, with only 7 percent working on-campus and 2 percent working both on-campus and off-campus (Table 4). Descriptive analyses of undergraduates who worked off-campus while enrolled in two-year and four-year higher education institutions in Washington State during the 1997-98 academic year showed that the five most common off-campus employers were restaurants or bars; health, business, or education services; and retail (Harding & Harmon, 1999). Although the most common source of employment, eating and drinking establishments averaged lower hourly wages than other off-campus employers: $6.07/hour for eating and drinking establishments versus $7.50/hour overall (Harding & Harmon, 1999).

Table 4. Location of employment for undergraduates who work by institutional type and dependency status: 2003-04

| | Location of Job | | |
Characteristic	On campus	Off campus	Both on and off campus
Total	6.8	91.1	2.1
Institution sector			
Public 4-year	11.4	85.2	3.5
Private 4-year	12.7	84.2	3.1
Public 2-year	2.9	95.9	1.2
Private for-profit	3.0	96.0	1.0
Dependency status			
Dependent	10.2	86.9	3.0
Independent	3.8	94.9	1.3

Note: Analyses are weighted by WTA00 study weight
Source: Analyses of NPSAS: 2004 Undergraduate Students.

Why Do Students Work?

To identify the most appropriate responses to student employment, institutional administrators and leaders must also understand the reasons that students work while enrolled. This section describes four perspectives that offer insights into why many students work: public policy, economics, sociocultural, and demographic. Together, these four perspectives suggest that paying college prices is only one of several reasons that students work.

Public Policy Perspective
    From a public policy perspective, work may be required to pay college prices in at least two instances: (1) when a student receives some portion of financial aid in the form of Federal Work-study; and (2) when the student and his/her family cannot, or will not, pay the price of attendance less grants from current income, savings, and loans.
    The federally mandated needs analysis formula determines eligibility for federal financial aid. Financial need is defined as the difference between the cost of attendance and the expected family contribution (EFC). Cost of attendance includes tuition and fees, books, materials, and living expenses. EFC, or the amount a family is expected to contribute to a student's college costs, is determined by a formula specified under Part F of Title IV of the Higher Education Act of 1965 as amended (U.S. Department of Education, 2004). The EFC, calculated from data reported on the Free Application for Federal Student Aid (FAFSA), is based on such factors as family income and assets, family size, and number of other college students in the family (U.S. Department of Education, 2004). The federally mandated needs analysis formula is used to determine student eligibility for several federal financial aid programs, including Pell grants, subsidized Stafford loans, and campus-based aid.
    Along with Federal Supplemental Educational Opportunity Grants and Federal Perkins Loans, Federal Work-study is one of three forms of federal campus-based aid, i.e., aid that is funded by the federal government but is

administered by financial aid offices at individual colleges and universities. Campus financial aid administrators include Federal Work-study in a student's financial aid package based on a consideration of the student's financial need, the types and amounts of other financial aid in the student's package, and the availability of funds at the institution for Federal Work-study awards. The primary purpose of the Federal Work-study program is to ensure that students have worthwhile and manageable opportunities to acquire the resources that are required to pay the costs of attendance by engaging in paid community service and/or performing work that is related to their academic interests (Higher Education Act of 1965, Title IV, Part C, Sec. 441)

A second reason that students work, from a public policy perspective, is that working provides a mechanism for paying the costs of attendance. The Advisory Committee on Student Financial Assistance (2002) reports that, in the late 1990s, students from low-income families averaged substantial unmet financial need (i.e., costs of attendance less expected family contribution and financial aid) even at public two-year institutions. Consequently, in order to pay the costs of college attendance, low-income students and their families must rely on other sources, most commonly their own employment and loans (King, 2002; St. John, 2006). The Advisory Committee (2005) estimates that, for dependent students with family incomes below $50,000 who attended public four-year institutions in 2003-04, the average work and loan burden for that year exceeded $7,300. Defined as the difference between total costs of attendance and all grant aid, the "work and loan burden" may be the best label for "the true net price of college and the [financial] barrier that must be overcome" for individuals to enroll and persist in higher education (Advisory Committee on Student Financial Assistance, 2002, p. 11).

Table 5. Percentage of undergraduates who cannot afford to attend college without working by institutional type and dependency status: 2003-04

Characteristic	Dependent	Independent
Total	71.3	91.9
Institutional type		
Public 4-year	69.1	88.6
Private 4-year	72.0	92.0
Public 2-year	73.5	92.8
Private for-profit	77.8	93.5
Income – Dependent students		
Less than $20,000	78.2	--
$20,000 to $49,999	76.6	--
$50,000 to $69,999	71.8	--
$70,000 to $99,999	68.3	--
More than $100,000	62.0	--
Income – Independent students		
Less than $10,000	--	85.9
$10,000-$29,999	--	91.8
$30,000-$49,999	--	95.0
$50,000 or more	--	95.1

Note: Analyses are weighted by WTA00 study weight
Source: Analyses of NPSAS: 2004 Undergraduate Students.

Descriptive analyses suggest that a substantial share of students work in order to pay the costs of college attendance. Working was the second most common strategy (after applying for financial aid) that low-income undergraduates in 1995-96 reported using to reduce college expenditures, while working was the most common strategy reported by middle- and upper-income undergraduates (King, 2002). Table 5 shows that, in 2003-04, 71 percent of working dependent undergraduates and 92 percent of working independent undergraduates reported that they had to work in order to pay the costs of attendance. Half (56%) of dependent undergraduates and three-fourths (77%) of independent undergraduates reported that the most important reason for working was to pay tuition, fees, and living expenses (Table 6).

Table 6. Main reason for working among working undergraduates by dependency status: 2003-04

Dependency status	Total	Earn spending money	Pay tuition, fees, or living expenses	Gain job experience	Other
Total	100.0	24.2	63.4	7.3	5.1
Dependent	100.0	32.3	55.8	7.6	4.2
Independent	100.0	9.2	77.4	6.7	6.7

Note: Analyses are weighted by WTA00 study weight
Source: Analyses of NPSAS: 2004 Undergraduate Students.

Economic Perspective

Economic theories also inform our understanding of the reasons that students work. Rational models of human capital investment assume that individuals decide to "invest" in higher education (i.e., enroll and persist in college) based on a comparison of the expected lifetime benefits with the expected costs (Becker, 1962, 1993; Ellwood & Kane, 2000; Paulsen, 2001). Individuals are assumed to act rationally in ways that maximize their utility, given their personal preferences, tastes, and expectations (Becker, 1962, 1993). Human capital theory assumes that individuals consider both monetary and non-monetary benefits in their calculation of the total expected benefits of higher education (Becker, 1993). The theory predicts, and research shows, that individuals realize a number of benefits from an investment in higher education. Among the long-term benefits of higher education are increased lifetime earnings, more fulfilling work environments, better health, longer life, more informed purchases, and lower probability of unemployment. Individuals who attend college also realize such short-term consumption benefits as enjoyment of the learning experience, involvement in extracurricular activities, participation in social and cultural events, and enhancement of social status (Baum & Payea, 2004; Bowen, 1997; Leslie & Brinkman, 1988).

The costs of investing in a college education include the direct costs of attendance (e.g., tuition, fees, room, board, books, and supplies) less financial aid, the opportunity costs of foregone earnings and leisure time, and the costs of traveling between home and the institution (Becker, 1993). Foregone earnings, i.e., the opportunity costs of college attendance, are defined as the earnings that the student would realize if they were not attending college. Therefore, from an economic perspective, students may work while enrolled in college not only to pay the direct costs of attendance, but also to reduce the costs of foregone earnings. In a simulation of the rate of return of working while enrolled, Stern and Nakata (1991) showed that, unless a student is certain that s/he will not graduate or will require additional time to complete their degree, working while enrolled increases the rate of return to their investment in college by reducing the costs of attendance.

Sociocultural Perspectives

By emphasizing the ways that socioeconomic and other background characteristics influence student decisions (Perna, 2006a; Terenzini, Cabrera, & Bernal, 2001), sociocultural perspectives offer insights into differences across groups in the frequency and amount of working while attending college. These perspectives predict that different groups of students engage in different levels, amounts, and types of employment because of differences in such preferences and tastes as parental willingness to pay the price of the student's college attendance; student willingness to borrow to pay the price of attendance; and student preferences for particular lifestyles.

One type of sociocultural preference that may shape students' decisions about work is parental willingness to pay college prices. Ruling out such potential explanations as increased cost of attendance relative to family income, reduced availability of financial aid, growth in financial aid awards in the form of work, and increased earnings of college student workers compared to other workers, Stern and Nakata (1991) concluded that growth between the 1960s and the 1980s in the share of college students who work was most likely attributable to changes in preferences. More specifically, while acknowledging a lack of data or research to support this explanation, Stern and Nakata argued that growth in working could be explained by such changes as increased student interest in financial independence and reduced parental willingness to pay students' price of attendance.

Over the past decade, students have become responsible for a relatively larger share, while parents have become responsible for a relatively smaller share, of the price of college attendance (Hearn, 2001; Stringer, Cunningham, O'Brien & Merisotis, 1998). Although many factors (e.g., increased consumer debt, inadequate savings, slow personal income growth) may contribute to parents' reduced ability to pay college prices (Perna & Li, 2006), a reduced willingness to pay may also explain the decline in the share of costs covered by parents (Stringer et al., 1998).

Parental willingness to pay appears to vary across racial/ethnic groups. Using national data and multinomial logit analyses, Steelman and Powell (1993) found that, even after controlling for parents' education, parents' marital status, number of children, and family income, African American, Hispanic, and Asian parents were more likely than White parents to perceive college prices to be the responsibility of parents rather than students.

Parental willingness to pay may also vary based on socioeconomic status, although observers offer conflicting views about the direction of the relationship. Based on their analyses of data describing high school seniors in the National Educational Longitudinal Study and High School and Beyond, Ellwood and Kane (2000) concluded that college enrollment rates may be positively related to family income, at least in part, because parental willingness to contribute to college prices increases with family income. On the other hand, King (2002) speculated that rates of working are as high among students from middle- and higher-income families as among students from lower-income families in part because of middle- and higher-income parents' unwillingness to pay their entire expected family contribution.

Regardless, parental ability/willingness to pay college prices is inversely related to the likelihood that an undergraduate works full-time while enrolled. Nearly one-half (43%) of undergraduates whose parents did not help pay costs of tuition and fees worked full-time in 2003-04, compared with 13 percent of undergraduates whose parents did help pay the costs of tuition and fees (McMillion, 2005).

A second sociocultural perspective suggests that variation in student employment behavior may be attributable to differences in willingness to borrow to pay college prices. In other words, some students may work because they are unwilling to use loans to fund educational prices. As indicated by the growing share of aid that is awarded in the form of loans, the declining share of aid that is awarded in the form of grants, and the declining value of the Pell grant (The College Board, 2005b), the nation's current system of financial aid seems to require that students and/or their families' borrow to pay the costs of attendance. About one-half (44%) of the nearly $142.7 billion in non-family funds used by postsecondary education students nationwide in 2004-05 was in the form of federal loans and an additional 10 percent was in the form of non-federal loans (The College Board, 2005b). Moreover, low-income students are not exempt from the expectation to borrow (Perna, 2006b). Regardless of income, nearly half of full-time, full-year dependent undergraduates with family incomes below $100,000 borrowed in 2003-04 (Berkner, Wei, He, Lew, Cominole, & Siegel, 2005).

Willingness to borrow varies based on economic, cultural, and psychological perspectives (Perna, 2006b). For example, Trent, Lee, and Owens-Nicholson (2006) argue that locus of control may influence willingness to borrow. Other research suggests racial/ethnic group differences in willingness to borrow. Using data from the U.S. Census Bureau and the 1999/00 National Postsecondary Student Aid Study, ECMC Group Foundation (2003) concluded that differences in use of loans to finance costs contributed to lower college enrollment rates for Hispanics and American Indians than for Whites. African Americans, American Indians, and Hispanics were more likely than Whites to enroll in lower price postsecondary educational institutions without borrowing even after controlling for socioeconomic characteristics. Socioeconomic characteristics, particularly mortgage status and the householder's educational attainment, were important positive predictors of enrolling and borrowing (ECMC Group Foundation, 2003).

A third sociocultural perspective suggests that differences in student employment may be attributable to differences across groups in lifestyle choices and other preferences and expectations. For example, some upper-middle- and upper-income students may work because they want to support a particular lifestyle (e.g., own a car), not because they need to pay the costs of attendance (King, 2002). Students from low- and lower-middle-income families may also work for reasons other than paying costs of attendance, including an obligation to contribute to the financial well-being of their families (King, 2002).

Demographic Perspective

A final perspective for understanding the phenomenon of working students is changing demographics. In other words, growth in the number of students who work may reflect changes in the demographics of college students generally, and an increase in enrollment of adult students more specifically. Likely reflecting an interest in updating skills in the face of changing technologies, the number of older individuals who are enrolling in higher education is increasing (Berker & Horn, 2003). Nearly half (43%) of all undergraduates in 1999-2000 were age 24 or older (Berker & Horn, 2003). Federal financial aid regulations categorize students who are at least 24 years old as financially independent of their parents.

Compared to dependent students, independent students are more likely to work while enrolled and work a greater number of hours. As described earlier, 80 percent of independent undergraduates worked an average of 34.5 hours per week in 2003-04, while 75 percent of dependent undergraduates worked an average of 24.1 hours per week (Table 1). Table 7 shows that, in 2003-04, 15 percent of independent undergraduates worked more than 40 hours per week compared with only 4 percent of dependent undergraduates. About half (52%) of independent under-graduates worked more than 30 hours per week while enrolled compared with only 20 percent of dependent undergraduates.

What Are the Implications of Working for Students' Educational Experiences?

Institutional leaders must recognize that the effects of employment vary based on the quantity and quality of employment as well as the outcome of interest (Pascarella & Terenzini, 2005; U.S. Department of Education, 1998). This section reviews what is known from prior research about the effects of employment on the following aspects of students' educational experiences: cognitive skills and intellectual development, academic performance, community service and moral development, persistence to degree completion, time to degree, and post-college earnings.

Cognitive Skills and Intellectual Development
    A public policy perspective predicts that working, especially working a work-study job or other job that is related to students' academic program and/or career goals, is positively related to students' cognitive development. Nonetheless, based on their comprehensive review and synthesis of prior research, Pascarella and Terenzini (2005) concluded that the relationship between student employment and cognitive development is ambiguous. In an exploratory study, Pascarella, Bohr, Nora, Desler, and Zusman (1994) found that, among freshmen at one university, scores on tests of reading comprehension, mathematics, and critical thinking were unrelated to whether students worked, whether students worked on- or off-campus, or the number of hours worked after controlling for other variables. In a follow-up longitudinal study of freshmen attending 23 colleges and

Table 7. Percentage distribution of undergraduates by number of hours worked per week, dependency status, and type of employment: 2003-04

| Status | Total | None | Hours worked per week | | | | |
			1-15	16-20	21-30	31-40	41 or more
Dependent	100.0	24.6	21.9	14.1	19.7	15.3	4.3
Non-work-study	100.0	--	26.5	19.8	27.9	21.5	4.4
Work-study	100.0	--	77.7	13.5	4.9	3.9	0.0
Both	100.0	--	12.9	12.8	26.1	22.9	25.4
Independent	100.0	20.0	8.3	7.9	11.3	37.2	15.4
Non-work-study	100.0	--	9.6	9.5	14.3	48.0	18.7
Work-study	100.0	--	48.2	29.3	9.3	13.2	0.0
Both	100.0	--	6.1	6.0	14.8	21.2	51.9

Note: Analyses are weighted by WTA00 study weight
Source: Analyses of NPSAS: 2004 Undergraduate Students.

universities, Pascarella, Edison, Nora, Hagedorn, and Terenzini (1998) found that, after controlling for other variables, neither location of employment (i.e., on- or off-campus) nor intensity of working was consistently related to measures of cognitive development at the end of students' first or second years of college. Scientific reasoning at the end of the second year was inversely related to the number of hours worked. At the end of the third year, working up to 15 hours per week on campus or up to 20 hours per week off campus was positively related to such measures of cognitive development as reading comprehension and critical thinking, net of other variables, while working more than 15 hours per week on campus or more than 20 hours per week off campus was negatively related to these measures.

Few studies have tested the hypothesis that working promotes cognitive development when the employment is related to the student's major field or career goals (Pascarella & Terenzini, 2005). Based on their evaluation of the quality and range of available research, Pascarella and Terenzini concluded that employment has no effect on students' cognitive development.

Academic Performance

A public policy perspective suggests that working while enrolled may enhance academic performance, especially when students are employed in Federal Work-study (FWS) programs. The U.S. Department of Education (2005) states that students who are awarded Federal Work-study aid should perform work that is "related to the recipient's course of study," regardless of whether the student's FWS employer is on- or off-campus" (www.studentaid.ed.gov, Types of Federal Student Aid). Working while enrolled may enhance the educational experiences of some portion of students (Choy & Berker, 2003), especially students who hold jobs that are related to their major field of study or career interest

(Stern & Nakata, 1991). About one-fifth of 2003-04 working undergraduates believed that working had a positive effect on their grades (Table 8).

Nonetheless, most research suggests that working is unrelated to grades. Table 8 shows that about one-third of working undergraduates in 2003-04 believed that working was unrelated to their grades. Other research shows that the number of hours worked per week (regardless of whether worked on or off campus) is unrelated to academic achievement, at least when measured by performance on standardized tests (Pascarella & Terenzini, 2005) or grade point average (Ehrenberg & Sherman, 1987; Furr & Elling, 2000; Harding & Harmon, 1999; Stern & Nakata, 1991).

Working has been shown to be unrelated to academic achievement even though research consistently shows that working is negatively related to academic involvement and time spent studying (Furr & Elling, 2000; Pascarella et al., 1994; Pascarella & Terenzini, 2005). Descriptive analyses show that, as the number of hours worked per week increases, so does the percentage of undergraduates who report that working limited their choice of classes, class schedule, number of classes taken, and access to the library (Choy & Berker, 2003; King & Bannon, 2002). In a descriptive study of students at one urban public university, Furr and Elling (2000) found that, compared with students who did not work and students who worked less than 30 hours per week, students who worked 30 or more hours each week were less engaged with campus organizations. Students who did not work reported more frequent contacts, and more meaningful relationships, with faculty than students who worked (Furr & Elling, 2000). Pascarella and Terenzini

Table 8. Distribution of undergraduates who worked by perceived effect of working on grades, institutional type, and number of hours worked per week: 2003-04

Institutional type	Total	Positive	Negative	None
Total	100.0	18.4	48.0	33.7
Public 4-year	100.0	18.5	49.3	32.2
Private 4-year	100.0	23.4	42.1	34.6
Public 2-year	100.0	16.9	48.3	34.7
Private for-profit	100.0	17.7	45.1	37.2
Hours worked per week				
1-15 hours	100.0	20.0	40.3	39.7
16-20 hours	100.0	20.3	43.1	36.9
21-30 hours	100.0	17.8	49.2	33.0
31-40 hours	100.0	16.7	52.4	31.0
41 or more hours	100.0	18.6	54.4	27.1

Note: Analyses are weighted by WTA00 study weight
Source: Analyses of NPSAS: 2004 Undergraduate Students.

(2005) speculate that, together, these findings suggest that, on average, working improves students' "organizational skills and work habits," thereby enabling them to use available study time more efficiently (p. 133).

Community Service and Moral Development

A public policy perspective predicts that employment will be positively related to community service, at least for some proportion of students working in Federal Work-study programs. Effective July 1, 1994, all institutions are required to use at least 7 percent of their Federal Work-study funds to compensate students who are employed in community service jobs.

Research on the relationship between student employment and indicators of community service and/or moral development is limited in both quantity and scope. Anecdotal evidence suggests that working in a community service job may encourage students to pursue such careers as public school teaching (Cheng, 2004). Pascarella and Terenzini (2005) described two studies that showed a negative relationship between the number of hours worked per week off-campus and such indicators as participation in community service during college and principled moral reasoning. This negative relationship may be attributable to the negative impact of time spent working on time available for community service and other activities that promote moral development (Pascarella & Terenzini, 2005). Regardless, additional research is required to fully understand the implications of working for moral-ethical behavior and moral development (Pascarella & Terenzini, 2005).

Persistence to Degree Completion

Tinto's (1993) model of voluntary student departure suggests that a student's decision to leave an institution is a consequence of the interaction between the individual student and the college or university as an organization. The model suggests that working a substantial number of hours, especially off-campus, limits a student's ability to become academically and socially integrated into the campus, thereby weakening a student's commitment to the institution and degree completion, and consequently increasing the likelihood of leaving the institution. Working a "reasonable" number of hours on-campus is expected to reduce the likelihood that a student will leave an institution before completing a degree, while working a "high" number of hours, especially when the employment is off-campus, is expected to reduce the likelihood that a student will persist to degree completion.

Descriptive data are consistent with this hypothesis. Among 1995-96 beginning postsecondary students, observed bachelor's degree attainment rates were higher for students who worked between one and 15 hours per week than for other students. Table 9 shows that 82 percent of 1995-96 first-time freshmen who attended a public four-year institution and who worked between one and 15 hours per week had attained a bachelor's degree by 2001, compared with only 69 percent of those who did not work, 63 percent of those who worked between 16 and 20 hours per week, 51 percent of those who worked between 21 and 30 hours per week, and 29 percent of those who worked 30 or more hours per week (Beginning Postsecondary Students Longitudinal Study [BPS]:96/01). Similarly, 91 percent of 1995-96 first-time freshmen who attended a private four-year institution and who worked between one and 15 hours per week had attained a bachelor's degree by 2001, compared with 84 percent of those who did not work, 77 percent of those who worked between 16 and 20 hours per week, 63 percent of those who worked 21 to 30 hours per week, and 54 percent of those who worked more than 30 hours per week.

Consistent with these descriptive data, Pascarella and Terenzini (2005) concluded that the relationship between employment and retention is likely U-shaped: retention rates are lower for students who do not work and for students who work more than 15 hours per week than for students who work between one and 15 hours per week. Working no more than 15 hours per week is associated with higher levels of involvement and learning, while working more than 25 or 30 hours per week is associated with lower levels of involvement with faculty and peers (Furr & Elling, 2000; Lundberg, 2004). Research typically shows that working between one and 15 hours per week, especially if the employment is on-campus, promotes persistence, whereas not working or working more than 15 hours per week, especially off-campus, limits persistence (Beeson & Wessle, 2002; Ehrenberg & Sherman, 1987; King, 2002; Pascarella & Terenzini, 2005). Working on campus is generally associated with higher persistence rates, regardless of whether persistence is measured as year-to-year enrollment or degree completion (Pascarella & Terenzini, 2005; St. John, 2003).

Time to Degree

Students who work while enrolled generally average longer time to degree (King, 2002; Stern & Nakata, 1991), although some research suggests that the positive relation-ship between hours worked and time to degree exists for students who work off campus and not for students who work on campus (Ehrenberg & Sherman, 1987; Pascarella & Terenzini, 2005). Based on their review and synthesis of prior research, Pascarella and Terenzini (2005) concluded that the likelihood of shifting enrollment from full-time to part-time increases as the number of hours worked per week increases.

Aspects of the Federal Work-study program, as well as the types of employment that are available to working students, suggest that students who work while enrolled may require additional time to complete their degrees. According to the U.S. Department of Education (2005), the total amount of money that students may earn through FWS programs is capped and the hourly wages that students receive through this program may be as low as the federal minimum wage ($5.15/hour in 2005).

The financial inadequacy of work-study employment is suggested by the high shares of work-study students who hold both work-study and non-work-study jobs while they are enrolled. Among 2003-04 dependent undergraduates who held a work-study job, the share who also held a non-work-study job ranged from 49 percent at private four-year institutions, to 53 percent at public four-year institutions, to 61 percent at private for-profit institutions and 64 percent at public two-year institutions (analyses of data in Table 3).

Students who hold only work-study jobs tend to work 15 or fewer hours per week, while students who hold both work-study and non-work-study jobs tend to work more than 40 hours per week. Table 7 shows that 78 percent of working dependent undergraduates who held only work-study jobs worked 15 or fewer hours per week, compared with just 13 percent of working dependent undergraduates who held both work-study and non-work-study jobs. No dependent undergraduates who worked only work-study jobs, but one-fourth of dependent undergraduates who held both work-study and non-work-study jobs, worked more than 40 hours per week. The pattern is similar for working independent undergraduates.

Post-College Employment and Earnings

The economic theory of human capital suggests that working while enrolled in college promotes various post-college outcomes, particularly employment and earnings. Human capital theory assumes that investments in human capital (e.g., education, on-the-job-training) enhance a student's "mental and physical abilities," thereby increasing their productivity (Becker, 1962). Increases in productivity are expected to be rewarded by higher earnings (Becker, 1993; Paulsen, 2001). Therefore, a student who works while enrolled in college may be building his/her human capital through both formal education and on-the-job training. Most of the available research shows that students believe that working while in college promotes job-related skills and that employers believe that college graduates who work while attending college are more job-ready than college graduates who do not work (Pascarella & Terenzini, 2005).

Although less conclusive than research about the perceived labor market benefits, research generally indicates that students who work while enrolled in college are more likely than their non-working peers to secure employment soon after graduating and to obtain employment that requires a bachelor's degree (Pascarella & Terenzini, 2005). Students who engage in work that is related to their major field and/or career choice typically realize the greatest success in securing employment after completing their bachelor's degree (Pascarella & Terenzini, 2005).

Nonetheless, despite the predictions of human capital models, the relationship between employment during college and post-graduation earnings is ambiguous (Pascarella & Terenzini, 2005). Little is known about the relationship between employment as a student and long-term career earnings (Pascarella & Terenzini, 2005; Stern & Nakata, 1991). Some research suggests that early career earnings are higher for those who work while attending college (e.g., Gleason, 1993; Light, 2001; Molitor & Leigh, 2005; Stern & Nakata, 1991), but that the rate of return to in-school employment varies based on the type of institution attended (Molitor & Leigh, 2005). The effect on post-college earnings of in-school work experience appears to be larger for students attending community colleges than for students

Table 9. Percentage distribution of 1995-96 first-time students who planned to attain a bachelor's degree according to attainment or enrollment status in 2001, by hours worked in 1998 and institution last attended by 2001

Hours worked per week while enrolled	Attained bachelor's degree	Attainment or level of enrollment 2001		
		Attained associate's degree or certificate	Never attained, enrolled at 4-year	Never attained, not enrolled
Institution Last Attended by 2001: Pubic 4-year				
Total	59.4	4.4	18.6	17.6
0 Hours	68.7	3.1	16.9	11.4
1-15 Hours	81.5	2.7	8.0	7.7
16-20 Hours	62.8	5.1	20.0	12.1
21-30 Hours	50.5	7.8	23.9	17.9
30 Hours or More	29.2	5.2	33.3	32.2
Institution Last Attended by 2001: Private 4-year				
Total	77.9	3.3	8.2	10.5
0 Hours	84.3	4.1	4.5	7.1
1-15 Hours	91.3	0.4	2.9	5.4
16-20 Hours	76.8	5.3	9.2	8.7
21-30 Hours	62.7	7.6	16.9	12.9
30 Hours or More	53.5	4.2	25.0	17.2

Note: Analyses are weighted by WTC00 Longitudinal weight for 96, 98, 01 respondent
Source: Analyses of Beginning Postsecondary Students (BPS:96/2001).

attending other types of colleges and universities (Molitor & Leigh, 2005). Nonetheless, other research suggests that the positive effects of working while in college on subsequent wages are eliminated after taking into account endogeneity of working and unobserved person-specific heterogeneity (Hotz, Xu, Tienda, & Ahituv, 2002). In their econometric analyses of the returns to high school and college employment on earnings of men using data from the 1979 National Longitudinal Study of Youth, Hotz and colleagues concluded that the returns to full-time schooling exceed the returns to employment especially for Blacks and Hispanics.

What Can Institutions Do to Promote the Educational Experiences of Working Students?

The data and research presented in this paper suggest that, in order to promote the educational experiences of students who work, institutions should consider at least four strategies: (1) determine the characteristics and consequences of employment for students at their own institution; (2) reduce the financial need to work by controlling the costs of college attendance, maximizing the availability of need-based grants for low- and lower-middle-income students, and encouraging students to borrow responsibly; (3) improve the quality of students' employment experiences by expanding on-campus employment opportunities and supporting increases in Federal Work-study funding; and (4) adapt the delivery of education to better meet the needs of working students.

Determine the Characteristics and Consequences of Employment at This Institution

The data and research summarized in this paper describe student employment and educational experiences at colleges and universities in the aggregate. To identify the most appropriate institutional responses, individual college campuses should examine the characteristics and experiences of students who work while they are enrolled on their own campus. An institutional assessment of student-employment patterns should be designed to identify the characteristics of students who work, the amounts and types of employment in which students are engaged, and the reasons that students work. The descriptive analyses in this paper show that employment patterns vary based on various demographic characteristics, particularly financial dependency. Compared with students who are financially dependent on their parents, independent students are more likely to work, work more hours, and are more likely to view themselves as primarily employees who study rather than students who work. The descriptive analyses also show that, nationwide, students work different numbers of hours, in different locations, for different reasons.

Institutions should also identify the extent to which students who work perceive themselves to be primarily students or employees. One limitation of much of the prior research examining the consequences of working is the failure to consider the endogeneity of the measures of student employment (Stinebrickner & Stinebrickner, 2003). In other words, students make "choices" about the extent to which they work while they are enrolled. If this endogeneity is not taken into account, the results of the analyses may be biased. For example, a negative relationship between employment and educational outcomes is often interpreted as reflecting the negative consequences of working for integration, engagement, and involvement. However, if endogeneity has not been considered, then this negative relationship may really reflect a student's decision to be more committed to the labor market than to college performance, involvement, and persistence.

Descriptive analyses suggest that persistence and degree completion rates vary based on whether students view themselves primarily as students who work or employees who study (Hudson & Hurst, 2002). Using data from the 1995-96 BPS, Hudson and Hurst found that students who view themselves primarily as employees who study are less likely than other students to persist toward completion of an associate's or bachelor's degree after taking into account degree aspiration. They also observe that students who view themselves as employees who study have other character-istics that are associated with lower rates of persistence and degree completion (e.g., full-time employment while enrolled, being a single parent, not having a standard high school diploma, and lower parental educational attainment).

Thus, institutions must identify students' perceptions and goals in order to understand the reasons for, and consequences of, working and the appropriate institutional response to such employment. Nationwide, virtually all (90%) of working dependent undergraduates in 2003-04 viewed themselves primarily as students who work to meet educational expenses (Table 10). Only 10 percent of working dependent undergraduates viewed themselves primarily as employees who are enrolled in school. In contrast, the majority (56%) of working independent undergraduates in 2003-04 reported that they were employees who study, rather than students who worked (Table 10).

Table 10. Distribution of undergraduates who work by perceived role, institutional type, and dependency status: 2003-04

Characteristic	Total	Perceived role: Student working to meet expenses	Employee enrolled in school
Total	100.0	66.1	33.9
Public 4-year	100.0	81.8	18.2
Private 4-year	100.0	72.3	27.7
Public 2-year	100.0	56.5	43.5
Private for-profit	100.0	46.0	54.0
Dependent	100.0	90.0	10.0
Independent	100.0	43.9	56.1

Note: Analyses are weighted by WTA00 study weight
Source: Analyses of NPSAS: 2004 Undergraduate Students.

Reduce the Financial Need to Work

A public policy perspective suggests that one reason students work is because of the gap between the costs of attendance and their financial aid and other resources (i.e., their work and loan burden). An economic perspective suggests that students work to reduce the costs of foregone earnings. Sociocultural perspectives suggest that students are working because their parents are unwilling to pay college expenses and/or because students and their parents are unwilling to use loans. Supporting all three perspectives, most students report that they work to pay college-related expenses. Institutions may reduce the financial need for students to work by controlling the costs of college attendance, maximizing need-based grants for low- and lower-middle-income students, and encouraging students to borrow responsibly.

Control the Costs of College Attendance
By controlling the costs of attendance, institutions will reduce students' work and loan burden. Over the past decade, the costs of attending college increased dramatically. Between 1995-96 and 2005-06, tuition and fees increased in constant dollars by 54 percent at public four-year institutions, 37 percent at private four-year institutions, and 30 percent at public two-year institutions (The College Board, 2005a).

Sponsored by the Lumina Foundation for Education, the publication, *Course Corrections: Experts Offer Solutions to the College Cost Crisis,* includes several recommendations for institutions. These recommendations include outsourcing functions that are not central to the institution's mission (Bushman & Dean, 2005; Coplin, 2005), developing dual enrollment programs with high schools so that students can earn bachelor's degrees in less time, granting credit for programs conducted by student services (Coplin, 2005), and using technology to redesign the delivery of courses (Twigg, 2005). By identifying ways to effectively reduce college costs, institutions will likely reduce students' financial need to work.

Maximize Need-Based Grants for Low- and Lower-Middle-Income Students
Institutions may also reduce students' financial need to work by maximizing the availability of need-based grants for low- and lower-middle-income students (Baum, 2005; Perna & Li, 2006; Richards, 2003). Virtually all full-time, full-year dependent undergraduates from low-, lower-middle, and middle-income families had some amount of financial need

in 1999-2000 (Choy & Berker, 2003). While a majority of students from upper-middle-income and upper-income families also had some amount of financial need, the challenges that limit the ability to pay unmet financial need are greater for students from lower- and lower-middle-income families than for other students (Perna & Li, 2006).

Some institutions are devoting substantial resources toward reducing the work and loan burden facing low-income students. Over the past several years, Princeton University has gradually increased the availability of need-based grants to low- and lower-middle-income students. Beginning in fall 1998, Princeton has met 100 percent of financial need without the use of loans (i.e., through grants, scholarships, and work-study) for students with family incomes below $40,000 and reduced loan amounts for students with family incomes between $40,000 and $57,000 (*Chronicle of Higher Education*, 1998). Princeton expanded this effort, effective fall 2001, by meeting 100 percent of undergraduates' financial aid through sources other than loans (Olsen & Lively, 2001). In 1998 Princeton also eliminated home equity from consideration in financial needs analysis for students with family incomes below $90,000 (*Chronicle of Higher Education*, 1998). Princeton reports that these changes caused the share of students who receive financial aid to rise from 38 percent in 1998 to 52 percent today (Princeton University, 2005).

Although Princeton is one of a very small number of institutions that has the financial resources for such generous aid packages (Brownstein, 2001), several public universities now offer programs that ease the work and loan burden for the lowest-income students. For example, starting with the fall 2004 entering class, the University of North Carolina's Carolina Covenant ensures that, for low-income students, the costs of attendance are covered by a combination of federal, state, institutional, and private grants and scholarships as well as a 10-12 hour/week work-study job. The program was originally targeted to students with family incomes below 150 percent of the poverty level and now serves students with family incomes below 200 percent of the poverty level (University of North Carolina, 2005). Similarly, the University of Maryland's Pathways program guarantees that students who are residents of the state of Maryland who have zero EFC will have the costs of attendance covered through a combination of federal, state, and institutional grants and on-campus work-study employment (University of Maryland Office of Student Financial Aid, 2005). The University of Virginia's Access UVA program has several components. First, effective fall 2004, the program meets the financial need of students with family incomes below 150 percent of the poverty level with a combination of grants as well as work-study. Effective fall 2005, the university limits the amount of need-based loans to 25 percent of the cost of attendance for an in-state student and meets any remaining financial need with grants. In addition, the University promises to meet 100 percent of financial need of all students through a combination of grants, loans, and work-study (University of Virginia, 2004).

The effects of these programs on students' employment decisions have not been examined. Moreover, reflecting the high costs of need-based grants, these programs serve relatively low numbers of students (e.g., 225 Carolina Covenant Scholars enrolled in fall 2004, University of North Carolina, 2005). Nonetheless, by meeting 100 percent of financial need and providing students with a 10-15 hour per week work-study job, these programs likely reduce financial pressures to work excessive numbers of hours off-campus and promote the most beneficial type and amount of employment.

Encourage Students to Borrow Responsibly

A third strategy for reducing students' financial need to work is to encourage students to borrow responsibly. For most students, some amount of borrowing is an effective mechanism for financing educational costs. Based on her descriptive analyses of data from the 1995-96 Beginning Postsecondary Student survey, King (2002) observed that the financing strategy with the highest observed persistence rates had two components: borrowing and working between one and 14 hours per week. Yet, King (2002) found that only 6 percent of 1995-96 beginning postsecondary students chose this financing strategy; 45 percent choose the strategy with the lowest persistence rates (no borrowing and working 15 or more hours per week).

Therefore, institutions are likely to enhance students' educational experiences by offering counseling about the range of available options for financing the costs of their education and the "costs, benefits, and consequences" of pursuing different options (King, 2002, p. 31). This type of counseling may be provided to students as part of first-year experiences and/or orientation programs (Richards, 2003; Tuttle, McKinney & Rago, 2005).

Of course, a strategy that encourages borrowing must recognize the potential negative consequences of borrowing, especially for students who are at-risk of dropping out of college (Gladieux & Perna, 2005). About one-fifth of borrowers who first enrolled in a postsecondary educational institution in 1995-96 had dropped out by 2001. Compared with borrowers who completed a degree, borrowers who dropped out were less likely to be employed and more likely to default on their loan (Gladieux & Perna, 2005).

These patterns challenge institutions to identify the most appropriate approach to the "double-bind" for low-income students:

Borrowing can cause long-term negative financial consequences for those who fail to complete their programs. Yet avoidance of borrowing may push students to delay enrolling after high school, to enroll part-time in college, or to work full-time while in college, each of which is a known risk factor for dropping out of college. (Gladieux & Perna, 2005, pp. 11-12)

Improve the Quality of Students' Employment Experiences

Even if institutions are able to reduce students' financial need to work, some portion of students will continue to work. Sociocultural perspectives suggest that some students will work to finance life-style choices, a perspective supported by the finding that 70 percent of dependent students with family incomes of at least $100,000 work while enrolled (Table 2). A demographic perspective suggests that the growing number of older students will work to enhance their families' financial well-being. Because research suggests that the greatest negative consequences in terms of persistence and time-to-degree are associated with working more than 15 hours per week off-campus, administrators should identify ways to expand on-campus employment opportunities and support increases in the Federal Work-study program.

Identify Ways to Expand On-Campus Employment Opportunities

As recommended by others (e.g., Tuttle et al., 2005), colleges and universities may enhance educational experiences by encouraging more students to work on campus. This paper shows that virtually all (91%) working undergraduates are now employed in off-campus positions. Thus, institutions should attempt to increase both the availability and attractiveness of on-campus employment opportunities.

Institutions must recognize that, in order to attract students to these positions, they must compete with off-campus employment opportunities.

In order to determine the best ways to expand on-campus employment, institutions must first understand why the vast majority of students are currently working off- rather than on-campus. One potential explanation is that off-campus employment opportunities are more plentiful than on-campus opportunities. However, anecdotal evidence suggests that this explanation is insufficient, as some institutions have difficulty filling all on-campus positions. Thus, before identifying how to expand the demand for on-campus positions, institutions must determine whether students prefer off-campus to on-campus employment because off-campus employment provides greater financial compensation, stronger links to future career goals, or some other advantage.

While offering higher wages than off-campus employers may be the simplest way to increase the attractiveness of on-campus employment opportunities, institutions may be able to successfully attract students to these positions by promoting other benefits. Among the potential non-monetary benefits of on-campus employment relative to off-campus employment are greater convenience, congruence with academic coursework, and promotion of career goals. Institutions should also consider ways to develop employment opportunities that are related to students' academic and career interests.

Support Increases in Federal Work-study Programs

To further improve the educational experiences of students who work, institutions should actively support increased federal funding for work-study employment. This report shows that 85 percent of working dependent under-graduates and 95 percent of working independent undergrad-uates hold only non-work-study jobs.

Despite the benefits of work-study employment, only a small fraction of the nation's financial aid resources are awarded in the form of work-study. Specifically, less than 1 percent of all aid awarded to postsecondary education students from all sources in 2004-05 was in the form of Federal Work-study (The College Board, 2005b). In 2004-05, nearly 7 times more students utilized Stafford subsidized loans than received Federal Work-study (5,546,000 borrowers versus 826,000 recipients, The College Board, 2005b). Between 1994-95 and 2004-05, total funding for grants increased in constant dollars by 86 percent and funding for loans increased by 130 percent, but funding for work-study increased by only 24 percent (The College Board, 2005b).

Work-study programs should be expanded not only to serve a higher percentage of students, but also to compensate participating students at a rate above the federal minimum wage. In his review of research conducted in the late 1980s and early 1990s, St. John (2003) found that aid in the form of work-study was negatively related to persistence. He concluded that the negative relationship between work-study and persistence suggests either that work-study wages are too low to enable a student to pay the costs of attendance, and/or that the hours worked by work-study students are too high. In 2003-04, a majority of working dependent and independent undergraduates who held work-study jobs also held non-work-study jobs, further suggesting the financial inadequacy of work-study employment (Table 3).

Adapt the Delivery of Educational Services to Address the Needs of Working Students

In addition to reducing the financial need to work and expanding on-campus employment opportunities, institutions should adapt the delivery of instruction, as well as academic and support services, to address the needs of working students. The research reviewed in this paper shows that, while their academic performance may not be affected, students who work are less academically involved, have fewer choices of classes, and have less access to the library (Choy & Berker, 2003; Furr & Elling, 2000; King & Bannon, 2002; Pascarella et al., 1994; Pascarella & Terenzini, 2005).

Institutions should consider strategies that simultaneously address students' needs to both work and participate in high-quality educational experiences. One approach may be to expand opportunities for students to earn experiential learning credit (Coplin, 2005). While offered as a means for reducing instructional costs, this strategy may also generate benefits for working students. Coplin provides anecdotal support for this suggestion, stating that alumni of one program support the granting of credit for experience-based learning. A second potential strategy is to employ upper-level undergraduates as teaching assistants or tutors. Future research should examine the benefits and costs of these and other changes in the delivery of educational services.

Conclusion

For various reasons, nearly all college students, regardless of the type of institution that they attend or their socioeconomic status, now work some number of hours while they are enrolled. Working 15 or fewer hours per week typically enhances a student's educational experiences, especially if the employment is on-campus and/or related to the student's field of study or career goals. However, for many students, especially those who work off-campus, work more than 15 hours per week, and/or hold jobs that are unrelated to their academic or career interests, working negatively impacts postsecondary educational experiences and opportunities. Given the prevalence of working and the range of potential positive and negative consequences, institutions must examine student-employment patterns on their individual campuses, reduce the financial need to work, improve the quality of students' employment experiences, and adapt the delivery of educational services to better serve working students.

References

Advisory Committee on Student Financial Assistance (2005, Fall). Is financial aid adequate? What do the data show? *Access and persistence.* Washington, DC: Author.

Advisory Committee on Student Financial Assistance (2002). *Empty promises: The myth of college access in America.* Washington, DC: Author.

Baum, S. (2005). *Financial barriers to college access and persistence: The current status of student reliance on grants, loans, and work.* Paper prepared for the Advisory Committee on Student Financial Assistance, Washington, DC.

Baum, S., & Payea, K. (2004). *Education pays 2004: The benefits of higher education for individuals and society.* Washington, DC: The College Board.

Becker, G. (1993). *Human capital: a theoretical and empirical analysis with special reference to education* (3rd edition). Chicago: University of Chicago Press.

Becker, G. (1962). Investment in human capital: A theoretical analysis. *Journal of Political Economy,* 70(5), 9-49.

Beeson, M.J., & Wessel, R.D. (2002). The impact of working on campus on the academic persistence of freshmen. *Journal of Student Financial Aid, 32*(2), 37-45.

Beginning Postsecondary Students Longitudinal Study (BPS:94/01). Data analysis system. Washington, DC: National Center for Education Statistics.

Berker, A., & Horn, L. (2003). *Work first, study second: Adult undergraduates who combine employment and postsecondary enrollment.* Washington, DC: U.S. Department of Education, National Center for Education Statistics. (NCES 2003-167).

Berkner, L., Wei, C.C., He, S., Lew, S., Cominole, M., & Siegel, P. (2005). *Undergraduate financial aid estimates for 2003-04 by type of institution.* Washington, DC: National Center for Education Statistics. (NCES 2005-163) Retrieved October 12, 2005 from www.nces.ed.gov/pubsearch.

Bowen, H.R. (1997). *Investment in learning: The individual and social value of American higher education.* Baltimore: Johns Hopkins University Press.

Brownstein, A. (2001, February 16). Upping the ante for student aid: Princeton replaces loans with grants, and the rest of higher education struggles to keep up. *Chronicle of Higher Education,* p. A47.

Bushman, M.F., & Dean, J.E. (2005). Outsourcing of non-mission-critical functions: A solution to the rising cost of college attendance. In *Course corrections: Experts offer solutions to the college cost crisis* (pp. 6-19). Indianapolis, IN: Lumina Foundation for Education.

Cheng, D.X. (2004). *To Work or Not to Work: The impact of work on students' college experience.* Paper Presented at the Association for Institutional Research Annual Forum.

Choy, S., & Berker, A. (2003). *How families of low- and middle-income undergraduates pay for college: Full-time dependent students in 1999-2000.* Washington, DC: U.S. Department of Education, National Center for Education Statistics. (NCES 2003-162).

Choy, S., & Carroll, D. (2000). *Debt burden four years after college.* Washington, DC: U.S. Department of Education, National Center for Education Statistics. (NCES 2000-188).

Chronicle of Higher Education (1998, September 4). Note book: New financial aid policy makes more students pick Princeton. *Chronicle of Higher Education*, p. A67.

College Board, The (2005a). *Trends in college pricing.* Washington, DC: Author.

College Board, The (2005b). *Trends in student aid 2005.* Washington, DC: Author.

Coplin, B. (2005). Seven steps: Ways to reduce instructional costs and improve undergraduate and graduate education. In *Course corrections: Experts offer solutions to the college cost crisis* (pp. 20-31). Indianapolis, IN: Lumina Foundation for Education.

DesJardins, S.L., Ahlburg, D.A., McCall, B.P. (2002). A temporal investigation of factors related to timely degree completion. *Journal of Higher Education, 73,* 555-581.

ECMC Group Foundation. (2003). *Cultural barriers to incurring debt: An exploration of borrowing and impact on access to postsecondary education.* Santa Fe, NM: Author.

Ehrenberg, R.G. (1991). Academic labor supply. In C.T. Clotfelter, R.G. Ehrenberg, M. Getz, & J.J. Siegfried (Eds.), *Economic challenges in higher education* (pp. 143-260). Chicago: University of Chicago Press.

Ehrenberg, R.G., & Sherman, D.R. (1987). Employment while in college, academic achievements, and postcollege outcomes. *Journal of Human Resources, 22*(1), 1-23.

Ellwood, D.T., & Kane, T.J. (2000). Who is getting a college education? Family background and the growing gaps in enrollment. In S. & W.J. Danzinger (Eds.), *Securing the future: Investing in children from birth to college* (pp. 283-324). New York: Russell Sage Foundation.

Fox, M. (1992). Student debt and enrollment in graduate and professional school. *Applied Economics, 24,* 669-677.

Furr, S.R., & Elling, T.W. (2000). The Influence of Work on College Student Development. *NASPA Journal, 37*(2), 454-470.

Gladieux, L., & Perna, L. (2005). *Borrowers who drop out: A neglected aspect of the college student loan trend.* San Jose, CA: National Center for Public Policy and Higher Education.

Gleason, P.M. (1993). College student employment, academic progress, and postcollege labor market success. *Journal of Student Financial Aid, 23*(2), 5-14.

Harding, E., & Harmon, L. (1999). *Higher education students' off-campus work patterns.* Olympia, WA: Washington State Institute for Public Policy. (ERIC Document Reproduction Service Number ED 434 627).

Hearn, J.C. (2001). Access to postsecondary education: Financing equity in an evolving context. In M.P. Paulsen, & J.C. Smart (Eds.), *The finance of higher education: Theory, research, policy, and practice* (pp. 439-460). New York: Agathon Press.

Higher Education Act of 1965, Part C, Section 441. Retrieved November 27, 2004 from www.edworkforce.house. gov/publications/heacomp/hea65003.pdf.

Hotz, V.J., Xu, L.C., Tienda, M., & Ahituv, A. (2002). Are there returns to the wages of young men from working while in school? *Review of Economics and Statistics, 84*(2), 221-236.

Hudson, L., & Hurst, D. (2002). *The persistence of employees who pursue postsecondary study.* Washington, DC: National Center for Education Statistics. (NCES 2002-188).

King, J.E. (2002). *Crucial choices: How students' financial decisions affect their academic success.* Washington, DC: American Council on Education.

King, J.E., & Bannon, E. (2002). *At what cost? The price that working students pay for a college education.* Washington, DC: State PIRGs.

Leslie, L.L., & Brinkman, P.T. (1988). *The Economic value of higher education.* New York: American Council on Education, MacMillan Publishing Company.

Light, A., 2001. In-school work experience and the returns to schooling, *Journal of Labor Economics, 19*(1), 65-93.

Lundberg, C.A. (2004). Working and learning: The role of involvement for employed students. *NASPA Journal, 41,* 201-215.

McMillion, R. (2005). *The role of work and loans in paying for an undergraduate education: Observations from the 2003-04 National Postsecondary Student Aid Study (NPSAS:04).* Round Rock, TX: Texas Guaranteed Student Loan Corporation.

Molitor, C.J., & Leigh, D.E. (2005). In-school work experience and the returns to two-year and four-year colleges. *Economics of Education Review, 24*(4), 459-468.

National Postsecondary Student Aid Study (NPSAS:04). Data analysis system. Washington, DC: National Center for Education Statistics.

Olsen, F., & Lively, K. (2001, February 9). Princeton increases endowment spending to replace students' loans with grants. *Chronicle of Higher Education,* p. A32.

Pascarella, E.T., Bohr, L., Nora, A., Desler, M., & Zusman, B. (1994). Impacts of on-campus and off-campus work on first-year cognitive outcomes. *Journal of College Student Development, 35,* 364-370.

Pascarella, E.T., Edison, M., Nora, A., Hagedorn, L., & Terenzini, P. (1998). Does work inhibit cognitive development during college? *Educational Evaluation and Policy Analysis, 20*(2), 75-93.

Pascarella, E.T., & Terenzini, P.T. (2005). *How college affects students, volume 2: A third decade of research.* San Francisco: Jossey-Bass.

Paulsen, M.B. (2001). The economics of human capital and investment in higher education. In M.B. Paulsen & J.C. Smart (Eds.), *The finance of higher education: Theory, research, policy, and practice.* (pp. 55-94). New York: Agathon Press.

Perna, L.W. (2006a). Studying college choice: A proposed conceptual model. In J.C. Smart (Ed.), *Higher Education: Handbook of theory and research.* New York: Agathon Press.

Perna, L.W. (2006b). Understanding the relationship between information about college costs and financial aid and students' college-related behaviors. *American Behavioral Scientist, 49,* 1620-1635.

Perna, L.W. (2004). Understanding the decision to enroll in graduate school: Sex and racial/ethnic group differences. *Journal of Higher Education, 75,* 487-527.

Perna, L.W. (2001). Undergraduate borrowing at the federal limit before and after the 1992 reauthorization of the Higher Education Act. *Journal of Student Financial Aid, 31*(1), 25-38.

Perna, L.W., & Li, C. (2006). College affordability for middle-income students: Implications for college opportunity. *Journal of Student Financial Aid, 36*(1), 7-24.

Princeton University (2005). *Undergraduate financial aid.* Princeton, NJ: Author. Retrieved October 13, 2005 from www.princeton.edu.

Richards, H.N. (2003). The effects of work on students' academic persistence and overall collegiate experience. *Journal of Student Affairs, 13.* Retrieved from www.sahe.colostate.edu/journalarchive.asp#0304.

St. John, E.P. (2006). Contending with financial inequality: The theory problem in research on college access and persistence. *American Behavioral Scientist, 49,* 1604-1619.

St. John, E.P. (2003). *Refinancing the college dream: Access, equal opportunity, and justice for taxpayers.* Baltimore: Johns Hopkins University Press.

Steelman, L.C., & Powell, B. (1993). Doing the right thing: Race and parental locus of responsibility for funding college. *Sociology of Education, 66,* 223-244.

Stern, D., & Nakata, Y.F. (1991). Paid employment among college students: Trends, effects, and possible causes. *Journal of Higher Education, 62,* 25-43.

Stinebrickner, R., & Stinebrickner, T.R. (2004). Time-use and college outcomes. *Journal of Econometrics, 121*(1/2), 243-269.

Stinebrickner, R., & Stinebrickner, T.R. (2003). Working during school and academic performance. *Journal of Labor Economics, 21*(2), 473-491.

Stringer, W.L., Cunningham, A.F., O'Brien, C.T., & Merisotis, J. (1998). *It's all relative: The role of parents in college financing and enrollment.* Indianapolis, IN: Lumina Foundation for Education, New Agenda Series.

Terenzini, P.T., Cabrera, A.F., & Bernal, E.M. (2001). *Swimming against the tide: The poor in American higher education.* (Report No. 2001-1). New York: College Entrance Examination Board.

Tinto, V. (1993). *Leaving college: rethinking the causes and cures of student attrition.* Chicago: University of Chicago Press.

Trent, W.T., Lee, H.S., & Owens-Nicholson, D. (2006). Perceptions of financial aid among students of color: Examining the role(s) of self-concept, locus of control, and expectations. *American Behavioral Scientist, 49,* 1739-1759.

Tuttle, T., with McKinney, J., & Rago, M. (2005, April). College students working: The choice nexus. *IPAS (Indiana Project on Academic Success) Topics Brief.*

Twigg, C. (2005). Improving quality and reducing costs: The case for redesign. In *Course corrections: Experts offer solutions to the college cost crisis* (pp. 32-49). Indianapolis, IN: Lumina Foundation for Education.

University of Maryland Office of Student Financial Aid (2005). *Maryland pathways.* College Park, MD: Author. Retrieved October 13, 2005 from www.financialaid.umd.edu.

University of North Carolina (2005). *Carolina covenant.* Chapel Hill, NC: Author. Retrieved October 13, 2005 from www.unc.edu/carolinacovenant.

University of Virginia (2004, October 15-28). *Inside UVA online.* Charlottesville, VA: Author. Retrieved October 13, 2005 from www.virginia.edu/insideuva.

U.S. Department of Education (2005). *Federal student aid: Students, parents, counselors.* Washington, DC: Author. Retrieved November 7, 2005 from www.studentaid.ed.gov.

U.S. Department of Education (2004). *The EFC formula, 2004-05.* Washington, DC: Author. Retrieved November 29, 2004 from www.ifap.ed.gov/efcinformation.

U.S. Department of Education (1998). *Indicator of the month: Working while in college.* Washington, DC: National Center for Education Statistics. (NCES 98010).

Weiler, W.C. (1991). The effect of undergraduate student loans on the decision to pursue postbaccalaureate study. *Educational Evaluation and Policy Analysis, 13,* 212-220.

CHAPTER 5

SEEKING EQUAL EDUCATIONAL OPPORTUNITY: DESEGREGATION OF HIGHER EDUCATION AND THE TOPS SCHOLARSHIP PROGRAM IN LOUISIANA

Masamichi Inoue and Terry G. Geske

Historical under-representation of minority groups in higher education, combined with the expected shifts in the demographic makeup of the general population in the United States, pose a significant challenge to the higher education community (Bowen and Bok, 1998). Finding ways to accommodate the increasing number of minority students at colleges and universities has become a daunting task for many states in the South. These states typically have higher concentrations of minority populations and they also have a more limited history of institutional accommodation of minority students at their predominantly white institutions (Kim, 2002).

Recently, an important issue of chronic under-representation of students coming from low income brackets in colleges and universities has been raised (Bowen, Kurzweil & Tobin, 2005). Since the early 1980s, enrollments at colleges and universities have increased steadily, whereas state appropriations to higher education have not kept up with inflation (Advisory Committee on Student Financial Assistance, 2002). At the same time, the average

161

Copyright ©2007 AMS Press, Inc. All rights reserved.

Pell Grant, which is need-based and funded by the federal government, has not kept pace with escalating college attendance costs (Kane, 1999). Hence, affordability of higher education has been seriously eroded (College Board, 2005a & 2005b), and minority students who predominantly come from low income brackets now experience even greater difficulties in attaining a college education. The plight of these low-income minority students has now been compounded by the recent efforts by various states to fund scholarship programs which are strongly biased toward merit-based programs rather than need-based programs (National Association of State Student Grant and Aid Programs [NASSGAP], 2005).

A new chapter in the history of higher education in Louisiana began in 1989 when the U.S. District Court of the Eastern District of Louisiana ordered a remedial plan for the ongoing desegregation effort of the higher education system in Louisiana. This new remedial plan followed a 40-year legacy of attempts to desegregate higher education, and it ultimately led to a new 10-year desegregation settlement in 1995. Every major initiative or implemented change in education in Louisiana has to be considered in the context of the state's history of desegregation. St. John and Hossler (1998) emphasized the need to consider the interconnectedness of various policy issues in higher education and the ongoing desegregation efforts in the South.

Thus, it becomes important to recognize and examine the interplay between the implementation of the ongoing desegregation settlement (*United States vs. Louisiana*, 1994) and the enactment of any new policy initiatives in education in Louisiana. Three years after a settlement was agreed upon in the desegregation case, Louisiana enacted in 1997 a merit-based scholarship program, entitled Tuition Opportunity Program for Students (TOPS), which was implemented for the 1998-99 school year. This broad-based merit-aid program pays for full or partial tuition costs at the state's public and private universities for those high school graduates who meet the required set of academic standards. Since its inception, total state funding for TOPS has increased rapidly, surpassing $116 million for school year 2004-05 (Louisiana Office of Student Financial Assistance, 2005).

Because the issue of improving equal educational opportunity or access to higher education is an inherent goal of both the desegregation settlement and the TOPS program, there is an opportunity for Louisiana to optimize the effectiveness of its merit-based scholarship program. As pointed out by St. John and Hossler (1998), statewide coordination is required in order to address the issue of accessibility to higher education as it relates to deseg-regation, student grants, and direct subsidies to institutions. In order to untangle the many complex issues intertwined in desegregating higher education in the South, a critical-empirical perspective is needed (St. John and Hossler, 1998). This chapter attempts to provide such a perspective by beginning with a brief history of both the ongoing desegregation efforts and the TOPS program in Louisiana. The chapter then examines who benefits from the TOPS program, and how these findings on the effects of the TOPS program serve to impact the desegregation settlement agreement.

Desegregation of Higher Education

Louisiana's first state university, then known as the Louisiana State Seminary of Learning and Military Academy was founded in 1861, (Arceneaux, 1995). Today it is known as Louisiana State University (LSU). The school remained a segregated institution until it admitted six African American students in 1964 (Louisiana State University, 2005, May 25). Following the period of Reconstruction after the Civil War, a dual system of higher education, based on the principle of "separate but equal" educational facilities for black students and white students, was firmly established. In Baton Rouge, the state's capitol, for example, LSU-BR and Southern University-BR, a historically black institution, both offered virtually the same types of programs.[1] Similar arrangements were found in Shreveport, New Orleans, and Lincoln Parish (Arceneaux, 1995). Arceneaux (1995) states:

> These universities, both black and white in each area, have since taken root and flourished as educational institutions. This has created what can correctly be called Louisiana's proximate college dilemma, in which universities in the same geographical area offer the same programs to racially different student bodies but with each university becoming an important part of the community in which it exists. (p. 1284)

In 1954, *Brown vs. Board of Education* signaled the end of the legal principle of "separate but equal," the theoretical underpinning of the dual system. The U.S. Court of Appeals for the Fifth Circuit examined the Louisiana school system using *Brown* in *Bush vs. Orleans Parish School Board*, a class action suit brought by black school children who wished to be admitted to Orleans Parish schools on a non-segregated basis. In *Bush*, the Fifth Circuit ruled that Louisiana's laws were unconstitutional. The *Bush* ruling spelled the end to Louisiana's de jure system of segregation, but not the state's open efforts to maintain the segregation of the races (Arceneaux, 1995).

Segregationist politicians in the 1950s and early 1960s refused to accept the U.S. Supreme Court's mandate in *Brown*. It was not until the late 1960s, after numerous federal law suits and increasing political pressure, that truly race-neutral admissions standards were established, and black students and white students were actually free to attend other-race schools. The racial structure of Louisiana's colleges and universities, however, remained virtually unchanged. There had been no affirmative action by the predominantly white institutions to recruit black students, and white students were not encouraged to attend black institutions because black institutions remained underfunded compared to their white counterparts.

In the case initially named *Adams vs. Richardson* (1972), the federal circuit court identified ten states as having dual systems of higher education and required them to submit desegregation plans to the federal government (Brown, 1999). Although *Adams vs. Richardson* (1972, 1973, & 1973) did clarify many of the questions central to collegiate desegregation, there had been little direct Supreme Court guidance on the issue of segregation in the higher education context using a post-*Brown* rationale until 1992 when it ruled on *United States vs. Fordice* (Byrd-Chichester, 2000).

In 1974, the U.S. Justice Department sued the State of Louisiana and its various governing boards of higher education for their lack of plans to change the formally de jure segregated system (Arceneaux, 1995). Also in 1974, Louisiana enacted a new state constitution that included a change for the governance of higher education. The new governance system, which was approved by the voters and implemented in 1975, consists of the following four boards: 1) the Board of Regents, a coordinating board; 2) the Louisiana State University Board of Supervisors, which oversees the LSU system; 3) the Southern University Board of Supervisors, which manages the SU system; and 4) the Board of Trustees for State Colleges and Universities, which has authority over the remaining universities (Arceneaux, 1995).

The parties to *United States vs. Louisiana* (1981) initiated settlement discussions in 1980 that eventually led to a consent decree the following year (Arceneaux, 1995). The decree had the following three basic goals: 1) to reshape the process of admissions and recruitment in Louisiana's public universities, with an emphasis on the recruitment of other-race students, 2) to eliminate some program duplication and to create entirely new programs at the predominantly black universities so as to enhance their academic standings, and 3) to remedy the financial disadvantages historically suffered by the predominantly black universities. Subsequently, in 1981, the consent decree was approved and adopted by the federal district court. The plan was to operate for six years.

A three-judge panel of this district court ruled in 1988 that the state was still operating "clearly racially identifiable" colleges and universities. The district court ordered a Special Master Plan to be prepared by the court's appointed expert. The remedial order consisted of four provisions. The first would eliminate the current governing system consisting of four separate boards and adopt a single governing board for all higher education. The second provision called for the classification of the state's universities into three levels with differing admissions standards for each. The highest classification would consist solely of LSU, which would become the state's "flagship institution." LSU would have the most selective admissions policy and a complete offering of doctoral and other graduate programs. The second level would consist of intermediate institutions having slightly less rigorous admissions standards than LSU. The third level contains the remaining universities with the least selective admissions policy or open admissions. The third provision of the order called for the creation of a comprehensive community college system. These community colleges would concentrate on remedial courses in an attempt to prepare students for four-year institutions. The final provision dealt with program duplication and management, including the immediate merger of the Southern

University Law Center and the LSU Law Center into one institution.

In 1989, the Southern University Board of Supervisors appealed to the U.S. Supreme Court to stay enforcement of the district court's rulings on liability and remedy pending appeal, and a stay was granted. This delay would play an important role in the litigation because the law was about to change within the Fifth Circuit regarding the desegregation of colleges and universities (Arceneaux, 1995). Prior to 1992, the U.S. Supreme Court had never specifically addressed the issue of segregation in the higher education context using a post-*Brown* rationale (Arceneaux, 1995). The law was not clear concerning what exactly comprised a state's affirmative duty to desegregate former de jure systems of higher education. To clarify this ambiguity, the Court granted certiorari in *Ayers vs. Allain*, a suit arising out of Mississippi for desegregation of their higher education system, under the name of *United States vs. Fordice*.

In discussing the specific situation in Mississippi, the court raised issues that could be applied to other states. The court noted that in the higher education context, the affirmative duty to desegregate should not mean that there can be no degree of racial imbalance. The duty to desegregate does not require any restriction of choice to achieve some specified level of racial balance. Quotas are not appropriate because a person's right to choose which college to attend should be respected. In addition, a state cannot meet its burden by solely enhancing its predominantly black universities to the level of predominantly white universities. A state must totally abandon its former practices and policies that promoted segregation to the full extent allowable within the parameters of sound educational practices.

Justice Thomas's concurring opinion in *Fordice* raised an important point for Louisiana's situation. He wrote separately to emphasize that *Fordice* does not demand the termination of historically black universities that have remained predominantly black because these universities no doubt serve sound educational goals, and for practical reasons, cannot be eliminated. Subsequently, the district court ruled to reinstate the 1988 liability order, along with the 1989 remedial plan, in light of the requirements set forth in *Fordice*. The only major amendment to the remedial order was the removal of the requirement to merge the LSU Law Center with the Southern University Law Center. It was believed that the LSU Law Center had made genuine good faith efforts to have a more racially balanced student body, and the Southern University Law School had already been fully integrated with a student composition of about 53 percent black and 47 percent white at that time.

United States vs. Louisiana (1992) reached the Fifth Circuit in 1993 (Arceneaux, 1995). If affirmed, it stood to make radical changes to Louisiana's higher education system. These changes were unanimously opposed by almost the entire state government and educational community. The court held that the district court properly analyzed the problem of Louisiana's proximate college dilemma and the program duplication it produced. The existence of proximate colleges and program duplication was found to be clearly traceable to the state's prior de jure system as a direct result of the "separate but equal" era. Despite this violation, the Fifth Circuit Court was unable to affirm the Eastern District Court on this basis because of issues of disputed fact concerning which programs were unnecessarily duplicative.

Regarding the governance issue, the appellate court found that the district court incorrectly analyzed the issue. Since the four board system of governance was not established until 1974, it could not be traced back to Louisiana's prior de jure policies or practices. In the remedial order, the court found that Louisiana's open admissions policy could not be traced back to a practice or policy of the de jure system. The court concluded by reversing the summary judgment ruling of the 1988 order, vacating the remedial order, and remanding the case for a determination of liability and resolution of the issues. Finally on November 4, 1994, the U.S. Justice Department and the state reached a settlement agreement. The settlement agreement was designated as Consent Decree II (CDII) (*U.S. vs. Louisiana*, 1994).

The CDII's main purpose was to create some measure of fiscal equality between the state's predominantly white universities and predominantly black universities (Arceneaux, 1995). The CDII pledged about $60 million dollars for a number of new programs at both Southern and Gambling Universities, while forbidding creation of duplicate programs at any proximate institution. The intent was to improve the quality of the predominantly black universities and thus make them more attractive to white students. Regarding the issue of the admissions criteria, the CDII allowed each institution to set its own criteria according to its own mission and goals. The plan clearly stated that an institution may not rely on one single measure, such as ACT test scores. The plan also allowed for a ten-percent exception for other-race students in the hopes of nurturing integration.

The agreement also established a community college in Baton Rouge. The Baton Rouge Community College would be run jointly by LSU's and Southern University's Boards and would target remedial students, while also providing vocational training for those who do not wish to attend a four-year institution. The joint operation was designed to ensure a racial balance from inception. The plan also included a commitment by the state to encourage the employment of other-race faculty, coupled with a plan for other-race recruitment and retention of students.

In the area of graduate programs, the plan called for LSU and Southern University to formulate an arrangement that would channel their respective graduates to the graduate and professional programs at each other's school as other-race students. Furthermore, scholarships would be created at the graduate level for both schools for other-race students at each school. The LSU Law Center would continue the process of attracting and graduating other-race students, while the Southern University Law Center would commit to a plan of improvement concerning both its facilities and academic standards.

The CDII went into effect in 1995, and was scheduled to end on December 31, 2005. It mandated that a three-member Monitoring Committee, approved by the court, be responsible for evaluating the state's compliance and filing an annual evaluation with the court. The governing board of higher education was restructured in 1998 when the voters of Louisiana revised its state constitution creating a fourth management board, the Louisiana Community and Technical College System (LCTCS). Thus, the governing system necessary to run the structure of higher education required by the settlement was satisfied.

The latest annual report available is the ninth-year report submitted to the court in 2004. According to the ninth-year report, mandates accomplished to date include the following:

- Creation of the Baton Rouge Community College
- Implementation of four Ph.D. programs, three masters programs, one baccalaureate program, and one associate program at Southern University
- Implementation of all mandated masters program at Southern University at New Orleans
- Implementation of one doctoral program, two masters program, one baccalaureate program, and one associate program at Grambling State University

- Implementation of joint, dual, and cooperative programs at proximate institutions
- Completion of fifteen of twenty-one capital outlay projects
- Improvement of physical facilities at Southern University Law Center
- Awarding of sixty-six doctoral degrees through the other-race doctoral scholarship funding at predominately white universities
- Awarding of 564 degrees through programs implemented through the settlement

TOPS Program

The origin of TOPS (Tuition Opportunity Program for Students) can be traced back to an idea originally proposed to Louisiana legislators by the late Patrick Taylor, a philanthropic petroleum industrialist, to provide funding for a free college education for every financially needy child who studied hard and made good grades. Taylor's plan resulted in the establishment of a new state-funded tuition program for financially needy students in 1989. This new scholarship program became the Louisiana Tuition Assistance Plan (LTAP) in 1992. Also at this time, a new merit-based program, the Honors Scholarship Program, an idea devised by then LSU Chancellor William "Bud" Davis, was established by the legislature. This Honors Program offered a full tuition waiver to all high school graduates who ranked in the top five percent of each graduating class at public and private schools in the state.

About a dozen states adopted state-funded, broad-based, merit-aid scholarship programs during the late 1990s after the HOPE (Helping Outstanding Pupils Educationally) program was enacted in Georgia in 1993 (Heller, 2004a). A significant feature of many of the merit-based scholarship programs implemented across the country was the absence of any income cap. A new state-funded merit-based program was adopted by the Louisiana Legislature in 1997 by removing the income cap from the TAP program and merging it with the Honors Program. The newly merged program was called TOPS, and it included four basic awards, namely the Honors, Performance, Opportunity, and Tech awards. In order to qualify for TOPS, students have to satisfy minimum academic requirements, including a minimum test score (either ACT or SAT) and a minimum high school grade point average (HSGPA) based on the required 16.5 units of a core curriculum. Table 1 summarizes the required academic qualifications, and the value and the duration of each type of TOPS award.

Table 1. Eligibility Requirements, Value, and Duration of TOPS Awards.

Award	Curriculum	Core GPA	ACT (SAT)	Value	Duration
Honors Award	College Prep Core 16.5 units	3.5	27 (1210)	Tuition + $800 stipend	4 years
Performance Award	College Prep Core 16.5 units	3.5	23 (1060)	Tuition + $400 stipend	4 years
Opportunity Award	College Prep Core 16.5 units	2.5	20 (940)	Tuition	4 years
Tech Award	Modified College Prep Core	2.5	17 (810)	Tuition	2 years

Source: Louisiana Board of Regents, 2004, p. 4.

The TOPS program was implemented with the fall 1998 entering freshman class. Although the legislation that created TOPS does not directly establish the goals of the program, the following four objectives are generally accepted as the objectives of TOPS (Louisiana Board of Regents, 2004):

- To provide financial incentives as a reward for good academic performance;
- To promote academic success by requiring completion of a rigorous high school core curriculum;
- To keep Louisiana's best and brightest in the state to pursue postsecondary educational opportunities; and
- To promote access to postsecondary educational opportunities.

Students eligible for a TOPS award may elect to attend any accredited public or approved private college and university within the state. TOPS awards provide an amount equal to undergraduate tuition for full-time attendance. For 2004-2005, the value of the TOPS tuition award varied from $764 at L.E. Fletcher Technical Community College to $3,232 at LSU. For students who attend private colleges and universities, the TOPS tuition award was set at $2,582. In addition to tuition, students are also assessed additional fees. The gap between the TOPS tuition award and the actual tuition costs, plus any mandatory fees, varied from $186 at River Parishes Community College to $964 at LSU. For private colleges and universities, this gap varied from $3,054 at Our Lady of the Lake College to $28,628 at Tulane University.

In 2001, the legislature assigned responsibility to the Louisiana Board of Regents to develop and implement a monitoring program for the TOPS program. Subsequently, the first report on TOPS was published by the Board of Regents in the fall 2004 (Louisiana Board of Regents, 2004).

Since the implementation of TOPS, the number of students participating in TOPS has increased from 23,509 to 42,035, while the corresponding total program cost has increased from $54,030,455 in 1998 to $113,651,660 in 2004 (Louisiana Office of Student Financial Assistance, 2005). Table 2 shows the distribution of the different types of awards for the 2003 entering cohort. Most TOPS recipients received Opportunity awards, while the Tech award was least utilized. In terms of institutional type, most TOPS recipients attend public 4-year institutions and some students at private institutions also benefit from TOPS.

Table 2. Distribution of TOPS Awards by Category and Institutional Type, 2003 Cohort.

Award	% Recipients
Honors Award	13%
Performance Award	18%
Opportunity Award	68%
Tech Award	1%
Institutional Type	
Public 2-year	6%
Public 4-year	88%
Private	6%

Source: Louisiana Board of Regents, 2004, p. 11.

Table 3 displays the number of high school graduates in 2003 and 2004 who completed the TOPS core curriculum and who qualified for TOPS. Slightly less than 60 percent of high school graduates completed the TOPS curriculum, and slightly less than 60 percent of those who completed the TOPS curriculum qualified for TOPS. It is important to recognize that the Board of Regents implemented new minimum admissions criteria for its public four-year universities, effective fall 2005 that included the completion of the Regents' high school core curriculum, currently identical to the TOPS core (Louisiana Board of Regents, 2001). More than 40% of high school graduates who completed the TOPS core curriculum did not qualify for TOPS because they did not attain the minimum ACT test score and/or minimum GPA required for TOPS. Despite the efforts and the willingness on the part of students to complete the TOPS core curriculum, students from low-income families are experiencing great difficulty in securing a minimum test score or minimum GPA.

Table 3. Number of High School Graduates, Number Completing TOPS Core Curriculum, and Number Eligible for TOPS, by Graduating Class.

	2003 High School Graduates	2004 High School Graduates
Graduates	45,226	44,569
With TOPS Core	25,546	26,111
Eligible for TOPS	14,797	14,961

Source: Louisiana Board of Regents, 2004, p. 10.

Based on a survey conducted using a small group of undergraduate students at LSU, Smothers (2004) concluded that many African American students are meeting the GPA requirements, but their low ACT scores are making them ineligible for TOPS awards. This finding is in line with other recent studies which suggest that when only courses, grades, and test scores are used as criteria, more prepared low-income students do not have the opportunity to enroll in college (Fitzgerald, 2004; Lee, 2004). Examples in Louisiana include Istrouma High School in Baton Rouge (with 99% black student enrollment, and 81 percent of student body qualify for free or reduced lunch program) where only 18 percent of those who completed the TOPS curriculum qualified for TOPS, and Southern University Lab School in Baton Rouge (with 100% black student enrollment, and 63 percent qualify for free or reduced lunch program) where only 21 percent qualified for TOPS (Louisiana Board of Regents, 2004).

It is well known that there exists a significant test score gap in standardized tests between students coming from wealthier families and those from poorer families and between white students and black students (Jencks and Phillips, 1998). The mean ACT score of all high school graduates in Louisiana who took the ACT has not increased much in recent years, from 19.5 in 1998 to 19.8 in 2005 (Louisiana Department of Education, 2005a), suggesting that as long as TOPS requires a minimum ACT score of 20 (slightly higher than the state's mean), a little more than half of the high school graduates who take the ACT would not qualify for TOPS. Moreover, the mean ACT score of African American students remains much lower, 16.9 for the 2004 Louisiana's high school class (Louisiana Department of Education, 2005a), suggesting that most of these students would not meet the necessary ACT minimum score to qualify for a TOPS award.

The college-going rate can be measured as the percentage of high school graduates who became first-time freshman in colleges and universities in Louisiana. Figure 1 suggests that, except for a temporary dip in 2001, there appears to be a general increasing trend in the college-going rate, which coincides with the implementation of the TOPS program since 1998. Previous studies in other states indicate that college-going rates do increase in response to state merit-based scholarship programs (Cornwell, Mustard & Sridhar, 2003; Dynarski, 2000). Part of the observed increasing trend in the college-going rate in Louisiana, however, is due to a decreasing trend in the number of high school graduates leaving the state for out-of-state colleges and universities.

If the college-going rate is defined as percent of high school graduates going directly to any college in the U.S., it increased from 54.2 percent in 1992 to 57.6 percent in 2002 in Louisiana (NCHEMS Information Center, 2002). The percent of college-going high school graduates staying in Louisiana has increased from 86.8 percent in 1996 to 91 percent in 2002 (Louisiana Board of Regents, 2004). It appears that more high school graduates in Louisiana are going directly to college overall, and more of them are staying in the state to attend college. The net impact of TOPS, however, appears to be minimal, primarily because the TOPS program appears to target the student population which would have gone to college even without TOPS awards. Figure 2 shows the percentage of the first-time freshman class who enrolled in developmental courses (remedial courses) in colleges and universities in Louisiana. A definite declining trend in the participation in developmental courses is evident, suggesting that more of the incoming freshmen are increasingly academically better prepared.

In order to retain their TOPS awards, students must maintain continuous full-time enrollment (24 credits over two semesters) and attain a specified GPA by the end of each academic year. Students must maintain a minimum cumulative GPA of 3.0 for the Honors and Performance awards, and a GPA of 2.3 for the first academic year, and a 2.5 for subsequent years for the Opportunity award. The percentage of students who lost their TOPS awards after the first year because they did not maintain the necessary GPA or carry the required course load was 20.4 percent and 13.8

percent for the 2002 cohort and 17.2 percent and 12.1 percent for the 2003 cohort, respectively (Louisiana Board of Regents, 2004, p. 15).

Figure 1. Percent of graduates who became first-time freshman in Louisiana.

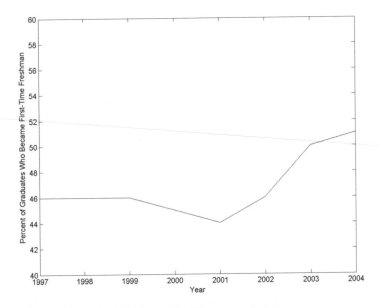

Source: Louisiana Department of Education, 2005b.

Graduation is usually measured at the rate in which first-time entering students earn their degrees within 150 percent of the time required—six years for baccalaureate degrees. The first cohort to receive TOPS awards was the fall 1998 entering class. The six-year graduation rate was 58 percent for TOPS recipients and 21 percent for non-TOPS students (Louisiana Board of Regents, 2004). TOPS recipients graduated at better rates and sooner than non-TOPS students. This may, however, simply be a reflection of the fact, that the TOPS recipients were better prepared than the non-TOPS students.

Figure 2. Percent of the first-time freshman class that enrolled in developmental courses.

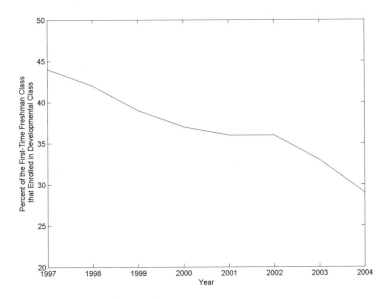

Source: Louisiana Department of Education, 2005b.

If freshman retention is used to measure the impact of TOPS on students' initial persistence in college, freshman retention at four-year institutions has been steadily increasing since 1994 (see Figure 3).   Freshman retention improved at Southern University from 66 percent in 1994 to 77.2 percent in 2005, and at LSU from 84.5 percent in 1994 to 90.6 percent in 2005 (Louisiana Board of Regents Statewide Student Profile System, 2005b).

In contrast, freshman retention at two-year institutions has been stagnant, perhaps reflecting the state's emphasis on improving the quality of higher education at four-year institutions, while two-year institutions have been primarily relegated to providing remedial courses to those who do not qualify for admission to four-year institutions. The vast majority of TOPS awards have gone to students at four-year institutions (see Table 2). A number of factors appear to be contributing toward improving freshman retention at four-year institutions. These factors include tightening the minimum admissions requirements at four-year institutions as mandated by the desegregation settlement while two-year institutions were allowed to maintain open admissions. A potentially troublesome development is that most of the students who do not qualify for admission to four-year institutions also do not qualify for TOPS, which severely curtails, from a financial perspective, their access to any type of postsecondary education.

Who Benefits from TOPS?

A requirement of the TOPS program is that every applicant must complete and submit the Free Application for Federal Student Aid (FAFSA) form, despite the fact that there is no income cap in order to qualify. Once submitted, FAFSA automatically estimates Expected Family Contribution (EFC) which is defined as the amount of financial contribution a student's family is supposed to make. Colleges and universities determine the amount of financial need as the difference between the expected total attendance costs minus EFC. Therefore, EFC can be used to estimate the amount of financial need of a student.

Since 2001, when the Board of Regents was given the task of archiving the relevant data on TOPS, individual student data have been collected by the Student Transcript System (STS) developed by the Louisiana Department of Education (LDE), the Louisiana Office of Student Financial

Assistance (LOSFA), and Louisiana's Board of Regents (BOR). A data set for the 2003 TOPS cohort of high school graduates (13,449) was provided by the Board of Regents for the analyses in this chapter, including data at the individual student level by family income, by EFC reported on the FAFSA form, by parish, by high school, by race, by ACT score, by eligibility for TOPS, by specific TOPS award, by enrollment with TOPS, and by postsecondary institution attended (Louisiana Board of Regents, 2005a). A preliminary analysis of the individual student data for the 2003 entering freshman cohort of TOPS recipients follows.

TOPS Findings

Table 4 displays the distributions of TOPS awards by different family income brackets and by race for all TOPS recipients. Median family income was $66,524 for all TOPS recipients while it ranged from $72,687 for white recipients to $31,764 for African American recipients. More than 40 percent of TOPS recipients came from families with income of more than $75,000/year. This high income bracket expanded to more than 50 percent for white TOPS recipients, whereas it accounted for only 17.7 percent for African American TOPS recipients. White students received 77.1 percent of all TOPS awards, while African Americans received 12.3 percent, Asian Americans 2.6 percent, and Hispanics 1.9 percent. These numbers are contrasted to their respective share of the state's total enrollment in higher education, with white students at 62.4 percent, African Americans at 29.6 percent, Asians at 2.1 percent, and Hispanics at 2.3 percent (Chronicle of Higher Education, 2005).

African American students are significantly under-represented among TOPS recipients, while white students are overrepresented. Table 5 shows the distribution of different TOPS awards among different racial groups. The more lucrative awards tend to go to white students and Asian students than to African American students.   The only difference in the qualification requirements between the top two awards, honors and performance awards, is in the minimum ACT score required, 27 and 23 respectively (see Table 1).   The observed inequity in the distribution of different TOPS awards is primarily impacted by differences in socioeconomic status.

Figure 3. Freshman retention rates at public two-year and four-year institutions in Louisiana. Retention includes transfer students if they transfer to other public institutions.

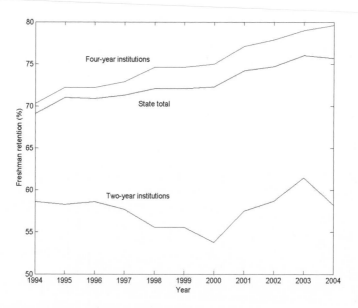

Source: Louisiana Board of Regents Statewide Student Profile System, 2005b.

Table 4. TOPS Recipients by Family Income and by Race, 2003 Cohort.

Family Income	All TOPS Recipients		Whites		African Americans		Asians		Hispanics		Others	
	Number	(%)	Number	(%)	Number	(%)	Number	(%)	Number	(%)	Number	(%)
Less than $20,000	1,784	(13.26%)	1,048	(10.09%)	493	(29.65%)	90	(26.23%)	54	(20.77%)	99	(12.34%)
$20,000 - $30,000	939	(6.98%)	279	(2.69%)	128	(7.70%)	21	(6.12%)	13	(5.00%)	69	8.58%)
$30,000 - $40,000	958	(7.12%)	702	(6.76%)	155	(9.32%)	33	(9.62%)	14	(5.38%)	54	(6.72%)
$40,000 - $50,000	963	(7.16%)	708	(6.82%)	136	(8.18%)	31	(9.04%)	21	(8.08%)	67	(8.33%)
$50,000 - $75,000	2,605	(19.37%)	2,112	(20.35%)	203	(12.21%)	58	(16.90%)	53	(20.38%)	179	(22.26%)
$75,000 - $100,000	2,374	(17.65%)	2,006	(19.33%)	166	(9.98%)	28	(8.16%)	33	(12.69%)	141	(17.54%)
$100,000 - $150,000	1,940	(14.42%)	1,687	(16.25%)	104	(6.25%)	28	(8.16%)	34	(13.08%)	87	(10.82%)
$150,000 - $200,000	528	(3.92%)	470	(4.53%)	21	(1.26%)	12	(3.50%)	2	(0.77%)	23	(2.86%)
More than $200,000	622	(4.62%)	566	(5.45%)	4	(0.24%)	9	(2.60%)	7	(2.69%)	36	(4.48%)
No income listed	736	(5.47%)	497	(4.79%)	158	(9.50%)	10	(2.92%)	22	(8.46%)	49	(6.09%)
Total	13,449	(100%)	10,379	(100%)	1,663	(100%)	343	(100%)	260	(100%)	804	(100%)
Median family income	$66,524		$72,687		$31,764		$39,766		$55,069			

Source: authors' calculations.

Table 5. Distribution of TOPS Awards by Race, 2003 Cohort.

	All TOPS Recipients	White Students	African Americans	Asians	Hispanics	Others
	Number (%)	Number (%)	Number (%)	Number (%)	Number (%)	Number (%)
Honors	1,474 (10.96%)	1,297 (12.50%)	44 (2.65%)	44 (12.83%)	21 (8.08%)	68 (8.45%)
Performance	2,040 (15.17%)	1,618 (15.59%)	214 (12.87%)	67 (19.53%)	33 (12.69%)	108 (13.47%)
Opportunity	9,933 (73.87%)	7,464 (71.91%)	1,405 (84.49%)	232 (67.64%)	206 (79.23%)	626 (78.05%)
Total	13,447 (100%)	10,379 (100%)	1,663 (100%)	343 (100%)	260 (100%)	802 (100%)

Source: authors' calculations.

Table 6 shows the EFC of TOPS recipients by race. Median EFC was $10,681 for all TOPS recipients. It ranged from $12,947 for white recipients to $1,950 for African American recipients. For 2003-2004, when the 2003 cohort graduates were college freshmen, the average full-time resident (in-state) undergraduate expenses at LSU were listed as $12,520 (tuition and fees $3,940, room $3,150, board $2,066, books and supplies $1,000, and other expenses $2,364) (Louisiana State University, Office of Budget & Planning, 2006, March 29). LSU is the most expensive public institution in the state. Any students with EFC of more than $15,000 at LSU were determined to have zero financial need. Accordingly, 42 percent of all TOPS recipients did not need financial aid in 2003. This increased to 48 percent of white students. Moreover, more of the well-to-do students qualified for more lucrative awards. On the other hand, over half of the TOPS recipients in every minority group had an EFC of less than $5,000, thus making them well qualified to receive TOPS awards. Nonetheless, a significant number of TOPS recipients (17%) had EFC of more than $30,000. They would not have qualified for financial aid even at most Ivy League schools.

Table 7 shows the characteristics of TOPS recipients at four different representative universities in Louisiana, LSU (public PWI), Southern University (public Historically Black College and University [HBCU], Tulane (private PWI) and Xavier (private HBCU). The dominance of LSU in benefiting from TOPS is evident. Most of its freshmen (80%) receive TOPS, and this single campus accounts for 32.1 percent of all TOPS awards in the state. The family economic background of many LSU TOPS recipients is very similar to that of their counterparts at Tulane. This is somewhat surprising since Tulane is a private institution which charges tuition approaching $30,000 a year. This simply suggests that LSU draws many students from the higher income brackets in the state. These students

Table 6. Expected Family Contribution (EFC) of TOPS Recipients by Race, 2003 Cohort.

Expected Family Contribution	All TOPS Recipients Number (%)	White Students Number (%)	African Americans Number (%)	Asians Number (%)	Hispanics Number (%)	Others Number (%)
Less than $5,000	4,250 (31.60%)	2,614 (25.19%)	1,056 (63.50%)	199 (58.02%)	147 (56.54%)	274 (34.08%)
$5,000–$10,000	1,891 (14.06%)	1,508 (14.53%)	187 (11.24%)	38 (11.08%)	29 (11.15%)	118 (14.67%)
$10,000–$15,000	1,573 (11.69%)	1,298 (12.51%)	121 (7.28%)	17 (4.96%)	19 (7.31%)	108 (13.43%)
$15,000–$20,000	1,230 (9.14%)	1,041 (10.03%)	88 (5.29%)	17 (4.96%)	24 (9.23%)	65 (8.08%)
$20,000–$30,000	1,570 (11.67%)	1,372 (13.22%)	79 (4.75%)	14 (4.08%)	13 (5.00%)	81 (10.07%)
$30,000–$40,000	804 (5.98%)	702 (6.76%)	33 (1.98%)	13 (3.79%)	7 (2.69%)	43 (5.35%)
$40,000–$50,000	406 (3.02%)	364 (3.51%)	9 (0.54%)	7 (2.04%)	3 (1.15%)	19 (2.36%)
$50,000–$75,000	538 (4.00%)	483 (4.65%)	16 (0.96%)	9 (2.62%)	6 (2.31%)	27 (3.36%)
More than $75,000	506 (3.76%)	453 (4.36%)	4 (0.24%)	11 (3.20%)	7 (2.69%)	32 (3.98%)
No EFC listed	681 (5.06%)	544 (5.24%)	70 (4.21%)	18 (5.25%)	12 (4.61%)	37 (4.60%)
Total	13,449 (100%)	10,379 (100%)	1,663 (100%)	343 (100%)	260 (100%)	804 (100%)
Median EFC	$10,681	$12,947	$1,950	$2,814	$7,311	

Source: authors' calculations.

probably could have gone to Tulane in terms of financial affordability.

Moreover, more than half of the TOPS recipients at LSU, based on their EFCs, do not need financial aid. Attendance costs at Tulane are more expensive ($39,302 in 2003) because of its high tuition; hence a typical TOPS recipient at Tulane still would have qualified for some financial aid. The number of students who qualify for TOPS is comparable at the two HBCUs, Southern and Xavier Universities. Xavier, however, is a private institution which draws nearly half of its students from out-of-state, suggesting that half of their in-state students qualify for TOPS. In contrast, at Southern, 86 percent of the students come from in-state (National Center for Educational Statistics [NCES], 2006), and only 16 percent of them qualify for TOPS. TOPS recipients at Xavier are slightly more competitive in terms of high school GPA and test scores than their peers at Southern.

TOPS and LSU

The TOPS impact in terms of the state's objective of keeping the best and the brightest in Louisiana is somewhat mixed thus far. First, more high school graduates appear to be remaining in the state. The number of high school graduates leaving the state has decreased slightly since the implementation of TOPS, from 3,182 in 1994 prior to TOPS to 2,753 in 2002 (Louisiana Board of Regents, 2004). The percent of high school graduates staying in Louisiana has increased from 86.8 percent in 1996 to 91 percent in 2002. Among the better-scoring students with ACT scores of 23 to 27, more students are staying in Louisiana to attend in-state institutions, from 69 percent in 1997 to 79.7 percent in 2003 (Louisiana Board of Regents, 2004). TOPS, however, does not appear to be impacting the best and the brightest students, with ACT scores of 28 to 36, with only a marginal

Table 7. Selected Characteristics of TOPS Award Recipients by Different Types of Universities, 2003 Cohort.

Selected Characteristic	LSU (PWI)[a]	Southern (HBCU)[b]	Tulane (PWI)	Xavier (HBCU)
Number of TOPS Recipients and as % of Total Freshman Class	4,323 (80.6%)	189 (13.9%)	206 (10.4%)	205 (27.3%)
Mean GPA of TOPS Recipients	3.37	3.22	3.60	3.46
Mean ACT of TOPS Recipients	24.54	21.76	28.88	23.02
Median Family Income of TOPS Recipients	$80,633	$36,966	$80,000	$35,474
Median EFC of TOPS Recipients	$15,985	$1,951	$17,019	$2,798

Source: authors' calculations.

[a]PWI = Predominantly White Institution
[b]HBCU = Historically Black College and University

increase opting to remain in Louisiana, from 58.7 percent in 1997 to 60.5 percent in 2003 (Louisiana Board of Regents, 2004). The HOPE program in Georgia, in contrast, appears to encourage the "best and brightest" students, who used to go out-of-state, to remain in the state and preferentially attend the two flagship institutions (Cornwell and Mustard, 2002).

Nonetheless, although TOPS does not appear to have much effect on the retention of the best and the brightest, the quality of students at LSU appears to have improved in recent years. The mean ACT score of the entering freshman at LSU has improved steadily since the implementation of TOPS, while the mean ACT score for the state as a whole barely moved during the same period (Figure 4). More students with ACT scores of 23 to 27 are remaining in state to attend its flagship university because of TOPS. It should be remembered that LSU has gradually tightened its admissions requirements during the same period, in part in response to the flagship agenda arising from the ongoing desegregation settlement (Davies, Jennifer & Toll, 2004).

One of the major unintended consequences of the HOPE program is that Georgia's public colleges and universities appear to have increased tuition and mandatory fees in the wake of HOPE (Long, 2002). If any university in Louisiana felt comfortable in raising tuition and fees, it would be LSU where 80 percent of the entering freshmen hold TOPS awards, thus making the majority of its students less price sensitive to tuition and fee increases. There appears to be some evidence of this occurring at LSU (see Figure 5). After the implementation of TOPS, any tuition and fee increases at the state's public universities had to be approved by two-thirds majority in the legislature. As a result, since 1999, LSU has resorted to significant fee increases (called an "academic excellence fee") because fee increases not covered by TOPS tended to be viewed more favorably by legislators compared to tuition increases.

Figure 4. Mean ACT score of entering freshman class at LSU and state average.

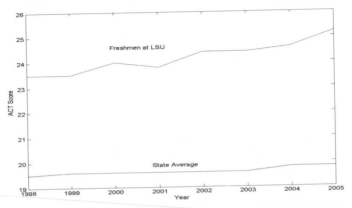

Sources: For mean ACT score of freshmen at LSU: Louisiana State University, Office of Budget & Planning, 2005, October 3. For mean ACT score for State: Louisiana Department of Education, 2005a.

Figure 5. Full-time undergraduate tuition and fees at LSU.

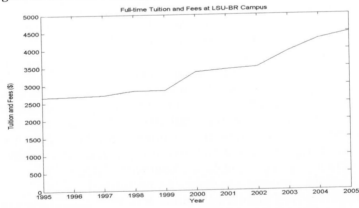

Source: Louisiana State University, Office of Budget & Planning, 2006, March 29.

As noted by Long (2002) for HOPE in Georgia, the real losers are the nonrecipients of the scholarship aid. Potentially this could lead to a widening gap between LSU and neighboring Southern University in terms of availability of funding. At Southern University, raising tuition and fees is more difficult because only a limited number of its students are receiving TOPS awards. These students need aid since most come from lower-income brackets with 80 percent of them qualifying for a Pell Grant (NCES, 2006). Furthermore, since fewer African American students (56%) qualify for TOPS awards than do white students (78%), any tuition and fee increases, even at LSU, would place an undue burden on nonrecipients of scholarship aid who are primarily minority students.

Admissions Criteria and Quality of Desegregation

Louisiana's "Master Plan for Public Postsecondary Education: 2001" stipulates that undergraduate admissions at each four-year institution shall require completion of the Regent's high school core curriculum (currently the TOPS core curriculum), combined with other requirements which may include high school grades, class rank, or standardized test scores (Louisiana Board of Regents, 2001). The "Master Plan" stipulates that all four-year institutions complete the process of implementing admissions criteria by fall 2005. Grambling State University and Southern University at New Orleans were exempt, however, and can remain as open admissions institutions until fall 2010. With the opening of the Baton Rouge Community College, Southern University began using selective admissions criteria for entering freshmen in fall 2001. Southern University's new admissions criteria include a prescribed high school curriculum of 13 units (3.5 units less than the TOPS core curriculum) and one of the following requirements, ACT of 17/SAT of 830, or high school GPA of 2.2.

The CD II settlement requires that each institution with selective admissions criteria have 15 percent of its entering class set aside for admissions exceptions. Ten percent is to be used for admitting other-race students, with the remaining 5 percent used for other institutional interests, students such as athletes, students with specific or unique talents, and children of alumni. In fall 2004, all institutions with selective admissions requirements exceeded the mandate of 10 percent enrollment of other-race entering freshmen, except LSU and Southern University (Davies et al., 2004). In fall 2003, African American students comprised 8.5 percent of the entering freshmen at LSU, and white students accounted for 0.6 percent of the entering freshmen at Southern University (Davies et al., 2004).

This confirms the observations of St. John and Hossler (1998) that HBCUs located in states and regions with higher concentrations of African American residents will usually enroll fewer white students. It is somewhat unsettling that the percent of African American freshman at LSU has declined since 1999 (see Figure 6), immediately after the implementation of TOPS, despite the efforts to recruit other-race students under the desegregation settlement. To some degree, this declining enrollment of African American freshman at LSU may be a reflection of the higher admissions standards (see Figure 4), and also of the increased tuition and fees (see Figure 5).

It is unfortunate that the settlement adheres to 10 percent other-race in the entering freshman classes at every institution. In their total respective institutional enrollments, for example, including graduate and professional schools, African American students accounted for 8.9 percent at LSU and white students accounted for 2.5 percent at Southern University. Southern University Law Center was already desegregated prior to the implementation of the current settlement, and during the fall 2004, its racial breakdown of the student body was 35.3 percent white, 63.4 percent

African American, 1.1 percent Hispanic, and 0.2 percent Asian (NCES, 2006). At the LSU Law Center, despite its active minority recruitment efforts, enrollment of African Americans remained at 7.8 percent of the first-year class in fall 2003. It appears that Southern University Law Center is expected to continue to attract white applicants. Its collaborative efforts with LSU Law Center in assisting each other in recruitment efforts and in sharing resources should be useful in the long-term.

Figure 6. Percent of freshmen enrolled at LSU who are African American.

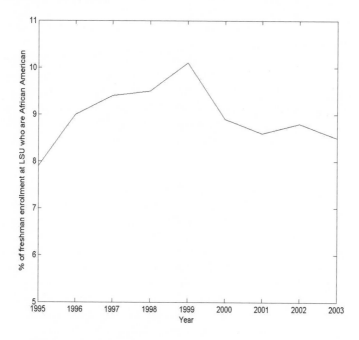

Source: Davies et al., 2004, p. 13.

Newly created doctoral programs in Public Policy and Nursing at Southern University, as well as a doctoral program in Educational Leadership and Master's program in Nursing at Grambling University, have enrolled a significant number of white students, and these programs hold great promise toward meeting the goals of the desegregation settlement (Davies et al., 2004). The creation of these types of programs confirms the suggestion proposed by St. John and Hossler (1998) that HBCUs can concentrate their new investments in locally situated high-demand programs that may have potentially high returns. It also confirms their hypothesis that for large HBCUs, such as Southern and Grambling Universities, there may be a sufficient enrollment base to begin a more focused effort to successfully implement doctoral and professional programs.

At LSU, graduate enrollment of African American students reached 10.5 percent of all graduate and professional enrollment (U.S. citizen and permanent residents only) in fall 2004 (LSU Office of Budget & Planning, 2005, September 30). Particularly noteworthy is the Department of Chemistry where African American enrollment accounted for 20 percent of total graduate enrollment, including a large contingency of international students. Within the pool of domestic students, African American students accounted for 43 percent of the total. This department, in recent years, has been the largest producer of African American Ph.D.s in chemistry in the entire country.

A prominent African American chemistry professor, recruited from Emory University in 1992, brought five African American graduate students with him, thus doubling the number of African American students in the department instantly (Collins, Stanley, Warner, & Watlins, 2001). The department's extensive minority recruitment programs have apparently worked in achieving a critical mass (Malcom, 2000;

Collins et al., 2001). Interestingly, most of these African American graduate students in chemistry do not conduct their dissertation research under the direction of an African American faculty member. Apparently, a good mentor does not have to be of the same ethnic or gender as the student:

> A critical component of the mentoring activity is that the mentor expects the student to adhere to high standards, that is, the same standards as all students. In addition, it is imperative that the mentor believes in the student. The student also must believe that the mentor is concerned about his or her well-being. It is desirable, however, that a faculty member of the student's ethnicity or gender be available as a potential secondary mentor or counselor (Collins et al., 2001, p.41).

As evident in the case of chemistry at LSU, a single department can make a difference once a serious commitment has been made toward desegregating its graduate program. This success at the graduate level is due primarily to the fact that while minority undergraduate persistence and attrition at PWIs have to focus on how well a student is integrated into overall campus life and its subcultures (Hurtado, Milem, Clayton-Pedersen, & Allen, 1999), the academic department is the relevant community for graduate students (Golde, 2000).

Louisiana is currently in the tenth year of its ongoing desegregation settlement, and it is necessary to reflect on the quality of the desegregation implementation so far. The contribution of public HBCUs with traditional open admissions policies toward educating leaders in the African American community has been rarely recognized compared to those contributions of the more selective and prominent private HBCUs (e.g., Gandara & Maxwell-Jolly, 1999). It is reasonable to assume that African American students who receive TOPS awards are the most academically competitive group relative to the nonrecipients.

For the 2003 TOPS cohort, there were 311 African American freshmen who qualified for TOPS at LSU, while there were 186 qualifiers at Southern University. If this is any indication of the size of the pool of competitive African American students at these two campuses, it is reasonable to expect LSU to be producing more African American students who go on to graduate programs, provided learning outcomes for African American students are at least comparable between the two campuses. On the basis of the number of African American baccalaureate degree recipients who went on to earn doctorates for the period 1994 to 2003, LSU falls far short in its production (36 doctorates) compared to Southern University (146 doctorates) (National Science Foundation, 2005). Despite the availability of an academically qualified pool of African American students, as measured by the number of African American TOPS recipients, Southern University also has to deal with a large pool of less academically competitive African American students because of its open admissions policy as recently as 2001. Southern University produced more African American students who went on to earn doctorates (146) than did Xavier University of Louisiana (81), Morehouse College (114), Tuskegee University (120), University of California-Berkeley (109), and Harvard University (97), and comparable to North Carolina Agricultural and Technical State University (153) for this time period (National Science Foundation, 2005).

The present situation in Louisiana can be contrasted to the status of desegregation of higher education in North Carolina. Strong leadership in North Carolina was able to implement statewide coordinated desegregation efforts, and was able to transform its higher education system. Consequently, its HBCUs and PWIs were able to desegregate, while these institutions were able to maintain their original institutional missions. For example, for the five-year period 1999-2003, both North Carolina A&T (HBCU) and North Carolina State (PWI) ranked among the top producers of African American doctorates in engineering, as well as among the top baccalaureate origins for African Americans who went on to earn doctorates in engineering (National Science Foundation, 2005).

At LSU, the graduation rate within six years for African Americans (33.3% for the 1998 cohort) significantly lags that for whites (57.1%) (NCES, 2006). Often poor academic preparation has been singled out as one of the primary reasons for high attrition and poor academic success of minority students (e.g., Choy, 2002). This conventional wisdom, however, has been challenged (see Fullilove & Treisman, 1990; Gainen & Willemsen, 1995; Seymour & Hewitt, 1997; St John, Carter, Chung, & Musoda, 2006). Recent efforts to reform teaching methods targeted at minimizing academic isolation of minority students at PWIs, rather than resorting to a remedial approach, have been very successful in reducing attrition and increasing persistence of minority students at PWIs, in particular in science and engineering (Fullilove & Treisman, 1990; Treisman, 1992; Bonsangue & Drew, 1995; Selvin, 1992; Tien, Roth & Kampmeier, 2002; Drane, Smith, Light, Pinto, & Swarat, 2005).

These efforts at reforming teaching methods are in line with the "wise" schooling advocated by Steele (1997) to improve the schooling of stereotype-threatened groups. Specifically, the three issues that need to be addressed are: 1) optimistic teacher-student relationships; 2) challenge over remediation; and 3) stressing the expandability of intelligence. There have been some efforts along the line of this approach suggested by Steel's "wise" schooling in the form of "wise" mentoring of minority graduate students, as can be found in the Department of Chemistry at LSU. Institutional level efforts, however, will be required in order to address persistence and academic success of minority undergraduate students at PWIs in the South by reforming teaching methods with the best practice available that has been successfully used elsewhere.

Baton Rouge Community College

Under the desegregation settlement, Baton Rouge Community College (BRCC) was founded in 1998 to provide open admissions, two-year postsecondary public education, designed to be accessible and affordable. Its mission is to offer collegiate and career education, allowing for transfer to four-year colleges and universities, community education programs and services, life-long learning, developmental education, distance learning, and workforce and continuing education programs (Davies et al., 2004). BRCC enrollment has increased significantly since its opening, and was 5,700 in fall 2004, with 62.1 percent white students, 31.3 percent African American, 2.2 percent Asian, and 1.6 percent Hispanic (NCES, 2006). Only 51 of the entering freshmen at BRCC qualified for TOPS awards in 2003, with the overwhelming majority of them being white students (47 out of 51). As the state's HBCUs, including Southern University, gradually tighten their admissions standards, it is expected that increasing numbers of their traditional applicant pool will be forced to matriculate at community colleges. There is a serious concern as to the ability of community colleges to educate minority students as well as HBCUs, since community colleges are not patterned after HBCUs, and their educational approach mimics that of PWIs. Although, difficulty of estimating the graduation rate at two-year institutions is well known, the three-year graduation rate at Baton Rouge Community College was 2.7 percent for African American students (NCES, 2006). This should be contrasted to a two-year HBCU, Southern University at Shreveport, which has a 15.7 percent graduation rate for African American students.

Discussion and Conclusions

The present status of the TOPS program indicates some good news, including some indication that more high school students are enrolling in more challenging curricula in order to qualify for TOPS. Without question, the TOPS program has served to strengthen the academic preparation of high school students throughout the state for study at postsecondary institutions. This is occurring not only because of the TOPS program, but also because the TOPS high school core curriculum is now required by the Board of Regents as the minimum admissions criteria at all four-year public universities in Louisiana, effective fall 2005. This is reflected in the declining trend in the percentage of the first-time freshman class enrolled in developmental courses.

The college-going rate in Louisiana has increased slightly in recent years. This has been occurring, however, because more students are choosing in-state schools due to the availability of TOPS awards. The overall college-going rate may not have increased due to TOPS, primarily because the current eligibility requirement involving a minimum ACT score may not provide sufficient encouragement to those who would not have considered college an option without TOPS. According to NCES statistics, high school completion rates at public high schools in Louisiana increased slightly from 60.4 percent in 1997-98 to 64.1 percent in 2002-2003 (NCES, 2002 & 2005). Unlike the situation in Michigan, where its merit scholarship program had some discernible positive impact on the high school graduation rate (Bishop, 2004), if there were any impact in Louisiana, TOPS was probably one of several reasons behind the observed increase.

TOPS awards are distributed very unevenly, going primarily to white students who come from higher-income brackets. The data on the 2003 cohort indicate that approximately 40 percent of all TOPS recipients, and nearly one half of white TOPS recipients, did not have financial need based on their EFCs. These students who come from higher-income families could have gone to college without TOPS. Of the minority students, however, 50-60 percent who received TOPS awards had financial need. These findings are consistent with similar studies on state-funded merit-based scholarship programs in other states, including Georgia, Massachusetts, and Florida (e.g., Heller & Marin, 2002; Heller, 2004a and b). Figures 7 and 8 represent a total of 14 4-year public colleges and universities in Louisiana with the corresponding percentage of students who qualify for TOPS and the percentage of students who qualify for Pell Grants (Figure 7), and the percentage of students who are African American (Figure 8). Strong negative correlations with correlation coefficients of -0.86 and -0.81, respectively, are found between the percentage of students who qualify for TOPS by institution and the two measures—financially needy status represented by Pell Grant qualification and minority status.

Minority students are not qualifying for TOPS at the same rate as white students, despite their efforts to complete the required high school curriculum, due to the required minimum ACT score. The present minimum test score automatically eliminates slightly more than 40% of those high school graduates who complete the TOPS core curriculum. It is well recognized that there is a significant gap in standardized test scores between students coming from wealthier families and those from poorer families (Jencks & Phillips, 1998). By requiring a minimum test score, TOPS contains a built-in bias against minority students and low-income students. In this regard, TOPS may be more biased against minority students and lower-income students than the HOPE program, which does not require a minimum test score while requiring a higher minimum GPA (3.0 versus 2.5 required for the most basic TOPS award). Furthermore, HOPE includes the HOPE Grant option, basically an entitlement with no academic qualification requirement (Georgia Student Finance Commission, 2006, February 21).

Figure 7. Correlation between percent of students who qualify for TOPS and percent of students who qualify for Pell Grants at each of the four-year public colleges and universities in Louisiana. Each data point represents a campus.

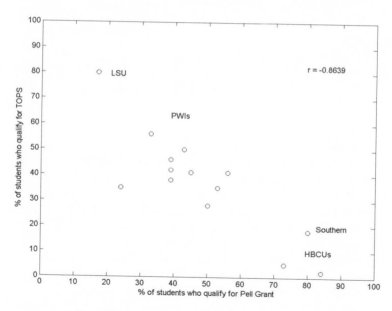

Source: NCES, 2006.

Figure 8. Correlation between percent of students who qualify for TOPS and percent of students who are African American at each of the four-year public colleges and universities in Louisiana. Each data point represents a campus.

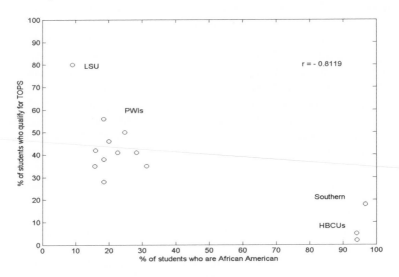

Source: NCES, 2006.

While the ACT test does contain a built in bias favoring well-to-do families, the ACT test requirement also serves as a standard to offset the considerable variation in the quality of the different curricula in the state's numerous high schools in preparing graduates for college. As such, the ACT test requirement is one useful factor in predicting college success, even though high school GPA has proven to be a stronger predictor of college freshman grades than has achievement scores on standardized tests. Considering the overwhelming evidence of the disadvantages that minority students have in securing TOPS awards, at least some modification of the required ACT minimum test score should be seriously considered.

Goggin (1999), for example, proposed a merit index constructed by subtracting the mean SAT score of the student's high school from the student's own score. This index provides a means of evaluating the performance of high school students in relation to their high school peers by adjusting test scores to the quality of high schools. St. John and Chung (2004) demonstrated that if this merit-aware index were used in the college admission process, it could predict college persistence about as well as the SAT, while the use of the index could increase diversity in the student body better than SAT scores. Other options include the Twenty Century Scholars Program in Indiana and the Washington State Achievers Program, both of which are a combination of merit-aid and need-based aid, and do not require test scores (Emeka & Hirschman, 2006; St. John, Gross, Musada & Chung, 2006) These two scholarship programs have been shown to be effective in encouraging aspiring minority students from lower-income families, providing college-going opportunities so that these students can succeed in college (St. John & Hu, 2006; St. John, Gross, Musada & Chung, 2006).

The overwhelming majority of students receiving TOPS awards enroll at four-year institutions. This presents a complex issue related to the desegregation settlement. Under the settlement, community colleges are expected to provide remedial courses to those who cannot go to four-year institutions immediately after high school. The required implementation of selective admissions standards at HBCUs will inevitably force less competitive students to go to community colleges. Many of these students are financially needy students, requiring financial aid to attend college. A component of the TOPS program should be tailored to meet the expected increasing demand for these students who will be attending community colleges, who nonetheless aspire to complete a four-year college education.

It is uncertain that community colleges will be able to educate less competitive minority students as well as HBCUs. It is ironic that one of the outcomes of the desegregation settlement is a potential shift in the institutional mission of state-supported HBCUs, which have played a vital role in educating African Americans in the segregated South where historical disparity in the quality of pre-college education between white students and black students has persisted (Brown, 1999). Many African American students, who would have been admitted to HBCUs under the old open admissions policy, will be forced to attend elsewhere once the new stricter admissions standard is fully implemented. The real contribution of HBCUs should be recognized in educating minority students, many of whom are less academically competitive upon graduation from high school, to become leaders in many disciplines.

Consideration of educational outcomes should be part of the debate regarding the desegregation of higher education in the South (St. John & Hossler, 1998). Despite the availability of an academically qualified pool of African American students, as measured by the number of African American TOPS recipients, LSU is not educating minority students as much as it should,, compared with Southern University's effort. Ultimately, what matters is not necessarily how many minority students enter PWIs as freshmen, but rather how many complete college and succeed after graduation. Educational outcomes and persistence of minority students at PWIs need to be monitored in order to fully assess the true impact of desegregation.

In this respect, much more attention should be devoted to the role of graduate and professional programs in the desegregation process and in contributing toward increasing institutional diversity. LSU's graduate program in chemistry is one of the bright spots. Another example is Southern University's Law Center which was desegregated even prior to the implementation of the present desegregation settlement. It is interesting to note that the Huel Perkins Doctoral Fellowship program for African American graduate students established at LSU under the desegregation settlement was cited as one of the factors contributing toward the successful minority graduate program in chemistry at LSU (Collins et al., 2001).

The accessibility issue is particularly critical for Louisiana. In other states, state-supported merit-aid has served to increase inequality in enrollment and has widened the opportunity gap between white students and minority students (Dynarski, 2002). While TOPS has not resulted in improvement in access for low-income students, the funds for the state-funded need-based scholarship program have been drastically reduced in recent years, from $8.19 million in 1997-98 to $1.45 million in 2003-04 (NASSGAP, 2005). Consequently, the state-run need-based student aid program is dwarfed by the state-run merit-based programs ($145 million in 2002-03) in Louisiana. Unless the state can devise new ways to use TOPS funds to improve accessibility for low-income students, state funds going into need-based aid program should be increased significantly.

It is only a matter of time before the state's legislators have to face the prospect of restructuring the TOPS program. The expected restructuring could include implementation of a cap based on EFC, thus making the TOPS program a combination of merit-aid and need-based grants. Currently, approximately one-third of high school graduates and about 46 percent of college going students qualify for TOPS awards. If a cap on EFC were implemented at $15,000, at the current funding level, approximately 7,000 additional financially needy students could be covered, instead of the same number of non-needy students currently receiving awards. Since many of these needy students are expected to be minority students, this would contribute toward greater diversity.

It appears that state-funded, broad-based, merit scholarship programs such as TOPS, if implemented on the heel of a desegregation settlement of higher education, might hinder desegregation efforts by curtailing access for minority students, especially at a state's flagship institution. The TOPS awards currently go primarily to white students from mid- and high-income brackets, many of whom could have gone to college without TOPS. Due to the required minimum ACT score requirement, TOPS currently handicaps disproportionately minority and low-income students, despite the fact that many of them are completing the TOPS core curriculum in high school.

The recent trend of rising tuition and fee charges, especially at the state's flagship institution, coupled with the increasing popularity of the flagship institution, appears to crowd out minority students at LSU. Despite the ten percent enrollment target agreed upon under the desegregation settlement for other-race students, LSU has been experiencing great difficulty in filling the allotted slots with African American students. The termination of the ongoing ten-year desegregation settlement will usher in a period of uncertainty and a pressing challenge for the state's flagship institution to continue toward a fully integrated higher education system, where the state-funded merit scholarship program can help improve access for financially needy and academically able students, many of whom are minority students.

Notes

[1] The LSU system and the Southern University system both have different campuses located throughout the state. In this chapter, our analysis and discussion are, for the most part, concerned only with LSU and Southern University at the Baton Rouge campuses. Thus, these institutions are simply designated as LSU and Southern University throughout the chapter. If there is a need to identify another institution from a different campus from one of these two systems, this chapter will include the other location involved, such as LSU-Shreveport or Southern University-New Orleans. The reader should also be aware that a third system, the University of Louisiana (UL) system, consists of eight regional institutions of higher education located throughout the state. The fourth postsecondary system in the state is the Louisiana Community and Technical College system (LCTCS).

It should also be noted that Southern University, as well as Grambling University in the UL system, are part of this country's system of Historically Black Colleges and Universities (HBCUs).

References

Adams vs. Richardson, 480 F.2d 1159 (D.C. Cir. 1973).

Adams vs. Richardson, 356 F. 2d 92 (D.C. Cir. 1973).

Adams vs. Richardson, 351 F. 2d 636 (D.C. Cir. 1972).

Advisory Committee on Student Financial Assistance. (2002). *An empty promise: The myth of college access in America.* Washington, DC.

Arceneaux, S.B. (1995). Chasing the dream: Higher education desegregation in Louisiana. *Tulane Law Review, 69*, 1281-1310.

Ayers vs. Allain, 914 Fed. 676 (CA. 5 1990).

Bishop, J.H. (2004). Merit scholarships for the many: Doubling the number of high school students who work hard in high school. R. Kazis, J. Vargas, and N. Hoffman (Eds.), *Double the numbers.* Cambridge, MA: Harvard Education Press.

Bonsangue, M.V.S., & Drew, D.E. (1995). Increasing minority students' success in calculus. In J. Gainen & Willemsen (Eds.) *Fostering student success in quantitative gateway courses.* San Francisco: CA, Jossey-Bass Publishers.

Bowen, W.G., & Bok, D. (1998). *Shape of the River.* Princeton, NJ: Princeton University Press.

Bowen, W.G., Kurzweil, M.A., & Tobin, E.M. (2005). *Equity and excellence in American higher education.* Charlottesville, VA: University of Virginia Press.

Brown, M.C., II. (1999). *The quest to define collegiate desegregation: Black colleges, Title VI compliance, and post-Adams litigation.* Westport, CT: Bergin & Garvey.

Brown vs. The Board of Education of Topeka, Kansas, 347 U.S. 483, (1954).

Bush vs. Orleans Parish School Board, 364 U.S. 500 (1960).

Byrd-Chichester, J. (2000). The federal courts and claims of racial discrimination in higher education. *The Journal of Negro Education,* 69(1/2), 12-26.

Choy, S.P. (2002). *Access & persistence: Findings from 10 years of longitudinal research on students.* Washington, DC: American Council on Education.

Chronicle of Higher Education, Almanac Issue, 2005-2006. (August 26, 2005). *The Chronicle of Higher Education,* LII(1).

College Board. (2005a). Trends in Student Aid 2005. Trends in Higher Education Series. New York: The College Board.

College Board. (2005b). Trends in College Pricing 2005. Trends in Higher Education Series. New York: The College Board.

Collins, S.N., Stanley, G.G., Warner, I.M., & Watlins, S.F. (2001). What is Louisiana State doing right? *Chemical & Engineering News: Science & Technology Perspective,* 79(50), 39-42.

Cornwell, C., & Mustard, D.B. (2002). Race and effects of Georgia's HOPE scholarship. In D.E. Heller, & P. Marin (Eds.), *Who should we help? The negative social consequences of merit scholarships.* The Civil Rights Project, Harvard University (p. 59-72).

Cornwell, C., Mustard, D.B., & Sridhar, D. (2003). *The enrollment effects of merit-based financial aid: Evidence from Georgia's HOPE scholarship.* Athens: University of Georgia.

Davies, G.K., Jennifer, F., & Toll, J.S. (2004). *Ninth annual evaluation of the desegregation settlement agreement: Implementation of the settlement agreement,* United States vs. State of Louisiana, Civil Action #80-3300A, Settlement Agreement Monitoring Committee.

Drane, D., Smith, H.D., Light, G., Pinto, L., & Swarat, S. (2005). The Gateway Science Workshop Program: Enhancing student performance and retention in the Sciences through peer-facilitated discussion. *Journal of Science Education and Technology, 14*(3), 337-352.

Dynarski, S. (2002). Race, income, and the impact of merit aid. In D. E. Heller & P. Marin (Eds.), *Who should we help? The negative social consequences of merit scholarships.* The Civil Rights project, Harvard University (p. 75-91).

Dynarski, S. (2000). Hope for whom? Financial aid for the middle class and its impact on college attendance. *National Tax Journal, 53,* 629-661.

Emeka, A., & Hirschman, C. (2006). Who applies for and who is selected for Washington State Achievers Scholarships? A preliminary assessment. St. John, E.P. (Ed.), *Public Policy and Educational Opportunity: School reforms, Postsecondary Encouragement, and State Policies on Postsecondary Education. Readings on Equal Education, Volume 21.* New York: AMS Press.

Fitzgerald, B. (2004). Federal financial aid and college access. In E.P. St. John (Ed.), *Readings on equal education: Volume 19. Public policy and college access: Investigating the federal and state roles in equalizing postsecondary opportunity* (pp. 1-28). New York: AMS Press.

Fullilove, R.E., & Treisman, P.U. (1990). Mathematics achievement among African American undergraduates at the University of California, Berkeley: An evaluation of the Materials Workshop Program. *Journal of Negro Education, 59*(3), 49-64.

Gainen, J., & Willemsen, E.W. (1995). *Fostering student success in quantitative gateway courses.* San Francisco: Jossey-Bass Publishers.

Gandara, P., Maxwell-Jolly, J. (1999). *Priming the pump: Strategies for increasing the achievement of underrepresented minority undergraduates.* New York: College Board.

Georgia Student Finance Commission. Georgia's HOPE Scholarship and Grant Program. (2006, February 21) Retrieved March 15, 2006, from www.gsfc.org/HOPE/Index.cfm.

Goggin, W.J. (1999, May). A "merit-aware" model for college admissions and affirmative action. *Postsecondary Education Opportunity Newsletter.* Mortenson Research Seminar on Public Policy Analysis of Opportunity for Postsecondary Education, pp. 6-12.

Golde, C.M. (2000). Should I stay or should I go?: Student descriptions of the doctoral attrition process. *The Review of Higher Education, 23*(2), 199-227.

Heller, D.E. (2004a). State merit scholarship programs: An overview. Heller, D.E., & Orfield, G. (Eds.), *State merit scholarship programs and racial inequality.* The Civil Rights Project, Harvard University (p. 15-23).

Heller, D.E., (2004b). The devil is in the details: An analysis of eligibility criteria for merit scholarships in Massachusetts. In E.D. Heller and P. Marin (Eds.), *State merit scholarship programs and racial inequality.* Cambridge, MA: The Civil Rights Project, Harvard University.

Heller, D.E., and Marin, P. (Eds.) (2002). *Who should we help?   The negative social consequences of merit* scholarships. Cambridge, MA: The Civil Rights Project, Harvard University.

Hurtado, S., Milem, J., Clayton-Pedersen, A., and Allen, W. (1999). *Enacting Diverse Learning Environments: Improving the Climate for Racial/Ethnic Diversity in Higher Education.* ASHE-ERIC Higher Education Report Volume 26, No. 8   Washington, D.C.:   The George Washington University. Graduate School of Education and Human Development.

Jencks, C., & Phillips, M. (1998). *The black-white test score gap.* Washington D. C: Brookings Institution Press.

Kane, T. (1999). *The price of admission.* Washington DC: Brookings Institution Press.

Kim, M.M. (2002).   Historically Black vs. White institutions: Academic development among Black students. *Review of Higher Education, 25*(4), 385-407.

Lee, J.B. (2004). Access revisited: A preliminary reanalysis on NELS. In E.P. St. John (Ed.), *Readings on equal education: Volume 19. Public policy and college access: Investigating the federal and state roles in equalizing postsecondary opportunity* (pp. 87-96). New York: AMS Press.

Long, B.T. (2002). Do state financial aid programs cause colleges to raise prices? The case of the Georgia HOPE scholarship. In D.E. Heller, & P. Marin (Eds.), *Who should we help? The negative social consequences of merit scholarships*. The Civil Rights Project, Harvard University (p. 95-109).

Louisiana Board of Regents (2005a). *Data set for the 2003 entering freshmen cohort of TOPS recipients*. Baton Rouge: LA.

Louisiana Board of Regents Statewide Student Profile System. (2005b). First-Time Full-Time Freshman Student Retention/Transfers Reports. Retrieved November 10, 2005, from www.regents.state.la.us/Reports/transfers.htm.

Louisiana Board of Regents (2004). *TOPS reporting system. Report to the house of education committee*. Baton Rouge: LA.

Louisiana Board of Regents (2001). *Master plan for public postsecondary education: 2001*. Baton Rouge: LA.

Louisiana Department of Education. (2005a). Louisiana ACT Reports. Retrieved November 10, 2005, from www.doe.state.la.us/lde/pair/1635.html.

Louisiana Department of Education. (2005b). Louisiana First-Time College Freshmen State Reports. Retrieved November 10, 2005, from www.doe.state.la.us/lde/pair/1635.html.

Louisiana Office of Student Financial Assistance. (2005). TOPS payment summary by award level for academic year 2004-2005. Retrieved December 11, 2005, from www.osfa.state.la.us/osfa.nsf/main?openframeset&Frame=Content&SRC=/infoindx.htm.

Louisiana State University, Office of Budget & Planning. (2006, March 29). Trend Data: General Information, Tuition and Fees. Retrieved April 10, 2006, from www.bgtplan.lsu.edu/trend/geninfo/tuition/fttuit&fees.htm.

Louisiana State University, Office of Budget & Planning. (2005, October 3). Trend Data: Students, Admissions and Entering. Retrieved November 10, 2005a, from www.bgtplan.lsu.edu/trend/students/admissions/avgact.htm.

Louisiana State University, Office of Budget & Planning. (2005, September 30). Trend Data: Students, Enrollment and Student Attributes. Retrieved November 10, 2005, from www.bgtplan.lsu.edu/trend/students/enrollment/GradRace.htm.

Louisiana State University. (2005, May 25). History of LSU. Retrieved May 18, from www.lsu.edu/aboutht.htm.

Malcom, S.M. (2000). Minority Ph.D. Production in SME Fields: Distributing the Work? Making Strides published by *American Association of Advancement of Science*, 2(3).

National Association of State Student Grant & Aid Programs. (2005). *NASSGAP 35th annual survey report on state-sponsored student financial aid 2003-2004 academic year*. Springfield: Illinois Student Assistance Commission.

National Center for Educational Statistics. (2006). Search for Schools, Colleges and Libraries. Retrieved March 15, 2006, from http://nces.ed.gov/globallocator/.

National Center for Educational Statistics. (2005). The Averaged Freshman Graduation Rate for Public High Schools from the Common Core of Data: School Years 2001-02 and 2002-03.

National Center for Educational Statistics. (2002). Public high school dropouts and completers from the Common Core of Data: Schools years 1991-92 through 1997-98.

National Science Foundation. (2005). Integrated Science and Engineering Resources Data System. Retrieved November 22, 2005, from http://caspar.nsf.gov/.

NCHEMS Information Center for State Higher Education Policy Making and Analysis. (2002). Participation: College-Going Rates of High School Graduates — Directly from HS. Retrieved March 22, 2006, from www.higheredinfo.org/dbrowser/index.php?submeasure=63& year=2002&level=nation&mode=data&state=0.

St. John, E.P., Carter, D.F., Chung, C-G., & Musoda, G.D. (2006). Diversity and persistence in Indiana higher education: The impact of preparation, major choices, and student aid. St. John, E.P. (Ed.), *Public Policy and Educational Opportunity: School reforms, Postsecondary Encouragement, and State Policies on Postsecondary Education. Readings on Equal Education, Volume 21.* (pp. 343-388). New York: AMS Press.

St. John, E.P., & Chung, C-G. (2004). Merit and equity: Rethinking award criteria for the Michigan Scholarship Program. In E.P. St. John and M.D. Parsons (Eds.) *Public Funding for Higher Education: Changing Contexts and New Rationales* (124-140). Baltimore: Johns Hopkins University Press.

St. John, E.P., Gross, J.P.K., Musada, D., & Chung, A.S. (2006). Postsecondary encouragement and academic success: degree attainment by Indiana's twenty-first century scholars. E.P. St. John (Ed.), *Public Policy and Educational Opportunity: School reforms, Postsecondary Encouragement, and State Policies on Postsecondary Education. Readings on Equal Education, Volume 21.* (pp. 259-294). New York: AMS Press.

St. John, E.P., Hossler, D. (1998). Higher education desegregation in the post-*Fordice* legal environment: A critical-empirical perspective. In R. Fossey (Ed.), *Readings on Equal Education: Volume 15, Race, the courts, and equal education: The limits of the law* (pp. 123-156). New York: AMS Press.

St. John, E.P., & Hu, S. (2006). The impact of guarantees of financial aid on college enrollment: An evaluation on the Washington State Achievers Program. In E.P. St. John (Ed.), *Public Policy and Educational Opportunity: School reforms, Postsecondary Encouragement, and State Policies on Postsecondary Education. Readings on Equal Education, Volume 21.* (pp. 213-257). New York: AMS Press.

Selvin, P. (1992). Math education: Multiplying the meager numbers. *Science, 258,* 1200-1201.

Seymour, E., & Hewitt, N.M. (1997). *Talking about leaving: Why undergraduates leave the sciences.* Boulder, CO: Westview Press.

Smothers, R.L. (2004). The influence of state merit-based aid on access and educational experiences: An exploration of the Louisiana Tuition Opportunity Program for students (TOPS). (Doctoral Dissertation, Louisiana State University, 2004).

Steele, C.M. (1997). A threat in the air: How stereotypes shape intellectual identity and performance. *American Psychologist, 52,* 613-629.

Tien, L.T., Roth, V.S., & Kampmeier, J.A. (2002). Implementation of a peer-led learning instructional approach in an undergraduate organic chemistry course. *Journal of research in Science Teaching, 39,* 606-632.

Treisman, U. (1992). Studying students studying calculus: A look at the lives of minority mathematics students in college. *The College mathematics Journal, 23*(5), 362-372.

United States vs. Fordice, 112 S. Ct. 2727 (1992).

United States vs. Louisiana, Consent Decree II, (No. Civ. 80-3300) (E.D. La. 1994).

United States vs. Louisiana, 811 F. Supp. 1151, 1156 (E.D. La. 1992), vacated, 9 F.3d 1159 (5th Cir. 1993).

United States vs. Louisiana, 718 F. Supp. 499, 514 (E.D. La. 189).

United States vs. Louisiana, 527 F. Supp. 509, 512 n.2 (E.D. La. 1981).

CHAPTER 6

STATE VALUATION OF HIGHER EDUCATION: AN EXAMINATION OF POSSIBLE EXPLANATIONS FOR PRIVATIZATION

Amy S. Fisher

Federal and state governments seemed to strike a balance in higher education financing in the late 1960s and 1970s by providing equal opportunity for higher education through reasonable tuition and sufficient aid to meet need.[1] However, the 1980s have brought a change, shifting aid strategies from grants to loans. Economic recession has led institutions to increase tuition. The result moves the cost burden of higher education to individuals and away from the government. What is an appropriate role for the states in higher education financing? One can argue that public funding of higher education is necessary to maintain the social contract.

This chapter examines factors associated with state governments' financial commitment to the social contract as it relates to postsecondary funding and privatization. First, a conceptual framework based in a philosophy of justice which also considers aspects of the economy and the political environment is proposed, followed by four questions related to causes and effects of privatization. Next is a description of the data, methodology, and findings. After results are presented, they are interpreted in relation to the conceptual framework, concluding with implications for the future.

219

Copyright ©2007 AMS Press, Inc. All rights reserved.

Conceptual Framework

John Rawls's *Theory of Justice* (1971) can be used to frame a philosophical understanding of funding policy in higher education (e.g., St. John, 2004, 2006a, 2006b). The first element of the theory, the distribution principle, states that every individual may lay claim to basic rights that should be applied equally. The second aspect, the difference principle, asserts that social and economic inequalities exist, but these inequalities must be accessible to everyone through the notion of equality of opportunity applied in a just manner; that is, because of equality of opportunity, everyone has access to the benefits and disadvantages of society and the economy — inequalities. Part of this principle asserts that the least advantaged must benefit the most from overcoming those inequalities. While the difference principle applies within a generation, a third principle exists — known as the just savings principle — that holds between generations. Just savings addresses "how far the present generation is bound to respect the claims of its successors" (Rawls, 2001, p. 159). Rawls uses this principle to understand systems of taxation. The constructs behind these principles speak to the idea of social mobility, a fundamental guiding principle of American culture. Horatio Alger stories[2] are emblematic of this idea.

One can consider a democratic society through a Rawlsian lens. In fact, Rawls (2001) himself claims that justice as fairness is framed for a democratic society that espouses that its citizens should be free and equal and "tries to realize that idea in its main institutions" (p. 39).[3] That is to say, a truly democratic society provides a voice for each person, thus establishing one layer of equality of opportunity. While the United States operates a representative government, the basic democratic dogma still applies.

A final element to consider is the economy. Rawls (1971) examines economic systems in relation to issues of morality and justice. In this section of his theory, he specifically distinguishes between a socialist, more public sector type of economy, and a private-property economy. He further debates about public goods — who is responsible for them and in what ways — concluding that each society develops a system to satisfy those needs. A thriving nation maintains a robust economy, and in today's world, that means leaving room for industrial positions, even while focusing more heavily on knowledge creation and intellectual pursuits.

Where does higher education fit into this frame composed of justice, the social contract, and the economy? Zumeta (2004) refers to the connection between a nation's educational attainment and its economic development. Particularly in today's current knowledge market, increased levels of education lead to a stronger economy, suggesting that higher education benefits society. Postsecondary education benefits society in more than just economic ways, however. Citizens who achieve even some level of postsecondary education are more likely to think critically and in more complex ways. In order for democracy in the United States to function effectively, the citizenry require enough education to be able to partake in decision making on any level, including to be informed about issues relevant to electing their representatives. Expanding this idea further, individuals' responses to a variety of local, state, and national issues range from liberal to conservative. For example, people who are more fiscally conservative would vote for lower tax rates because they prefer to reduce the scope of government control, while those who are more liberal would increase taxes to fund social welfare programs. Political ideologies play into the complex and critical thinking necessary to participate in democracy, as individuals must be able to evaluate not only their opinions and responses to governmental action, but how they came to feel the way they do and to act on those feelings. Consequently, participation in a democratic society along with the economic advantages of receiving postsecondary education leads to the notion of higher education as a public good.

However, one cannot forget the ideas of equality of opportunity and social mobility — the Horatio Alger notion. Higher education provides the tools necessary to increase one's income potential and advance in the social strata (Hearn, 2001). In this manner, higher education becomes a basic right according to the *Theory of Justice*. Thus, it is also clearly a private benefit as well.

Human capital theory elucidates this idea. Paulsen (2001a) defines this theory as the "productive capacities — knowledge, understandings, talents, and skills — possessed by an individual or society" and adds that "investment in human capital refers to expenditures on education, health, and other activities that augment these productive capacities" (p. 56). Based on this definition, one can conclude that both individuals and the government consider investment in human capital important due to increased lifetime earnings for the individual and expansion of the workforce capacity with resulting impacts on the economy.

Individual investment in higher education as human capital has been found to be predicated on habitus, attitudes and values acquired from the individual's environment; cultural capital, symbolic wealth transmitted through generations, typically among middle- and upper-income groups; discrimination; and access to funds, which is strongly connected to socioeconomic status (SES) (Paulsen, 2001a). The individual investment in human capital thus relates directly back to Rawls's difference and just savings principles.

Looking at the public sector, Paulsen (2001b) notes several benefits of higher education. However, he also points out that individuals underestimate the external benefits, what he also calls the public good, of higher education when deciding on their investment in higher education. Paulsen argues that without public policy in the form of subsidies to either students or institutions (or both), students would invest less in higher education. Subsidies make it possible for students to "internalize these external benefits" (p. 100). Furthermore, Paulsen's argument that public subsidy for higher education makes it possible for low-income students to participate speaks to Rawls's distribution and difference principles.

With this lens set, we can turn to the debate about how much investment each party should make, based on the private economic benefit versus the public economic good. This all leads to a policy framework for investing in higher education that strikes a balance between higher education as a private benefit and as a public good and finds an intersection between these two notions.[4] In order to maintain justice, Rawlsian ideas may inform policy decisions surrounding higher education, and thus access and equity should be considered in every policy set forth. "Society must establish, among other things, equal opportunities of education for all regardless of family income." (Rawls, 2001, p. 44). However, policy makers also must consider what is best — and most efficient — for the economy and democracy.

Instead of focusing on a more interconnected approach to higher education, the financing outcome comparing state allocations and public tuition indicates an emphasis on the private benefits. Bypassing this approach has long-term effects for low-income and minority students who are priced out of higher education both personally, as a lack of postsecondary education limits their social and economic mobility, and publicly, as it limits their ability to contribute to economic development as well as reducing their opportunities to be involved citizens. A brief overview of privatization follows in an effort to begin understanding what contributes to the formation of privatization policies that oppose the principles in Rawls's *Theory of Justice*.

Privatization

In his historical overview of federal aid policy, Hearn (2001) shows that the federal government plays a large role in student aid. Zumeta (2004) points out that states have also maintained a degree of budgetary responsibility for higher education. Increasingly, aid for students has become a large part of the states' domain, particularly in the debate over need-based versus merit-based aid. As recently as the fall of 2005, university officials have claimed that public colleges and universities have a mission of serving the public good (Dillon, 2005 October 16). Given the previous discussion about the principles of justice, the economy, the political environment, and the public good–private benefit debate, it follows that one would question to what degree states should be involved in the financing of higher education, particularly since the U.S. Constitution leaves authority over education to the states.

Parsons (2004) argues that postsecondary education benefits individuals to an extent so much greater than it does society that policymakers must take those benefit into account when developing their funding plans. Alternatively, one must keep in mind that with the establishment of the Morrill Act in 1862, one of the core missions of public universities has been to provide services that promote the well-being of communities and states. Some consider privatization a force on universities to abandon this social contract (Dillon, 2005 October 16). In an environment of increasing privatization, the next logical step would be to transfer the costs of higher education completely to individuals, instead of continuing with state government sponsorship on some level. However, that would void the social contract, a key tenet of U.S. society. In order to maintain this basic democratic right, governments ought to continue funding higher education, and not only that, but make it attainable for all citizens. Policy can ensure that is so. The direction of the market makes it impossible for higher education not to move toward privatization, particularly when considering the high personal benefit for individuals to obtain a postsecondary degree. Nonetheless, in an effort to uphold their end of the social contract, governments should continue to subsidize the costs of higher education in an equitable manner. However, politics, taxes, and other social welfare programs complicate maintenance of the social contract.

An appropriate proxy measure for the extent of privatization is the percentage of costs per student of providing public higher education paid for by state subsidies. The cost of public higher per full time equivalent student (FTE) can be constructed from the sum weighted average public tuition charges within a state and the weighted average subsidy in public colleges per FTE.[5]

What might be some of the causes of the reduction in the percentage of education costs subsidized by states? A framework suggesting several influences on privatization appears in Figure 1. The framework adapts a logical model developed by St. John (2006b) in his effort to reconceptualize the state role in promoting improvement in preparation for, access to, and retention in higher education. This assumes that the percentage of educational costs subsidized by states is influenced by:

- Demographic characteristics and wealth in the state,
- Extent of private sector of higher education in the state,
- Political context (including government ideologies),
- Constraints on the state budget, and
- Tax rate.

Figure 1. Framework for Assessing Influences on Privatization

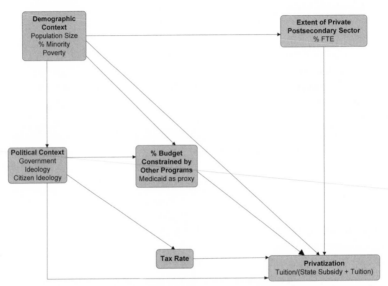

Source: Adapts logical model presented by St. John (2006b). The work focused on variables related to tuition and state subsidies as intermediate variables associated with rates of college enrollment. Political context and public constraints are additional variables considered in the adaptation of the model presented by St. John (2006b).

Based on this framework, the analyses that follow focus on the following research questions:

• What impact do mandatory expenditures, in combination with state revenue sources, have on higher education financing strategies? Heller (2006) argues that such constraints lead to pressure for tuition prices to increase. He claims that Medicaid, corrections, and K-12 funding have become "*de facto* entitlements." Other researchers have noted that these programs have put the squeeze on higher education funding (e.g., Hossler, Lund, Ramin, Westfall, & Irish, 1997). Does that factor into the perception of public versus private good when states develop their higher education financing approaches?

• In what ways does political ideology influence policies leading toward or away from privatization? Hossler et al. (1997) suggest that political context plays a role in funding decisions.

• What are some of the implications of the shift toward privatization, particularly on access for low-income and minority students?

• Will an interconnectedness of higher education for the public good remain possible?

Methods

To address these research questions, I have adapted the basic indicators model set forth by St. John in *Education and the Public Interest* (2006a). They use the state indicators tracking demographic, political, economic, social, and policy characteristics as control variables in analyses of the effects of policy reform. Whereas St. John uses the indicators to examine the effects of various policies on student outcomes, this analysis uses the indicators to elucidate influences on policy decisions. To that end, several new variables are included, including the percent of Medicaid expenditures (serving as a proxy for budget expenses constrained by law) and variables that speak to the political context of the state, specifically noting the effect of liberal or conservative leanings.

Data

Using state-level data provides an approach for examining the influence of state characteristics on privatization. Privatization here is measured by a ratio of weighted average tuition rates to state subsidies for higher education (direct budget allocation and state grants) weighted per FTE and tuition rates as the outcome.

St. John (2006a) created a database culled from numerous sources, including the U.S. Census Bureau, the NCES Common Core of Data, and the Integrated Postsecondary Education Data System (IPEDS). These data are available for multiple years, allowing for analyses that can consider changes over time relative to policy formation. Data from 1992, 1994, 1996, and 1998 were years that contained the most complete data for the variables used in this study. Other variables were added, including Medicaid expenditures[6] from the Annual State Expenditure Reports by the National State Budget Officers (NSBO) and two variables measuring political ideology[7] (created by Berry, Ringquist, Fording, & Hansen, 1998) from a publicly available source (through the Inter-University Consortium for Political and Social Research at the University of Michigan).

Measures

The top half of the ratio is calculated by measuring (per FTE) the aggregate tuition state rate. The bottom half of the ratio is calculated by taking the sum of the direct state allocation to public institutions as well as need-based and non-need-based grants to determine the total amount of money devoted to higher education in the state budget added to the aggregate tuition rate. Because the privatization variable is highly skewed to the right, and regression — my analytic technique — requires a normally distributed outcome, I took the natural log of privatization and used that more normally distributed transformation as my outcome. Five major groupings of independent variables emerge: demographic information about the state, capacity for private higher education in the state, political climate of the state, state tax rates, and the percent of the state budget constrained by law. I explain the rationale for using each group when I describe each measure below.

<u>Demographic indicators.</u> The main purpose for including demographic indicators is to control for state characteristics such as the population level, percentage of minorities,[8] and poverty rate. This will reveal if a relationship between characteristics of state residents and privatization exists.

<u>Capacity of private education.</u> I include a measure of the proportion of the postsecondary sector that is private in nature (as measured by FTE) in the state because it may indicate both citizens' and the government's attitudes toward higher tuition. For example, states that have a large capacity for private higher education may be more likely to move toward privatizing public postsecondary institutions.

<u>Political climate indicators.</u> There is a relationship between party affiliation, ideology, and policy (Doyle, McLendon, & Hearn, 2005; McLendon, Heller, & Young, 2005). I chose variables measuring ideology as opposed to party affiliation because the dominant political parties exhibit different ideologies depending on the region (e.g., Southern Democrats tends to be more conservative than Northern Democrats). Taking into account ideologies of both governments and citizens of states may help explain the adoption of more conservative financing strategies (indicated by the outcome of a high ratio of tuition to state subsidy). Berry et al. (1998) developed two variables, one measuring citizen ideology on a continuum of liberal to conservative, the other measuring government ideology along a similar continuum. Their algorithm for calculating ideology is complicated; refer to their article for how it is constructed.

<u>Tax rate.</u> Just as the political climate influences policy, so does the tax rate. If citizens do not want to pay high taxes, state budget allocations for a variety of needs and services will have to be reduced. Tax rates no longer provide an accurate indication of the wealth of the state. However, they can reflect what the citizens of the state

value, which influences policy development. St. John (2006a) calculated the tax rate by taking the total taxes collected by a state divided by personal income.

Percent of the budget constrained by law. In most state budgets, higher education is a discretionary item, while several other programs — such as Medicaid, prisons, and K-12 funding — can require mandatory allocations. As a result of a tight economy, there may be less discretionary money available in a given year. It is important to control for this aspect of the budget when determining state's conceptualization of higher education in order to prevent invalid interpretations of the outcome. Because Medicaid is the fastest growing mandatory expenditure, it serves as an adequate proxy for non-discretionary state budget items. Table 1 displays descriptive statistics for variables included in the model. Table 2 contains information about the trend of privatization, that is, the increasing percentage of a student's education paid for by the student through tuition, rather than by the state.

Analytic Strategy

Regression is appropriate for an analysis of the impact of state characteristics and budgets on the ratio of state subsidies to tuition because the outcome variable is a ratio. I used STATA 9.0 software to conduct my analyses.

Table 1. *Descriptive Information about Variables Included in Model Predicting Privatization*

	Mean/%	Std. Deviation	N
Natural Log of Privatization Ratio (a)	-0.95	0.56	204
Privatization Ratio (b)	0.29	0.11	255
Total Population	5098627.95	5642362.41	561
Minority Percentage of the Population	0.22	0.16	561
% in Poverty	0.13	0.04	561
Extent of Private Education in Postsecondary Sector/FTE	0.26	0.16	199
Tax Rate	0.07	0.01	450
% Medicaid Expenditure	0.16	0.06	635
Citizen Ideology	48.98	14.49	700
Government Ideology	50.12	24.37	700

a. Outcome Variable

b. This is the ratio measuring privatization using real numbers. Because it was not normally distributed, the natural log was used as the outcome variable

Table 2. *The Privatization Trend: Change over Time*

Year	Average % Paid by Tuition(SD)	Change in Percentage Points
1992	.28(.11)	
1994	.29(.11)	+1
1996	.30(.12)	+1
1998	.29(.11)	-1

Ordinary least squares (OLS). Regression can be used in an exploratory manner to identify a group of variables that may predict an outcome (Cohen, Cohen, West, & Aiken, 2003). Ordinary least squares regression requires a normally distributed, continuous outcome. Using the natural log of the privatization variable meets this assumption. All of the indicators in the model are continuous, which also supports the use of regression.

Fixed effects.[9] Fixed effects models are similar to OLS in that they, too, require continuous outcomes. However, one distinctive feature is that the model accounts for time. In these models, cases represent a state in a given year; there are also cases that serve as a panel of multiple state-year cases. A variable is then included to control for the state, allowing one to consider the change in state characteristics over time. A fixed-effects version of regression to account for additional unspecified state characteristics and policies, controls for additional effects without actually specifying them.

Limitations

Though some use regression to determine causality, in non-experimental and quasi-experimental research this technique can only provide information about influences on an outcome. A logical framework is used to select the variables in an effort to evince a stronger relationship to the outcome.

Furthermore, statistical significance typically refers to generalizing from a sample to the population. When using actual population parameters, statistical significance indicates a meaningful linkage between two variables, which is how it is applied in these analyses.

Analyses are limited by the time period studied. Changing political climates and implementation of new, innovative policies limit the implications of these analyses.

Findings

Each of the regression analyses yields results quite different from the other, both in the sign of coefficients and in significance of coefficients, as well as in total explanation of variance.

Ordinary Least Squares

Analyses using simultaneous OLS regression reveal that state-level demographic variables, political ideologies, and budgetary factors (tax rate and mandatory expenditures) all influence privatization of public higher education. The degree of private education in the postsecondary sector does not impact privatization of public colleges and universities. Results from the ordinary least squares analysis appear in Table 3.

The demographic variables yield generally expected results. Though the size of the population does make a difference, as indicated by the level of significance, it has virtually no influence on privatization as evidenced by the coefficient. However, specific characteristics of the population tell a more complete story. As the minority population and poverty rates in a state increase, privatization decreases.

Similar to the demographic variables, the direction of the effects of the tax rate and the percent of the budget constrained by law (using Medicaid expenditure as a proxy) are unsurprising. For each percent increase in the tax rate, privatization decreases by approximately 621 percent. As federally mandated state expenditures rise, so does the likelihood of privatization of public higher education.

Although the impact of political ideology remains low for both the government outlook and the citizen viewpoint, this result indicates differing influences. As the government becomes more conservative, less privatization occurs, but as citizens become more conservative, the opposite takes place. This model explains 58 percent of the variance in predicting privatization of public higher education ($F_{8, 179} = 30.9$, $p <$ .001).

Table 3. *Results of Ordinary Least Squares Regression Assessing Influences on Privatization of Public Postsecondary Education (N=188)*

	Unstand. Coeff.	Sig.
Total Population	0.000	*
Minority Percentage of the Population	-0.712	***
% in Poverty	-1.116	~
Extent of Private Education in Postsecondary Sector/FTE	0.303	
Tax Rate	-6.208	***
% Medicaid Expenditure	1.295	**
Citizen Ideology	0.002	***
Government Ideology	-0.004	***
Constant	-1.089	**
R2	0.583	***

$\sim p < .1;$ * $p < .05;$ ** $p < .01;$ *** $p < .001$

Fixed Effects

The results of the fixed effects regression differ markedly from the results of the OLS model, even though the only difference is the addition of the panel analysis. In the fixed effects analysis, only the extent of private education in the postsecondary sector and the state's tax rate bear significant relationships to privatization. Results are displayed in Table 4.

Table 4. *Results of Fixed Effects Regression Assessing Influences on Privatization of Public Postsecondary Education (N=188)*

	Unstand. Coeff.	Sig.
Total Population	0.000	
Minority Percentage of the Population	-1.222	
% in Poverty	0.351	
Extent of Private Education in Postsecondary Sector/FTE	1.812	**
Tax Rate	-2.585	**
% Medicaid Expenditure	0.199	
Citizen Ideology	-0.001	
Government Ideology	-0.001	
Constant	-1.445	***
R2	0.285	***
P-value for F test that all ui= 0		***

~ p < .1; * p < .05; ** p < .01; *** p < .001

Unlike the OLS analysis, as the extent of private education in the postsecondary sector rises, the ratio of tuition to state subsidy in the public sector increases when employing a fixed effects method of analysis. The impact of the tax rate follows the same direction in the fixed effects model that it does in the OLS model, but it is slightly less significant.

It also bears less influence on the degree of privatization; as the tax rate goes up one percentage point, privatization only decreases by approximately 259 percent, as opposed to the 621 percent decrease observed in the OLS analysis (Table 3). The fixed effects model explains 28.5 percent of the overall variance in predicting privatization ($F_{8, 132} = 4.4$, p < .000).

Discussion

Extreme differences in the results of each model require exploration of this disparity. Following that is a deeper discussion of the results from the fixed effects regression.

Disparity of Results

Not only is the change in R^2 from OLS to fixed effects a shock, I was quite surprised by how many variables lost significance in the more advanced model. I chose to focus my attention on understanding why the R^2 changed and why variables became insignificant, rather than on sign changes for variables that were no longer significant in the fixed effects model.

It is possible that a variable that has been omitted from the OLS model confounded the results. Because fixed effects regression controls for unobserved conditions and characteristics, the technique accounts for that missed variable. Although this hypothesis does not explain the drop in R^2 (after all, one would expect the R^2 to remain the same, if not actually increase, as a result of accounting for additional state characteristics), it does elucidate the loss of significance. Some of the unobserved conditions "grab" significance from the observed controls. The idea is similar to running a hierarchical regression with neighborhood safety in one model, and then including socioeconomic status in the next. Because neighborhood safety is so highly correlated with SES, introducing SES into the model reduces the influence of neighborhood safety, possibly making it insignificant altogether.

Proportion of Private Higher Education in the
Postsecondary Sector and Tax Rate

States with a higher percentage of private higher education also have higher levels of privatization in the public postsecondary sector, at least in the fixed effects model. There are several possibilities for this. One relates back to the notion of the market model. A market for high tuition/low subsidy postsecondary education not only exists in the states, it is sustainable. Based on that example, it is rational for policymakers to expect success with a similar model in the public sector. According to human capital theory, as long as the model is efficient and equitable, the market maintains the social contract.

Another option is that with the higher incidence of private educational opportunities, there are fewer students available to fill places in public institutions. In order to meet educational costs, states and institutions need to rely on tuition revenue and cannot afford large subsidies. In this case, the social contract may be unfulfilled.

As noted in the findings section, with increases in the tax rate, the extent of privatization decreases. This makes sense logically because higher taxes lead to more money in the budget, which means the state can subsidize the cost of public higher education, thereby reducing the ratio of tuition to subsidy plus tuition. Because of the influence of tax rate, it is somewhat surprising that the political ideology variables bear no impact on privatization. Tax rate is modestly but significantly correlated with both citizen and government ideology. As noted in the conceptual framework, conservative leanings tend to call for lower taxes, but the correlation between ideology and tax rate is not high enough that tax rate should take away all significance of political ideology. It is also surprising that Medicaid expenditures are not significant, but after reviewing that Medicaid and tax rate are somewhat strongly correlated ($r = -.454$, $p < .001$), it is possible that tax rate is taking the significance from Medicaid.

Nevertheless, it is concerning that the tax rate has such an influence on privatization, particularly since many states seek to keep taxes as low as possible. This outcome directly opposes all principles of Rawls's *Theory of Justice* and notions of the social contract. It denies the equal application of the basic moral right of education to some people and does not favor the disadvantaged in equality of opportunity. Finally, the just savings principle argues for taxation as a way to continue assurance of the first two principles for future generations.

Individuals' investment in human capital will not compensate for the government's disinvestment because fewer people will be able to participate in higher education. Without a fair tax rate, public higher education institutions will not receive the subsidies necessary either to keep tuition low or to provide grants to needy students, whichever method is more feasible, efficient, and equitable.

Arguably, the public good of higher education becomes devalued with this disinvestment because even though the trend toward privatization has not affected enrollment rates yet, it has affected who is enrolling. The gap between the wealthy and the poor will only widen because fewer low-income people will be able to participate in higher education. That means diversity in the workforce will diminish, and, potentially worse, diversity in the body politic will decrease. If fewer low-income people obtain the education needed to develop the critical and complex thinking required to consider political issues, participation in civic roles will not only be skewed, it may no longer fight for or represent the best interests of those the government is purportedly in existence to serve — all citizens in the democracy.

Conclusion

This chapter is not intended to debate the degree of investment individuals and the government should make in human capital. Rather, the goal is to understand drivers of privatization, the justice of those influences, and how justice relates to the outcome. To that end, the tax rate and the extent of the private sector in postsecondary education affect the degree of privatization in each state. Even though political ideology and the tax rate are related (or perhaps, because they are related), the political context of the state bears no influence on privatization, though Hossler et al. (1997) would argue differently.

The shift toward privatization results in dangerous implications for low-income and minority students. Because many states seek to keep taxes as low as possible, the fact that tax rate is such an important driver of privatization suggests a breach of the social contract and opposition to Rawls's *Theory of Justice.* That is, the just savings principle proposes that taxation assures equal application of basic moral rights (in this case, education) and that equality of opportunity favors the disadvantaged. However, if the just savings principle is violated, it becomes harder to uphold the first two principles in Rawls's theory. The outcome is that low-income and minority students end up farther behind their peers when it comes to their access to higher education.

My final research question asks: Will an interconnect-edness of higher education and the public good remain possible? Though my analysis predicts a gloomy outcome, I believe it is still possible. A trend toward privatization does not have to mean the end of the social contract, as long as public higher education does not become completely private. If movement in the direction of privatization follows an arc of justice, all prepared members of society will be able to participate equally in higher education, which means they all will be able to experience personal benefits and contribute to the public good. Privatization does not have to disentangle the interconnection between higher education and the public good. Since there is no stopping this trend, policymakers simply need to be aware of the impact of their decisions and act in a just, equitable manner.

Notes
[1] See Heller (2006) for a historical overview of support for higher education, focusing on state support, but

also considering federal contributions.   Also see Hearn (2001) and Mumper (2001).

[2] Horatio Alger wrote "rags-to-riches" stories emphasizing the ability to overcome adversity through perseverance, honesty, and hard work.

[3] Public higher education can easily be viewed as one of those main institutions.

[4] For a more complete discussion about the interconnected conceptualization of higher education for the public good, please see Pasque's typology and analysis (2005).   In this paper, she analyzes three typologies developed by the Institute for Higher Education Policy and develops a fourth that specifically looks at the interconnections between public and private benefits of higher education.

[5] As discussed below, these measures were derived from a state indicators database developed by St. John (2006b).

[6] Chris Baldwin located this information and compiled it into a clean form for addition to St. John and Associates' data set.

[7] Variables provided to me by Michael McLendon through Chris Baldwin. Nathan Daun-Barnett assisted me in adding the Medicaid and ideology variables to the indicators data set created by St. John (2006).

[8] I created a continuous variable that measures the total percentage of minorities — specifically members of Black, Hispanic, Indian, and Asian racial and ethnic groups — in the state.

[9] Special thanks to Anna Chung for providing guidance to me in this technique, and for helping me to understand disparate results comparing the OLS model to the fixed effects model. I discuss those results in greater detail in the Discussion section of the paper.

References

Berry, W.D., Ringquist, E.J., Fording, R.C., & Hanson, R.L. (1998). Measuring citizen and government ideology in the American states, 1960-93. *American journal of political science, 42,* 327-48.

Cohen, J., Cohen, P., West, S.G., and Aiken, L.S. (2003). *Applied multiple regression/correlation analysis for the behavioral sciences* (3rd ed.). Mahwah, NJ: Lawrence Erlbaum.

Dillon, S. (2005, October 16). At public universities, warnings of privatization. *New York Times,* p. 12.

Doyle, W.R., McLendon, M.K., & Hearn, J.C. (2005). Adoption of pre-paid tuition and savings plans in the American states: An event history analysis. Unpublished manuscript, Peabody College of Vanderbilt University, Tennessee.

Hearn, J.C. (2001). Paradox of growth in federal student financial aid. In M.B. Paulsen & J.C. Smart (Eds.) *Finance of higher education: Theory, research, policy, and practice.* (pp. 267-320). New York: Agathon Press.

Heller, D.E. (2006). State support of higher education: Past, present, and future. In D. Priest & E.P. St. John (Eds.), *Privatization and public institutions* (pp. 11-39). Bloomington, IN: Indiana University Press.

Hossler, D., Lund, J.P., Ramin, J., Westfall, S., & Irish, S. (1997). State funding for higher education: Sisyphean Task. *Journal of Higher Education, 68,* pp. 160-90.

McLendon, M.K., Heller, D.E., & Young, S.P. (2005). State postsecondary policy innovation: Politics, competition, and the interstate migration of policy ideas. *Journal of Higher Education, 76,* 363-400.

Mumper, M. (2001). Paradox of college prices: Five stories with no clear lesson. In D.E. Heller (Ed.) *States and public higher education policy: Affordability, access, and accountability* (pp. 39-63). Baltimore: Johns Hopkins University Press.

Parsons, M.B. (2004). Lobbying in higher education: Theory and practice. In E.P. St. John & M.D. Parsons (Eds.) *Public funding for higher education: Changing contexts and new rationales* (pp. 231-52). Baltimore: Johns Hopkins University Press.

Pasque, P.A. (2005). Typology and critical analysis of conceptualizations of Higher Education for the Public Good: Summary of the full paper. Unpublished manuscript, University of Michigan, Ann Arbor.

Paulsen, M.B. (2001a). Economics of human capital and investment in higher education. In M.B. Paulsen & J.C. Smart (Eds.) *Finance of higher education: Theory, research, policy, and practice.* (pp. 55-94). New York: Agathon Press.

Paulsen, M.B. (2001b). Economics of the public sector: Nature and role of public policy in the finance of higher education. In M.B. Paulsen & J.C. Smart (Eds.) *Finance of higher education: Theory, research, policy, and practice.* (pp. 95-132). New York: Agathon Press.

Rawls, J. (2001). *Justice as fairness: A restatement* (E. Kelly, Ed.). Cambridge, MA: Belknap Press of Harvard University Press.

Rawls, J. (1971). *Theory of Justice.* Cambridge, MA: Belknap Press of Harvard University Press.

St. John, E.P. (2006a). *Education and the public interest: School reform, public finance, and access to higher education.* Netherlands: Springer.

St. John, E.P. (2006b). Privatization and the public interest. In D.M. Priest & E.P. St. John (Eds.) *Privatization and public universities.* (pp. 247-80). Bloomington, IN: Indiana University Press.

St. John, E.P. (2004). Policy research and political decisions. In E.P. St. John & M.B. Parsons (Eds.) *Public funding for higher education: Changing contexts and new rationales* (pp. 231-252). Baltimore: Johns Hopkins University Press.

Zumeta, W. (2004). State higher education financing: Demand imperatives meet structural, cyclical, and political constraints. In E.P. St. John & M.B. Parsons (Eds.) *Public funding for higher education: Changing contexts and new rationales* (pp. 79-107). Baltimore: Johns Hopkins University Press.

CHAPTER 7

HIGH SCHOOL GUIDANCE COUNSELORS AS REPRODUCTIVE FORCES IN THE LIVES OF AFRICAN AMERICAN STUDENTS: A STUDY OF A GEORGIA HIGH SCHOOL

Ontario S. Wooden[1]

High school guidance counselors face numerous challenges related to ensuring the successful navigation of students not only through the academic areas of high school, but also that often complicated personal development stage of life. Students, especially those in urban schools, do not totally understand the challenges counselors face and, upon entrance into high school, present additional challenges to the counselors depending on the student's specific situation. Regardless of the challenges presented, high school guidance counselors are expected to provide support to all students with the desire and motivation to attend college. There are also those who feel that the support and motivation should not only be given to those who have made the decision to attend college, but that a goal of high schools should be to prepare all students for college. It is also important to note that college preparation is just as important as talking students through difficult personal challenges, administering standardized tests, and developing students' class schedules.

At the same time, educators are plagued with recent discussion pertaining to dismal high school completion rates and the number of students who enter college ill-prepared. Additionally, this same group of educators is also challenged

245

Copyright ©2007 AMS Press, Inc. All rights reserved.

by the continued lower college participation rates of African American students in comparison to their White peers. This paper is intended to assist in explaining how high school tracking and relationships with guidance counselors impact the college preparation and attendance process for African American students in a Georgia high school. Two questions guide the findings of this research: (1) How does tracking impact the college preparation experience for students in this school? (2) What assistance do high school guidance counselors provide in preparing these students for college?

Reframing Research on Preparation

In studying the college preparation experience and subsequent participation of African Americans in higher education, it is imperative that there is a strong theoretical underpinning for the study. Of equal importance is a proper cultural context in which to place this work. As defined by Freeman (1998), cultural context is "interrelated characteristics that provide a perspective — frame of reference — for understanding individuals' and/or groups' ways of knowing and being" (p. 2). Making these cultural considerations allow the researcher to present findings that are proper interpretations of the group under study (Freeman, 1998). Specifically, this analysis focuses on the role of counselors in the college preparation process considering the cultural context in which the students live.

Preparation for college has become a focal point in the literature on college access (Choy, 2002; Perna, 2005), including in studies of African Americans (Freeman, 2005). It has also been argued that the role of financial inequalities has been left out of arguments about preparation and access, and there is substantial evidence of this omission (St. John, 2006). While I acknowledge the central roles that both preparation and family concerns about college costs play, I argue that the frame used to study access for African Americans should be broadened to consider the African

American tradition of education. Specifically, in this study I
focus on the ways an understanding of this tradition can help
to untangle the role of tracking as a barrier to academic
preparation and college access.

African American Tradition
     The theoretical underpinnings for this study are based on
the African American tradition. This tradition has tenets
related to caring, cross-generational uplift, and faith
communities. In addition, cultural reproduction and social
reproduction are explored to better understand other influences related to college decision making.

     Carism. Contemporary work on care theory is most
often based on the work of Carol Gilligan (1982) who
defines care as "a web of interdependence, a concept of
being there, listening as a moral act, understanding, shared
responsibility for another's welfare" (Schrader, 1999, p. 42-
43). Noddings (1999) continues to say that as schools
respond to the needs of students, there may be a need to
design varying types of curricula and to carefully guide the
students through the web of possibilities. Differentiated
curricula are evidence that those who surround students
really care for them and curricular change is evidence of this
care. Care, as Noddings (1999) defines it, forces teachers to
look at students closely before remedies are recommended
and listen to those whose "aspirations, interests, talents, and
legitimate values" may differ from the teacher's (p. 15).
This is better than strict curricular offerings that "produce
resistance and weaken the relation." Noddings (1999) insists
that in addition to caring, students need adults in their lives
who "listen, invite, guide, and support them." According to
Allen-Hayes, St. John, and Cadray (2003), "the African
American tradition, which emphasizes care and community,
provides an important foundation for creating just and caring
learning environments in post-desegregation urban schools"
(p. 250). The authors go on to state that the ethic of care that

was an important part of African American schooling was nearly lost after desegregation. They explain, "To a large extent, this ethic of care that was experienced in African American schools prior to 1954, had its origin in the neighborhood school concept through which everyone in the school shared a common view of the world" (p. 251). These schools were effective because they fostered a strong sense of community and family cooperation. Teachers lived and worked in the neighborhood, thus the school was able to serve as a center for social activity. Because of the association, communication, and trust that developed between the parents and the school, it was not uncommon for teachers to stop by a parent's home or talk to the parent while at church on Sunday (Allen-Hayes, St. John, & Cadray, 2003).

The best example of the African American tradition is documented by Siddle Walker (1996). In her book on a segregated African American high school in the South, she found that students were successful because of the relationships that were developed between the school and the families in the community. Caring is the foundation of the African American tradition.

Cross-Generation Uplift. St. John and Mirón (2003) state, "The major social theory of educational and social attainment argues there is a pattern of cross-generation uplift, with gains in parent education and occupational status in one generation having a positive influence on the next generation" (p. 288). Further, St. John and Mirón (2003) note that the primary use of this theory related to education is "that African American families have aspirations for a better life for their children" (p. 288). Dilworth (2003/2004) points out that historically "the quests of African Americans for educational equality were framed around the struggle for racial uplift" (p. 8). It was imperative that those in the African American community who were able to be educated "reach back" and share their knowledge and resources with those that did not have the opportunity to do so. This theory makes a strong contribution to research related to high school students in predominantly African American urban high schools as it relates to college preparation and attendance.

If the student attends a high school where there are numerous African American teachers that have characteristics that relate to the African American tradition, there is the possibility that the student will be cared for and supported to the point that the student will take the proper courses to prepare for college. Additionally, there might be a chance that the student will gain some knowledge of the financial preparations needed in order for college attendance to become a reality. On the other hand, for those schools that are charged with educating multiracial populations, I offer that an introduction of tenets of the African American tradition can be helpful in increasing the academic achievement of those students and possibly increase the number of African American students who attend college.

Countervailing Social Forces

Since freed slaves began to advocate for their civil and educational rights, the basic inequality in American society has been well understood (Moses, 2001). In addition to facing an educational system that systematically excluded African Americans from the pathways commonly associated with academic success, advocates of justice for freed people had to contend with the patterns of class reproduction within society. As background to this study, I was particularly interested in the role of cultural and social reproduction, as social forces that reproduce class and potentially mitigate the efforts to use education as means of promoting cross-generation uplift.

   Cultural Reproduction. Cultural reproduction has been defined as the way schools, in collaboration with other social institutions, aid in maintaining social and economic inequalities across generations (Bourdieu, 1977). Carspecken (1996) offers that culture "is produced when people draw upon cultural themes they are already familiar with. They draw upon such themes in response to institutional settings and the constraints these settings exert upon them" (p. 18). Giddens (1997) acknowledges that cultural reproduction "refers to the mechanisms by which continuity of cultural experience is sustained across time. The processes of schooling in modern societies are among the main mechanisms of cultural reproduction, and do not operate solely through what is taught in courses of formal instruction. Cultural reproduction occurs in a more profound way through the hidden curriculum—aspects of behavior which individuals learn in an informal way while at school" (p. 581). Generally, cultural reproduction is the means by which class values are passed down and in extreme cases allow the poor to remain poor and the rich to remain rich.

   Social Reproduction. It is via social reproduction that schools are able to benefit some students while simultaneously oppressing others. Bourdieu (1977) provides a basis for thinking about social reproduction in the larger society and connects it with the oppressive practices in schools. He explains:

> By making social hierarchies and the repro-
> duction of these hierarchies appear to be based
> upon the hierarchy of "gifts," merits, or skills
> established and ratified by its sanctions, or, in a
> word, by converting social hierarchies into
> academic hierarchies, the educational system
> fulfills a function of legitimation which is more
> and more necessary to the perpetuation of the
> "social order" as the evolution of the power

relationships between classes tends more completely to exclude the imposition of a hierarchy based upon the crude and ruthless affirmation of the power relationship. (p. 496)

As it will be explained later, schools structure opportunity for students using the rationale that some students are academically superior to others, or that some students merit the right to special treatment over others. While these students receive this treatment due to their merit, there often remains a larger class of students who are oppressed. According to Bourdieu, the powerful group in society seeks to maintain social order by these practices. Further, Spring (2000) contends that school is where students' family backgrounds are converted into occupational and income opportunities.

Tracking. Tracking in schools is the means by which schools maintain a particular social order, or hierarchy. Tracking, also known as ability grouping, has long been a practice in education (Oakes, 1985; Spring, 2000). This grouping may take place as early as elementary school. One 1991 study found that 56 percent of elementary Math classes in the country were using tracking mechanisms (Spring, 2000). In middle schools, school officials usually make decisions with regard to student course placements, with parents often not being a part of the decision-making process (Oakes, 1985). Because of some parents' lack of involvement in the course selection process in middle schools, these parents are also often not involved in the processes in high schools as well. Yet, because of the social reproductive forces in schools, other parents are able to enroll their children in more rigorous courses than parents who do not have this advantage.

It has also been found that because school officials tend to mask tracking structures and are not totally forthcoming about the consequences of such structures, class differences in student placement and achievement are amplified (Oakes, 1985). This supports Rist's (1970) findings that the African American student failure rate can be attributed in part to ability grouping, which allows for downward, as opposed to upward, movement within an academic system. Thus, once students are placed into these tracks, it becomes difficult to be moved to another track, and few students are moved to higher tracks (Oakes, Guiton, Selvin, & Karoly, 1990). It also increases the possibility of failure for students placed in lower tracks where teachers often do not expect strong academic performance from students.

Framing this Study
The thesis in this exploratory study is that tracking decisions made by high school counselors are events that precede other interventions that aim to provide encouragement for preparation and information on student financial aid: as a social screening device, tracking not only serves to route students through high school in ways that denies opportunity to prepare for college, it also veils the sorting process from visibility of African American families, thus mitigating the role of cross-generation uplift. Rather than encouraging all students to achieve the most possible from their schools, tracking decisions made as early as middle school not only route students out of higher education, but also encourages dropping out of high school.

The cultural ecology model introduced by Tierney and Venegas (see Chapter One) provides a lens for integrating the role of information on student financial aid into the process of counseling students in high school, overcoming one limitation of extant theories of preparation and access. However, when researching student preparation by African American students in middle schools and high schools, it is also important to consider the role tracking, as a reproduction force, in relation to the carism that promotes cross-generation uplift among African Americans.

Methodology

The thick, rich description that qualitative research provides cannot be matched by the simple representation of numbers and figures that quantitative research offers. Qualitative research possesses the inherent ability to bring the research "alive." Further, with regard to the subject of the study, qualitative methods are appropriate because the voices of these African American students are rarely heard in debates regarding their lives, and oftentimes, the voices of disempowered students are even more inaudible (Nieto, 1992).

Qualitative research also has the ability to expound on how individuals experience events in order to grasp a firm understanding of how these events work together to inform life decisions. There are assumptions that meanings are developed in people's experiences and these meanings are made sense of through the investigator's own perceptions (Merriam, 1998). In defining qualitative research, Patton (1985) states:

> ... [qualitative research] is an effort to understand situations in their uniqueness as part of a particular context and the interactions there. This understanding is an end in itself, so that it is not attempting to predict what may happen in the future necessarily, but to understand the nature of that setting-what it means for participants to be in that setting, what their lives are like, what's going on for them, what their meanings are, what the world looks like in that particular setting.... (p. 1)

The most important concern in qualitative research is to see the phenomenon under study through the eyes of the study participants, not the eyes of the researcher.

This study involved mixed methods, combining case study techniques with the use of critical ethnography. The case study method was chosen because it allows findings to be bound to Urban City High School (UCHS), while critical ethnography was used in order to critically examine practices taking place in this school.

Case Study

Oftentimes much-needed information can be gleaned from studying one place or thing in order to answer research questions. When this is done, a researcher is said to be using a case study method. According to Bogdan and Biklen (1998), "a case study is a detailed examination of one setting, or a single subject, a single depository of documents, or one particular event" (p. 54). For this study, UCHS is the unit of study. When a researcher studies schools using case study methods, he "might visit the school on a regular basis, observing what goes on in classrooms, during recess periods, in the hallways and lunchroom, during faculty meetings, and so on" (Fraenkel & Wallen, 2000, p. 538).

In addition to the use of case studies, critical ethnography was also used. While the case study allowed for the examination of UCHS as one case, critical ethnography allowed a "critical eye" to be given to the practices which shape the lives of the participants, both inside and outside of school.

Critical Ethnography. Thomas and O'Maolchatha (1989) assert that critical ethnography refers to the reflective process of "choosing between conceptual alternatives and making value-laden judgments of meaning and method to challenge research, policy, and other forms of human activity" (p. 4). Critical ethnographers take on the responsibility of using their research to empower their participants by giving more authority to their voices. Tierney (1991) explains, "Critical theorists tie their investigations to a concern for social justice and democracy" (p. 41) and Fay (1987) points out "the role of the critical theorists is to explain the organizational world, criticize it,

and empower its audience to overthrow it" (p. 23).
Consequently, critical ethnographers invoke a call to action
and attempt to use knowledge gained for social change
(Thomas, 1993).

Critical ethnography is based on the understanding that
the structure and content of culture make life nastier, brutish,
and short for some people for unnecessary reasons (Quantz,
1992; Thomas, 1993; Tierney, 1991). For an increasingly
large number of African American high school students,
college is no longer a reality. Social science research must
address the hidden causes of this inequality. Critical
ethnography is grounded in explicit prior evidence of
debilitating conditions that provide avenues for research. It
is obvious that cultural forces have shaped the conditions
that have disadvantaged some groups more than others.
Simply put, "if critical ethnography is about anything, it is
about freedom from social repression and a vision of a better
society" (Thomas, p.71).

Site and Subject Selection

Patton (2002) states that cases can be individuals,
groups, neighborhoods, programs, organizations, cultures,
regions, or nation-states. For this study, the cases consisted
of African American high school students who were
participating in the college choice process, those with no
definite plans for college, and those who have dropped out,
thus a purposeful sample. According to Fraenkel and Wallen
(2000), purposeful sampling is the process of using personal
judgment to select a sample based on previous knowledge of
a population and the specific purpose of research.
Researchers assume they can use their knowledge of a
population to judge whether or not a particular sample will
be representative. The participants in this purposeful sample
were able to provide the information that the researcher
needed. Additionally, Patton (2002) states, "purposeful
sampling involves studying information-rich cases in depth
and detail to understand and illuminate important cases

rather than generalizing from a sample to a population" (p. 230).

The participants were identified as college going, those with no definite plans of going to college, and those who have dropped out. Once identified, these students were contacted in order to conduct an interview. Participants were given a copy of the Study Information Sheet according to Human Subjects guidelines. Over forty students, teachers, counselors, administrators, and parents participated in this research study. The names of these participants have been altered to protect their identity.

Data Collection

The primary method of data collection for this study was interviews. Patton (2002) introduces several interview approaches. A combination of two interview methods was employed for this study. The interview guide was used because it provided topics or subjects so that the interviewer was free to explore, probe, and ask questions that would expand that particular subject. The interview guide was used to assist in forming an outline for the subjects to be explored. The standardized open-ended interview, where carefully and fully worded questions are developed before the interview, completed the process of developing interview questions.

Data Analysis

These interviews provided a rich set of data to analyze and present in the analysis of this study. A thick, rich description of the data emerged as a result of audio taped interviews, field notes on thoughts and feelings during the course of the study, additional notes on the expressions and gestures of the participants, document analysis of attendance patterns, test scores, grades, and full transcriptions of the recorded interviews. Field notes included biases that existed going into the interviews and any perceptions that arose during the interviews, facial expressions and gestures from the participants, thoughts on the information received, thoughts on other emerging themes in the research, and any other thoughts related to the research design.

In Chism's (n.d.) article on *Analyzing Qualitative Data,* she explains:

> The analysis of qualitative data involves several activities, including: becoming familiar with the data, selecting certain parts of the data as most relevant, sorting the data into categories, displaying the data for review, reading within and across categories for themes, and synthesizing the information. (p. 1)

Data analysis was conducted during and after the data collection process. Field notes were often expanded immediately following the interviews and a transcriber immediately transcribed tapes. Following transcription of the interviews and expansion of the field notes, instances in the data were found that aided in the development of themes and the expansion of pre-existing themes.

After an initial review of the data, a list of categories and themes was developed. After a more in-depth analysis, themes were further expanded and new ones were created. This aforementioned process was much easier because of the use of a thick, rich description. Further, the Non-numerical Unstructured Data Indexing Searching & Theorizing (NUD*IST Vivo) was used to analyze the data collected. This data analysis program allowed for easy coding of data and made the data more manageable. It was interesting to use this software because it allowed for quotes to be placed in one or more categories, which aided in the analysis of data. The final product included well-analyzed data and easily disseminated research findings.

Limitations

The first limitation is the possible lack of trust participants may have had with the researcher and the research being conducted. It is possible that because the interviewer was also the researcher, there was information participants may not have been compelled to share. Further, because the research conducted was about their school and, in some cases, their place of employment, participants may have also been hesitant to share data or other information pertinent to the study.

Findings

High School Course Taking and Tracking Mechanisms

It was important to know if students had any idea of how they became enrolled in the courses in which they were currently enrolled. In addition to other variables, high school courses (Gandara, 2002; St. John & Musoba, forthcoming) have a large effect on the later success of high school students. First, the college preparatory students, then the vocational/career technical students responded to my query. All ten of the college preparatory students knew relatively well how they came to be enrolled in the college preparatory classes. Amber abruptly responded, "In the eighth grade we had to sign a paper, and they recommended that I be on College Prep because I want to go to college." Jeria explained:

> Ninth grade year I don't believe so, but after that they pretty much ask you. I don't know what they do with other kids, but counselors show favoritism because they don't call them to [the] office and ask them what they want, and then the next semester when classes start they have a lot of people in the office or whatever. But I've been asked every year what classes I want to take, and most of the classes were already assumed that I was going to take them, but they just make sure.

Antoine added:

> Coming from middle school and into high
> school they look at your GPA and what type of
> classes you have taken. And basically they place
> you in a class according to your performance in
> that class, and they move you up to a higher class
> or lower class.

These students had a pretty clear idea about how they
became enrolled in the courses they had taken and are taking
as high school students. This is an interesting point to note in
light of the fact that the vocational/career technical students
shared almost the opposite insights. It is also an early
glimpse at the social reproductive roles counselors play in
high schools, which, in a sense, help to maintain
stratification of social classes. In addition, counselors seem
to serve as sorting mechanisms for success at UCHS. Unlike
the ten vocational/career technical students, students who
were pursuing the college preparatory diploma exhibited
more confidence and control over their class schedules and
course taking habits.

The vocational/career technical students also shared
information with me regarding their graduation track and
their high school coursework. The stories these ten students
shared were very different stories from those the college
preparatory students shared. The first student interviewed
commented, "I'm on Vocational, I was on College but I got
off." I asked her for her reason for getting off the college
track and she answered:

> I made a decision. It was hard. I was in the 10th
> grade and it was hard. I wish I wouldn't have got
> off, but I wouldn't have gone to college anyway.
> But I wish I wouldn't have gotten off. I was going
> to go to college, but when I really thought about

it, there isn't any way because my dad died when I was in 8th grade.

Mark reported that he was on the "technical track," and when asked why he was on this graduation track, he offered:

> I was [on College Preparatory track] but I had flunked a class in 9th grade, which hurt me, and then I mentioned to my parents that I wanted to go ahead and get on the technical track. I could graduate on time and then attend a two-year college and then later on, a four-year university.

Other students were not as reflective on their graduation track, probably as a defense mechanism [there seems to some shame associated with preparing for a vocational/technical career], but their responses were brief and to the point. Dawn informed me that "I'm on Tech Prep" and Bryon added "Vocational."

To encourage the students to become more reflective about the graduation track they were currently on, students were asked how they got on the graduation track they were on. Because of the tracking mechanism in their school system students are assigned to a track based on their math placement and standardized test performance in eighth grade. I wanted to find out if students were aware of this. Only two of the ten vocational/career technical students reported that they knew how they became enrolled on this graduation track.

In having this discussion with John, he responded, "I really couldn't tell you, but I was thinking I was in the wrong place [wrong classes]. When asked if he knew that in eighth grade his high school graduation track had been decided by a standardized test, he responded, "Yeah, I think I knew that." On the other hand, Andrew offered, "We thought it [the standardized test] was just for classes, to decide your Math class like Algebra, Pre-Algebra…." Louis declared, "Naw [he did not know the test was deciding his graduation track] I remember taking that test too. You know, nobody was really making any big deal about it to me. I really didn't pay any attention to it."

Based on these comments, I became even more convinced that these students were not aware of issues relating to tracking and, if unchecked, how detrimental these decisions could be to a student's academic career. I probed further to get additional thoughts about their placements and how they thought it had impacted them.

Keith commented, "Yeah, I was placed on college prep but since I didn't pass that first class you are automatically put on technical track." John continued his comments to talk about the advice that he gives his peers and students that have come to the school after him. He stated, "I have friends. I tell them the mistakes I made and I got on this track and I want you all to do this. Don't be on this track, be on college prep so when you graduate you get to choose where you want to go to college." Andrew commented that he was also shocked by the courses that he was enrolled in upon arriving at the school. He lamented:

> When I first got here, I was like man. Because some of the people, they had different kinds of class, like Spanish. And I didn't have none of those classes. And then I went to the counselor and she told me I was on vocational track, I wasn't on college prep. You don't need a foreign language on the vocational track.

He continued, "I wish I had gotten college prep, [but] back then I wasn't even thinking about college. Now, I think a lot of classes could have gotten me ready for college."

Also important to this research are the academic experiences of dropouts before they left school. Research posits (LeCompte & Dworkin, 1991) that students who perform poorly where their academics are concerned are likely to be dropouts. The dropout students in this study represented both college preparatory and vocational/career technical students. This was a surprise to me, as I thought that students who dropped out of high school were those who were on the vocational/technical diploma track, not those who were seeking a college preparatory high school diploma. Of these students, two were on college preparatory track and two were on vocational/career technical. However, when I asked Jamillia which graduation track she was on before she left school, she responded, "I guess vocational. I have no idea." Actually, she was on the college preparatory track earlier in her high school career and after failing a class, she was placed on the vocational/career technical track.

There seemed to be a bit of embarrassment when she answered the question, as there was a frown on her face when she gave me her answer. Michael also exhibited some of the same behavior in that after informing me that he was on the vocational/career technical track, he added, "Most of my classes, they are senior classes because I was short some credits, but most of them are senior classes." This response was seemingly given to ensure me that even though he was on the vocational/career technical track; he was still a senior and was taking classes he needed to graduate.

Ms. Westbrook, a counselor, helped me to gain an understanding of the tracking processes at UCHS and in the school system. These processes often work against minority and low-income students' success (Gandara, 2002). For the most part, she confirmed my underlying assumptions:

> You see, for the most part the way the curriculum is structured now in the eighth grade, they just about determine whether they are college prep or tech route. If they miss it in eighth grade, when they come to us, if they are not in Algebra I in ninth grade, they're tech prep. There's no ifs, ands, or buts about it. But you have to take Algebra I in ninth grade, Geometry, Algebra 2,

and Advanced Math your senior year. If you are not prepared when you come from the eighth grade for Algebra I, then you are on tech prep.

It was clear that the eighth grade standardized test determined the fate of the students attending UCHS. I wondered why the students, at least a large majority of them, did not know about this.

These findings highlight some important issues related to school tracking processes. While 100 percent of the college preparatory students knew how they became enrolled on their graduation track, only 20 percent of the vocational/career technical students knew the reasons they became enrolled in their track. It appears that college preparatory students at UCHS have greater access to information regarding graduation tracks. What is compelling from these interviews is that so many of the students who were moved to the vocational track had lost their aspirations to enroll in college. In some instances, students pointed to poor performance in prior classes as a reason for being moved to a vocational track. It is apparent that the tracking mechanism denied opportunity for some students who aspired to enroll in college.

Counselor Practices

The support students in this study received for college from their counselor is consistent with that described by other researchers (Hossler, Schmit, & Vesper, 1999; McDonough, 1997) who reported that students who earned better grades were more likely to get strong support from their parents, siblings, and others to continue their education. In addition to talking with family members about college plans, students also discussed their involvement with their counselors regarding their college planning. While it may be expected that students who are seeking a college preparatory diploma are able to get the needed assistance from their counselors, this was not always the case. However, it should be noted that low-income students rely on their counselors for information about college (Leslie, Johnson, & Carlson, 1977). Yet, it becomes clearer that because of the social reproductive aspect of counselors, their practices continue to oppress most students while assisting only a few. Even among these students, there are still students who get more information than others. In discussing his interactions with his counselor, Antoine explained:

> Only a select few that the counselor talks to about different schools and you may have to be known in the school to have a counselor talk to you or speak with you on a regular basis about school. It's not easy because I know some counselors are so fed up they really don't want to have to take time out to deal with children. They have real bad attitudes and real nasty attitudes.

It was difficult to hear this from a college preparatory student with a 3.7 GPA. This is consistent, however, with Brantlinger's (1993) findings that because of the varied duties of high school counselors, they only give attention to those students who have superior academic skills. Other students shared similar experiences. Jolan added:

> [If] I need a transcript or something I have to keep coming back day after day. They tell you to come back the next day, but when they just say come back the following day and you know that following day you have to come back again. You just stop coming because you know they aren't going to give it to you. Before you see the counselor you have to talk to [the secretary] and she has her attitude every day and whatever she says, that's what goes.

Amber shared that while she rarely sees her counselor, she does attempt to be helpful:

> Right now I rarely do because she's busy most of the time. You have to get in when you can to talk to her. I've rarely even seen my counselor until like this year. When I transferred back over here she talked to me about my classes. She tried to see what classes I wanted to be in. Then she gave me my transcript, so I could see my ranking and all that stuff.

However, Amber does admit that to an extent, she is disappointed about the role her counselor plays in her plans for college. She thought that she would be able to get more support than what she has been given. Amber continued, "I expected the counselors to be more involved with us in our college education and that kind of stuff. It seems like no one seems to care as much as I thought they would."

On the other hand, one student shared a different story. Interestingly enough, other students who were interviewed had warned me that this would be the case. Jeria only had positive things to say about her counselor and the role that the counselor plays in her plans for college. Jeria, seemingly knowledgeable of this favoritism concluded, "We had a discussion about that in one of our classes last year and truthfully the smart kids they put more focus on you. If you're not in the top percentage they just throw you in a class." In telling me how often she sees her counselor she proudly responded, "Four times a week, I go to the counselor office every day." She wrapped her comments up by informing me that her counselor really cares about her. It is interesting that of all the college preparatory students, there is only one student who spoke at length about the positive impacts of her counselor on her college plans and she probably needed the counselor the least because not only was she set to be the class valedictorian, she had a strong support system, both at school and church, for college attendance.

The vocational/career technical students also spoke about the support they received, and did not receive, from their counselors. As was the case with college preparatory tracked students, there were differences in the amount of contact with counselors. These findings were also consistent with Howard's (2003) in that the students in his study questioned their potential for college sometimes because of their interactions with their counselors. Generally, vocational/career technical students did not receive the support they felt other students receive, as only 20 percent of them interact regularly with their counselors. Keith reported:

> I don't even know who my counselor is. I just don't have any reason to talk to my counselor over here. At [another high school he attended], I talked to my counselor two times and he told me I needed to go to summer school this year to take two classes and if I pass all my classes, I'll be on track to graduate.

However, there are some disadvantages of not speaking with his counselor, as he soon shared. He commented, "Basically, I know what I have to do as far as school, but as far as college, technical college I have no idea. I'm going to have to go to the [technical college admissions office] on my own."

John acknowledged that he did not talk to his counselor because he does not want to hear the bad news that he feels the counselor is always there to bear. He said:

> I don't talk to the counselor. The counselor, you know, you don't want to hear the same thing, if you want to go to this school, you probably can't go because of your grades or whatever, that's the reason I don't talk to them.

When I asked if he felt that it was the counselor's responsibility for him to make the grades he needs to make to get to college or his own, he answered, "I can't say that I messed up a whole lot, but I messed up like in the classes [college preparatory classes] I was supposed to be in. Andrew asserted, "I haven't talked to them in a while. Last time I talked to them was like last year because that was when we had that little conversation about the SAT."

Did the students who dropped out of UCHS know their high school counselor before they left? What were their interactions with their counselor like? As Brantlinger (1993) found, counselors are busy doing course schedules, dealing with students who have overt issues, and attempting to assist the students they know will be attending post-secondary education after graduation from high school. This case was no different. Only two of five dropouts reported favorable interaction with their counselors. Kendall told me that he did not know who his counselor was. When I asked if he had ever tried to talk with the counselor about his academic issues, he responded, "I wasn't the type of person to sit and talk to somebody about stuff like that."

This comment reminded me of the notion in the African American community that one does not talk to people outside the family and even sometimes outside one's home about issues or problems; what happens at home, stays there. Further, speaking with a counselor has a very negative connotation in the African American community. A follow up probe asked if he even asked the counselor about his schedule. He insisted, "Naw, I just took what they gave me." This comment supports Useem's (1992) study which found that parents and students from lower income families were less likely to challenge their child's course placements than students whose parents were more educated and possessed more wealth.

Michael shared a similar story to Kendall. He said that he did not talk to his counselor about his plans, but after I asked him the question for a second time, he confessed, "Not much at all unless I'm going to get my schedule changed, because usually they don't have time to sit and talk to you." While he recognized that his counselor was busy, he was still a bit bothered that he could not speak with her as much as he would have liked. He shared, "when I get ready to talk to her, it's [the conversation] kind of short...two or three words." To give him an opportunity to think about any other conversations with his counselor, a probe asked him if the counselor ever followed up with him when there was a moment. He declared, "no."

While using classroom teachers to support the advising efforts of counselors, it remains imperative that students have regular contact with someone in a guidance-counseling role. In addition to using the advisement program as a means for discussing classes, it is also important that someone is available to discuss career plans with students in order that they will enroll in the right classes. Yet, there was evidence that these relationships do not exist.

An administrator at UCHS shared that parents and students are often told needed information regarding course scheduling and graduation requirements, but they do not understand what they are told and the counselors do not take the time to explain things in detail. He shared:

> Once you give a parent some information, you have to be able to point out to a person this line means your child should have had ninth grade Literature and she didn't have it. It's an eye contact thing and it's a comfortable feeling. [This is important] because a person will come back at the end and say, "Nobody told me this." Yes ma'am you were told this on this day. You were told but you didn't understand.

Another administrator was also aware of the broken relationships between the students and the counselors. She suggested:

> I don't think they have good relationships with their counselors. I think they see the counselors as someone who calls them in and tells them what they need to do. Someone who says, "this is what you need to do. You are going into twelfth grade. You passed this. You failed this. You are going to have to make it up." But as far as somebody to talk to, "may I please go see Mrs. So and So?" I don't see that a whole lot.

Because of her former employment at a predominantly White school in the system, she offered that a benefit of being at a predominantly African American school is that there are other caring persons in the school who can provide support and direction. She continued:

> If you don't have a counselor's attention at a predominantly Black school...there are other people there to look out for you. You have more people who don't want to see you become a statistic so they ask, "what are you doing? Why are you doing this? What are you supposed to be doing?" And, as a matter of fact, [a teacher] told me just yesterday "I have five [students]. They're not doing well, and I need for you to talk with them. " And that's the kind of thing you're going to have at a Black school as opposed to a predominantly White school.

As has been expressed throughout the interviews, she noted the need for extra support for those students who are not the top students. When asked if she was aware that only the top students were being given the time needed with the counselors, the administrator responded, "This is supposed to be going on [the counselor should be calling all students in]. I don't check this as closely as I should." Given the multiple challenges she apparently has, this does not come as a surprise. However, one of the counselors feels that the students may be expecting too much of them. She insisted:

> I think they rely too much on us. They take away their power when they just rely on us. I mean we announce to anybody in the school. It's not like we hide this stuff. We announce the scholarships that we know about and the criteria. If they meet the criteria, then certainly they can apply. If they don't meet the criteria, then you don't need to apply if you don't have the grade point average or the SAT scores, you know what I'm saying? But there's a lot out there that our kids don't take advantage of. It's very rare that the kids do their search on their own. We spoil them, because I know when I was in school whatever you got you did it on your own and I don't remember talking to my guidance counselor. But there are a lot of things that they hear about that we don't have a clue about, you see what I'm saying? But we do help them in terms of providing all the addresses for the colleges in Georgia.

Clearly, one understands that there are many things students need to do and should possibly do on their own, but there is a need for stronger support from counselors for the students at UCHS. Their need for support is amplified given the backgrounds and family situations of many of these students. The counselor also seems to be projecting her own experiences with counselors on her students, which is definitely unfair given the context of UCHS. McDonough (1997) found that counselors can either uplift low-income students or act as gatekeepers. In this case, it appeared there was much more gatekeeping than uplifting.

Counselors also play a role in students' preparation for college. The parents shared sentiments much like the students. Parents spoke rather bluntly about the role their child's counselors played in their child's preparation for college. Ms. Price informed me that her son's interactions with his counselor are "pretty superficial." She added that his relationships with his counselors exist to the extent that they are:

> Telling him about graduation tests, schedules, as well as the study sessions. Talking to him about SAT, PSAT, and National Merit Scholar test, talking to him about some extra-curricular things like special leadership programs they might do, special Math or science programs that he might be eligible to attend. They have advised him about some recruiting, college-recruiting activities, off campus. So he's been involved in things like that. But again, there are a handful of students that get that attention, that get those notices, and I see the same ones. All the parents know each other.

Ms. Baxter spoke about her concerns related to the students who are not able to get the attention she feels they need from the counselors. She apprehensively shared:

> I might be wrong for thinking or saying it, but I've always had a problem with the kids that are caught in between. You know you get the kids that are caught between the 2.5 and the 3.0 grade point average. The kids at the 3.5 and above are going to excel anyway. They're going to get the scholarships. But then what about those kids that are caught between that 2.5 to 3.0 grade point average? I don't really think they were told that

your grade point average is going to follow you
until you become a senior. And I really think that
if SOME of them were told it's hard to pull up a
2.5 by the time [they graduate], unless every
semester from that point on you're just a straight
A student. And I think I've always had a problem
with those kids not getting the recognition or the
extra push.

Overwhelmingly, students on the college preparatory
track (60%) receive more attention from their counselors
than their vocational/career technical (20%) or dropout
(20%) counterparts. Many of the college preparatory
students who explained the counselors' interactions with
students are those who receive favoritism, but often fail to
realize it. The vocational/career technical students cited the
difficulties in talking with their counselors, who were always
busy when the students attempted to visit the office.
Counselors at UCHS clearly serve as gatekeepers to
information and oftentimes college enrollment.

Administrators are aware of the broken relationships
between students and counselors. They reported that policies
are often not explained to all students and, more often than
not, students with higher GPAs have more access to
information. Even among parents, only two of six offered
that their children have favorable interactions with their
counselors. The shocking thing about this is that these
comments are from parents who are largely involved in their
child's education. What is happening with the other students
who depend on their counselors to assist them in preparation
for college?

With regard to high school courses and tracking
mechanisms, it is clear that in middle schools, students
whose teachers feel they will be successful, who have
parents who are involved in their education, or those students
who have both formal and informal relationships with school
officials are those who are given the opportunity to be placed

in higher tracks. These courses also tend to be designed to ensure the student's success, thus giving this segment of students hope that they will be successful.

Social reproduction contributes largely to students being placed in these tracks, which determine their academic success. For the most part, counselors are the vehicles which ensure that one group of students are favored over another. The most troubling part of this favoritism is that the students who are oppressed continue to be oppressed and are usually the students who need the most assistance from counselors. While the efforts of teachers to counter the negative counselor practices are to be applauded, it does not overcome the devastating effects counselor practices have on student success. Truly, counselors are not solely responsible for the tracking systems. Yet, while they execute tracking systems, the other school officials support these systems

Additionally, given the plethora of responsibilities that high school counselors have, it becomes much easier for them to favor those students who come to high school as favored students from middle school. The students also perceived this favoritism among school administrators to a certain degree. Yet, where administrators are concerned, the students felt that not only the academically inclined students and the favored students received additional support and attention, but also the students who were athletes. For students who were not favored, there was diminished hope that they would be successful because the opportunity structures seemed to dictate the level of success for students at UCHS.

Therefore, the fact cannot be denied that tracking has contributed to African American student failure (Rist, 1970). And while the purpose of this work is not to assign blame, those responsible for placing students on these tracks without the students' and parents' knowledge should be held responsible. One might even ask the question, "why are there so many students on the vocational track when the principal and teachers know they can be successful in college?" The professional judgment of teachers should mean something. As noted above, both students and parents are very unaware of the way tracking takes place in schools. Even more important is that once students are on these tracks it is almost impossible to get out of them (Oakes, Guiton, Selvin, & Karoly, 1990). Considering the discussion of the African American tradition earlier in this paper and the limits to caring, it is difficult for unengaged parents to provide supportive care for their children when they do not even understand the different graduation tracks on which students are placed, not to mention the possibility of getting them on another track. This is yet another example of the limited access to information which takes place in schools.

The lack of care that some students claimed they received from their teachers and administrators demands that practitioners and researchers ponder why students' interests were not valued when tracking decisions were made. For some students, being frustrated about not being on the college preparatory track and not being aware of it can be enough to discourage them from attending high school. It is possible that many students have dropped out of school given the comments students made when they discovered they were not on the college preparatory track. Some of the students must have felt embarrassment and shame when their friends were enrolled in algebra and they were enrolled in applied math or when their friends were enrolled in biology and they were enrolled in botany. Students look to their peers for acceptance and support and anything that creates a differential in the friendship can be problematic. This also contributed further to the number of African American students who do not attend college.

Conclusions and Implications

This study of an urban high school serving mostly students of color further revealed some of the ways that tracking reinforces poverty. Tracking has serious implications in an environment in which college is linked to employment opportunities and denial of preparatory courses could seriously constrain future opportunity. In these interviews it was evident that most of the students who were not on the college preparatory track lamented about the lost opportunity. The valuing of cross-generation uplift, an integral part of the African American tradition, was evident in the widespread desire to attend colleges. The tracking system reinforced the underclass in a school community that valued uplift.

There are alternatives to the sorting mechanisms used in UCHS. For example, this school might benefit from the creation of a small school. The Bill and Melinda Gates Foundation is establishing small schools across the country with the purpose of preparing larger numbers of students for high school success and college enrollment. Fouts & Associates (2003a) offer that because of their size, current high schools "are failing to teach young people what they need to know to lead meaningful lives, succeed in college and earn a decent living" (p. 3). The purpose of these small schools is to provide a smaller learning environment and give students the opportunity to develop meaningful relationships with teachers and mentors. Early results show that the students in these schools react positively to the smaller learning environment by being "willing to ask questions and that the tone of the individual classrooms was more informal and relationship-oriented" (Fouts & Associates, 2003b, p. 20).

These smaller learning environments may also contribute to positive self-esteem and greater academic outcomes. In the second-year evaluation report found that students who attended the small schools which were well into implementation "report being more interested and more persistent in their schoolwork and having stronger academic self-concepts" among other things (National School District and Network Grants Program, 2004, p. 98). These are the types of changes needed to make UCHS more supportive of college enrollment.

The findings from this study suggest several implications for those committed to increasing high school academic achievement and college access for students attending predominantly African American urban high schools. Because of the challenges these students faced related to the lack of course offerings needed for a successful transition to college, higher education decision makers must take these differences into account when instituting polices related to college admissions. It is apparent that many of these students who graduate from high school will not be adequately prepared for the rigors of college work because of the lack of rigor in their high schools.

Institutions of higher education should partner with high schools, especially those located in urban areas, in order that all students, regardless of their backgrounds, have access to the information needed to make a successful transition to college. While visiting UCHS, there were definitely more military recruiters in this high school than college recruiters. This trend must change. It is likely that more students may aspire to college if given the opportunity to interact with college recruitment officers as well.

High schools should hire additional counselors or have specific counselors to support the college-going efforts of their students. In the case of students at Urban City High School, students' aspirations for college may be thwarted because of limited interaction with a high school counselor. While the teachers provide some support and encouragement, it is possible that students do not receive all the support they need or deserve because there is information available that certain students do not receive. It may even be necessary to shift the focus from high achieving and refocus some of those energies on students who have average academic performance. While these students do not have comparable high school academic records as the top students, the support and encouragement of a counselor may assist them in working harder to get into college

There must be increased pressure on administrators to see that a college-going culture is developed at urban high schools. As was the case in this study, due to the challenges the principal has to deal with each day, it can be difficult to keep up with counselor practices. If the principal is not able to monitor the services counselors are providing students, the responsibility for supervision should be shared with an assistant administrator. Ultimately, the success or failure of a school falls on the shoulders of the principal, and proper supervision of counselors might lead to increased student success at urban schools and alleviate some of the stress that teachers currently have placed on them.

The lack of research on student experiences with predominantly African American urban high schools creates a void in understanding. There needs to be more research to understand the relationship between the increasing number of African American students enrolled predominantly African American urban high schools and the increasing gap between White and African American college enrollments. There also must be continued research related to the role social class plays within predominantly African American environments with respect to student access to information on college-going.

While there is increased research on the role teachers play in urban high schools (e.g., Perna 2005; Freeman, 2005), more research should focus on how these teachers assist students in college preparation. This is imperative given the many challenges that the small number of counselors in urban high schools face and the roles of teachers to fill the gaps. For example, research should address what impact does the additional support provided to students have on a teacher's classroom performance with regard to their teaching? Do these additional responsibilities lead to teacher burnout? Does it encourage teacher departure from schools?

Clearly, the voices represented in this study inform readers that we are in a "crisis" state as it relates to the role guidance counselors play in the college preparation and choice experiences for African American students. While there is an existing understanding that there is a "pecking order" in which information is shared and support provided, we must diffuse this inequality. While there still exists the popular claim that all students have the opportunity to attend high school and experience success, this was not necessarily the case due to ways opportunities are structured for different segments of students in this school. Thus, the reproductive forces at UCHS and schools like it must be destroyed.

Notes
[1] The author thanks Edward St. John for reviews on earlier drafts of this paper and for service as chair of his dissertation. An earlier version of this paper was presented at the 2006 Association for the Study of Higher Education Conference in Anaheim, CA.

References

Allen-Hayes, L., St. John, E.P., & Cadray, J. (2003). Rediscovering the African American tradition: Restructuring in post-desegregation urban schools. In L.F. Mirón & E.P. St. John (Eds.), *Reinterpreting urban school reform* (pp. 249-275). Albany: State University of New York Press.

Bogdan, R.C., & Biklen, S.K. (1998). *Qualitative research in education: An introduction to theory and methods* (3rd ed.). Boston: Allyn and Bacon.

Bourdieu, P. (1977). Cultural reproduction and social reproduction. In J. Karabel & A.H. Halsey (Eds.), *Power and ideology in education* (pp. 487-511). New York: Oxford University Press.

Brantlinger, E.A. (1993). *The politics of social class in secondary school.* New York: Teachers College Press.

Carspecken, P.F. (1996). *Critical ethnography in educational research: A theoretical and practical guide.* New York: Routledge.

Chism, N. (n.d.). *Analyzing qualitative data.* Center for Teaching Excellence: The Ohio State University.

Choy, S.P. (2002). *Access & persistence: Findings from 10 years of longitudinal research on students.* Washington, DC: American Council on Education.

Dilworth, P.P. (2003/2004, Fall/Winter). Competing conceptions of citizenship education: Thomas Jesse Jones and Carter G. Woodson. *International Journal of Social Education, 18*(2), 1-15.

Fay, B. (1987). *Critical social science: Liberation and its limits.* Ithaca, NY: Cornell University Press.

Fouts & Associates. (2003a). *The Bill and Melinda Gates Foundation's Washington State Achievers Program — Year one evaluation summary.* Seattle, WA: The Bill and Melinda Gates Foundation.

Fouts & Associates. (2003b). *Classroom instruction in Achievers grantee high school — A baseline report.* Seattle, WA: The Bill & Melinda Foundation.

Fraenkel, J.R., & Wallen, N.E. (2000). *How to design and evaluate research in education.* Boston, MA. McGraw Hill.

Freeman, K. (2005). *African Americans and college choice: The influence of family and school.* Albany: State University of New York Press.

Freeman, K. (1998). Introduction. In K. Freeman (Ed.), *African American culture and heritage in higher education* (pp. 1-5). Westport, CT: Praeger.

Gandara, P. (2002). Meeting coming goals: Linking K-12 and college interventions. In W.G. Tierney & L.S. Hagedorn (Eds.), *Increasing access to college: Extending possibilities for all students* (pp. 81-103). Albany, NY: State University of New York Press.

Giddens, A. (1997). *Sociology*. London: Polity Press.

Gilligan, C. (1982). *In a different voice*. Cambridge: Harvard University Press.

Hossler, D., Schmit, J., & Vesper, N. (1999). *Going to college: How social, economic, and educational factors influence the decisions students make*. Baltimore: Johns Hopkins University Press.

Howard, T.C. (2003). "A tug of war in their minds": African American high school students' perceptions of their academic identities and college aspirations. *High School Journal*, 4-17.

LeCompte, M.D., & Dworkin, A.G. (1991). *Giving up on school: Student dropouts and teacher burnouts*. Thousand Oaks, CA: Corwin Press.

Leslie, L.L., Johnson, G.P., & Carlson, J. (1977). The impact of need-based student aid upon the college attendance decision. *Journal of Education Finance, 2,* 269-285.

McDonough, P.M. (1997). *Choosing colleges. How social class and schools structure opportunity*. Albany, NY: State University of New York Press.

Merriam, S.B. (1998). *Qualitative research and case study applications in education*. San Francisco: Jossey-Bass.

Moses, R.P. (2001). *Radical equations: Civil Rights from Mississippi to the Algebra Project*. Boston: Beacon Press.

The National School District and Network Grants Program. (2004). *Year two evaluation report*. Washington, D.C.: The American Institutes for Research.

Nieto, S. (1992). *Affirming diversity: The sociopolitical contest of multicultural education*. White Plains, NY: Longman.

Noddings, N. (1999). Care, justice, and equity. In M.S. Katz, N. Noddings, & K.A. Strike (Eds.), *Justice and caring: The search for common ground in education* (pp. 7-20). New York: Teachers College Press.

Oakes, J. (1985). *Keeping track: How schools structure inequality.* New Haven, CT: Yale University Press.

Oakes, J., Guiton, G., Selvin, M., & Karoly, L. (1990). *Tracking, counseling, and vocational education: The dynamics and consequences of high school curriculum decisions.* Paper presented at the annual meeting of the American Education Research Association. Boston, MA.

Patton, M.Q. (1985, April). *Quality in qualitative research: Methodological principles and recent developments.* Address to the American Educational Research Association, Chicago.

Patton, M.Q. (2002). *Qualitative research and evaluation methods.* Thousand Oaks, CA: Sage Publications.

Perna, L.W. (2005). The key to access: Rigorous academic preparation. In W.G. Tierney, Z.B. Corwin, & J.E. Colyar (Eds.), *Preparing for college: Nine elements of effective outreach* (pp. 113-134). Albany: State University of New York Press.

Quantz, R.A. (1992). On critical ethnography with some postmodern considerations. In M.D. LeCompte, W.L. Millroy, & J. Preissle (Eds.), *Handbook of qualitative research in education* (pp. 447-505). San Diego, CA: Academic Press.

Rist, R.C. (1970). Study of how teachers treat children differently. In *Final report on the schooling of young children: Cognitive and affective outcomes.* National Institute of Education.

St. John, E.P. (2006). Contending with financial inequality: Rethinking the contributions of qualitative research to the policy discourse on college access. *American Behavioral Scientist.* Tierney, W.G., Venegas, K., DeLa

Rosa, M.L., Issue Editors, *Financial aid and access to college: The public policy challenges.* 49(12).

St. John, E.P., & Mirón, L.F. (2003). A critical-empirical perspective on urban school reform. In L.F. Mirón & E.P. St. John (Eds.), *Reinterpreting urban school reform* (pp. 279-297). Albany: State University of New York Press.

St. John, E.P., & Musoba, G.D. (forthcoming). *Pathways to academic success: Using research to inform academic reform.* Albany, NY: SUNY Press.

Schrader, D.E. (1999). Justice and caring: Process in college students' moral reasoning development. In M.S. Katz, N. Noddings, & K.A. Strike (Eds.), *Justice and caring: The search for common ground in education* (pp. 37-55). New York: Teachers College Press.

Siddle Walker, V. (1996). *Their highest potential: An African American school community in the segregated south.* Chapel Hill: The University of North Carolina Press.

Spring, J. (2000). *American education* (9th edition). Boston: McGraw Hill.

Thomas, J. (1993). *Doing critical ethnography.* Qualitative Research Methods Series, Vol. 26. Newbury Park, CA: Sage Publications.

Thomas, J., & O'Maolchatha, A. (1989, June). Reassessing the critical metaphor: An optimistic revisionist view. *Justice Quarterly, 6,* 143-172.

Tierney, W.G. (1991). Ideology and identity in postsecondary institutions. In W.G. Tierney (Ed.), *Culture and ideology in higher education: Advancing a critical agenda* (pp. 35-57). New York: Praeger.

Useem, E.L. (1992). Middle schools and math groups: Parents' involvement in children's placement. *Sociology of Education, 65,* 263-279.

Part III

Making Change

CHAPTER 8

ACTIVIST RESEARCH, POST-KATRINA: ONE TOOL FOR RENEWAL?

Luis Mirón

It is evident to the world that New Orleans is in crisis. What is less evident to the United States is that this country may be in a state of chronic denial with respect to systemic racism (Feagin & Barnett, 2005). Furthermore, there is increasing class inequality, or a widening gap between the upper and lower socioeconomic groups. This chapter takes a cross-sectional look at one specific aspect of race and class issues in America recently expunged by the devastation caused by Hurricane Katrina and the attempts in the educational community in New Orleans to reconstruct urban schools using a model that may be described as quasi privatization— charter schools.

In what follows, I provide a brief pedagogical context to the multiple approaches of school reform and their embedded assumptions of teachers and teaching. I also out- line what I consider three different, yet somewhat interrelated views. The chapter is organized into three major sections. Part I provides a model of teaching anchored in action research and inquiry. This model informed much of educational reform in the 1990s, especially the *Accelerated Schools Movement.* Part II presents a case study of the second model of educational reform, depicted as "rapid fire educational transformation," which uses a more radical form of action research and participatory action research called *activism* (Fine,1994). I seek to both unpack the historical and

283

Copyright ©2007 AMS Press, Inc. All rights reserved.

discursive seeds of the paradoxical moves toward transformation and privatization, as well as highlight the everyday
cultural practices new school leaders are cultivating.   In
particular my goal in using activist-feminist methodological
stances is to privilege the reduction of social and educational
inequality, especially in places like New Orleans where the
brunt of racism and poverty have historically taken their toll.
Finally, Part III highlights the constraints on both research
models, as well as more explicit social activism methods
(Fine, 1994; Fine, Tuck, & Zeller-Berkman, 2006). The
paper concludes with an effort to explain why current
attempts at addressing the urban school crisis in New
Orleans do not bode well, even at this early start seven
months after the storm. I begin with the hallmarks of action
research—teacher inquiry and reflective practice.[1]

Part I. The Underpinnings of Action Research
and the Possibilities for Activism

In 1983, the *National Commission on Excellence in
Education* announced the educational system has become
steeped in mediocrity and rendered the country to be "A
Nation at Risk…" and that this situation demanded sweeping
reform in what was to be taught in our schools and how.[2]
The plethora of responses to this mandate include a
variety of restructuring configurations (Rich, 1991) such that
the decade that followed has been described as less
productive than the preceding one (Kohn, 2000).   In his
forward to *High Stakes: Children, Testing, and Failure in
American Schools* (Johnson & Johnson, 2002), Carl Grant
stated that the national reform craze that began in the late
1980s and has persisted to this time has been fueled by the
political belief that being tough on schools would "bring
about change and will win elections" (p. xii). What actually
has resulted, however, is an entrepreneurial atmosphere
where testing companies, test preparers and scorers,
instructional materials and software developers, and the

tutoring enterprise have benefited from the craze (Kohn, 2002; Mirón, 1996), while "teachers and administrators feel helpless and overwhelmed as the test-prep skilling-and-drilling consumes the schools day" (Johnson & Johnson, 2002, p. xii).

Yet, in the midst of the chaos described by Grant and many others, measurable change in academic improvement has occurred in many schools across the nation since the inception of the reform dialogue. In *Families in Schools: A Chorus of Voices in Restructuring*, St. John, Griffith, and Allen-Haynes (1997) present case studies of a statewide network of schools experiencing academic improvement through teacher action research and school/classroom-level inquiry. Each of these schools respond to state mandates for excellence, demands for restructuring, and the involvement of parents by adopting the *Accelerated Schools* model of the 1980s. Of the three guiding principles that the Accelerated Schools process conceive as the foundation of this model, *teacher empowerment with responsibility* has been shown repeatedly (St. John et. al., 1997) to be the more critical ingredient for success. Through an action research process labeled *inquiry*, "the decisions about what aspects of teaching and learning should be changed, how they should be changed, and who should comprise the agents of change, are made by the persons closest to the problem — classroom teachers." This paradigm of research methods informs a view of teaching, and the everyday practices of teaching and learning in particular, grounded in local knowledge (Gertz, 1983), and the idea that teachers are professionals engaged in both the science and art of instruction and learning.

Exactly how researchers were to enact inquiry methods—I and my colleagues discovered—was somewhat vaguely specified. Below I present a theory of methodology that may frame action research generally and activist research in particular.

Stances on Social Action: A Macro Method for
Transformation
    In this section, I gauge the transformative possibilities of
this, the first model of teaching and learning for engaging in
a most pesky of educational environments, inner-city public
schools.   In particular, I present a case study of the
development of charter schools in the Algiers neighborhood
of New Orleans post-Katrina, and examine both the potential
for and the ideological/structural constraints upon *activist*
research (Fine, Tuck, & Zeller-Berkman, 2006; Fine, 1994)
as   a   partial   vehicle   to   enact   sustained   educational
transformation in New Orleans. Before doing that I need to
provide the methodological and epistemological lens by
which I will assess these possibilities, as well as their
constraints. This is feminist standpoint theory and research
methods or what Fine (1994) calls *activist research.*
    Michelle Fine (1994) puts forth three stances qualitative
researchers may assume in relation to social action. These
stances are the *ventriloquist, voice,* and *activism.* Fine
argues, first and foremost, that all researchers, but especially
those feminist scholars and scholars of color, are "agents, in
the flesh...and in the collective, who choose, wittingly or
not, from among a controversial and constraining set of
political stances and epistemologies" (1994, p. 16).
    For feminist researchers especially, activism seeks to
unearth, interrupt, and open new frames for intellectual and
political theory and practice. The feminist activist researcher
not only explicitly acknowledges, but also embraces
research-as-politics. She or he desires to occupy the
knowledge space and ontological position of the political
domain. Fine asserts that feminist practitioners of this
research method in particular openly choose politics because
women, perhaps more so than men, may revolt most acutely
against domination and oppression. Fine (1994) extends the
feminist perspective to other marginalized researchers and
macro theoretical work leading to social change, such as

Critical Race Theory (see Parker, 2003). Such like-minded researchers, whether women, scholars of color, or youth activists, become critical participants in the discourses over power, and the concomitant restless struggle for domination, and the particular meaning that power holds for marginalized people. The narrative of oppression post-Katrina represents the new African American diaspora.

This stance of activism, in turn, is informed by three distinctions: (1) an explicit account about the space the researcher occupies wittingly — this knowledge space comprises both theoretical space and political ground; (2) the written research expresses a critical appraisal of the existing social order and the under girding ideological structures; and (3) the research text presents the images of new social possibilities resulting from reconstruction and the use of social imagination (Rizvi, 2006).

Through her sustained engagement with participatory action research (PAR), Fine (1994) has, perhaps more than any other educational researcher, shaped the contours of a radical methodology that challenges the very soul of science in its most gross form, positivist empirical research and epistemology. From its inception Fine notes that this method of knowledge inquiry has global roots, in Africa, Asia, Central, and South America (Fine, Tuck, & Zeller-Beckman, 2006). In this respect, the long roots of PAR parallel the theory and practice of Paulo Freire's (1970) *critical pedagogy* with one important distinction. Whereas Freireian methods emphasized the formation, and potential liberation, of adult peasants through the formation of dialogic groups and the production of "generative themes" in Brazil, Fine et al. (2006) specifically collaborate with and build coalitions among youth in the U.S. and across the globe. Put differently, Fine's use of PAR, and social activism resulting from the production of knowledge from those at the bottom of the research hierarchy, is concerned as much with new forms of knowledge and its production as it is with being merely a tool to aid practitioners to reflect critically about their professional practice.

Thus in the struggle to fight the spread of AIDS, and the exposure of human genocide in Darfur and elsewhere, for example, as well as prisons and schools in America, Fine (1994) has extended the context of her scholarship and advocacy of this research method, and theory of methodology, to engage with and join youth in their collective struggles across the globe, as they collectively resist multiple forms of oppression and domination by structures and agents of power.   This move I want to conceive as political agency grounded in the inversion of the subject-object of research relation (Mirón, 2007, forthcoming). This method of research, described below as "activist" embeds dimensions of performativity as well as performance. Feminist standpoint epistemology enables the research subject to potentially exercise her own will to power, thus becoming a producer of knowledge.   Social inquiry is both a research act or performance (Denzin & Lincoln, 2003) as well as a discursive practice that materially and bodily enact the very reality that it seeks to distantly describe through objective laboratory-like methods of science, for example the colonized racial other (McCarthy, 1996).

The Micro Level

The question of *how* scientific knowledge is rendered intellectually and also socially legitimate is arguably of equal importance from the standpoint of feminist researchers. One of my central concerns here is with the people affected (or disaffected as it were) with the outcomes of prior failed educational reform (Mirón & St. John, 2003). Put differently, those poor minority students left behind in the wake of Hurricane Katrina, now numbering approximately 20 percent of the total enrollment in New Orleans (Marsal, 2006; Mirón & Ward, 2006), are expected to perform at world-class standards of learning in order to compete in the global economy. Prescriptions for how such learning are to transact stem in large part from the dominant evidence-based research traditions such as school effectiveness research and practice, and the use of the foundational knowledge upon which it rests. Without a substantial voice in the production of knowledge standards, as part of the everyday politics of education on the material ground in places like New Orleans and elsewhere—the actual, as distinct from the merely symbolic spaces of knowledge (Fine, Tuck, & Zeller, 2006), I expect that transformation of teaching and learning is unlikely to occur. Next I wish to briefly highlight the data collection procedures and methods of analysis as I move through a tricky research path laid out by Fine and colleagues 15 years ago (see Fine, Tuck, & Zeller-Berkman, 2006).

The data sources relied on documents produced by the *Algiers Charter Association*, the *Mayor's Rebuilding New Orleans Commission*, newspaper accounts, and Louisiana State Department of Education reports. In addition I conducted informal telephone and email conversations with former New Orleans public school administrators, teachers, and parents. Finally I serve as a consultant to the *Algiers Charter Association*, where I engage in staff development activities to advocate on behalf of equity concerns for children left behind by the move toward a charter district in New Orleans.[3]

I used a quasi case study method informed by both action research and feminist standpoint epistemology to both describe and critically interpret the charter school phenomenon in New Orleans. I begin with what I perceive as the fundamental basis for the widespread advocacy for charter schools among elite groups in New Orleans, privatization (Mirón, 1992).

Part II: Echoes Of Privatization: The Charter School Movement and Rapid Fire Transformation

I want to argue that the exigencies caused by Katrina had one profound implication on the start-up of the five Algiers Charter schools. These could not be status quo schools; that is, they were to aspire toward, and ultimately achieve, world-class status. The reason was that the elite political and business community in New Orleans—bluntly stated—was fed up with the educational establishment. This elite community, backed by a plethora of community organizations and neighborhood groups, perceived the school system as bloated with bureaucracy, the teachers strapped by a recalcitrant union, the school board and superintendent incompetent and unqualified to govern and lead, educationally. Displaced parents interviewed on the national news networks lent credence to this widespread belief at public hearings when they shouted, "we want the schools to change." To be certain, the charges were laden with racial and class overtones (as was all social life in New Orleans as Katrina brought to the surface). However, based on 20 years experience and observations of the external relations and inner workings of the district, on balance I can attest that these charges were essentially correct (see Bogotch, Mirón, Biesta, & Reidlinger, 2006). They were not merely perceptions borne out of ignorance and prejudice.

Change was indeed in the air. As stated above, the New Orleans public schools had been engaged in chronic educational reform, "over and over again." The widely held perception on behalf of informed citizens, practitioners in and out of the system, and researchers were that, on balance, school reform had failed. Worse the children of New Orleans had suffered as a result. By most measures of achievement data, the system had failed. Put differently, the question was no longer how to "fix" a system that was chronically "broken." From the perspective of elite groups in particular, and their educational leaders like Scott Cowen, President of

Tulane University (see Bernofsky, 2006; Davis, 2006), the question was how to design a new system that would continually engage in sustained "transformation." After dismissal of the current superintendent for fiscal mismanagement, the question on the mind of the general citizenry was could *any* measure—short of fundamental overhaul—salvage a deeply dysfunctional educational system. Katrina provided this opportunity, both as a result of human caused disaster and devastation from nature.

The hope lay in the small cluster of charter schools, and selective admission schools or citywide access schools, the latter of which had a long history of promoting and realizing success in New Orleans. In Algiers the difference would be that the schools would not operate via selective admissions—they would enroll anyone if space allowed (see below for controversy). This put a somewhat undue burden on the principals, and it was this authors' impression that the dynamics of high educational expectations in New Orleans— if not statewide—that a possible self-fulfilling prophecy was in the making. The everyday school practices would revert toward the mean, thus potentially ending the vision of an educational utopia for New Orleans provided by Katrina. Worse, failure to achieve excellence, ideologically voiced by the discourse of world-class academic standards, would doom public schools to institutional failures. The long held fears of widespread vouchers, and broader privatization of education, would mark the course. These were the dynamics in the wider society as the researchers considered action steps at the educational summit, the first staff development session for new principals, their assistant principals, and the school leadership teams. The School Leadership Center and Algiers Charter Association co-sponsored these meetings.

The School Leadership Center
In the late 1990s the Baptist Convention Center of New Orleans established the School Leadership Center. The overriding goal of the Center was to provide ongoing

professional development for both existing principals and aspiring new building administrators.[4]

The somewhat unique design of the Center—at least as far as school reform in New Orleans was concerned—was the element of choice and selection. School leaders needed to apply for admission into the professional development programs or be selected as "fellows." This model of professional/staff development for educational leaders contrasted markedly with the "compliant" character of training most building principals or assistant principals. This traditional model of professional development was especially relevant for the New Orleans public schools in particular and the state of Louisiana in general. The reason was that with few exceptions, the more entrepreneurial leaders— instructional risk takers and fund raisers such as Reidlinger and Dr. Roslyn Smith[5] felt that the traditional model of staff development did not offer useful professional experiences.

From the outset the Board of Directors of Baptist Convention Center built in systematic program evaluation anchored in formative studies to redefine the already sophisticated model of leadership training and development aimed at increased student achievement and school improvement (Bogotch et al., 2006). It commissioned internationally recognized researchers whose work focused on educational leadership and school change to conduct program evaluations and provide feedback on performance to the staff of the School Leadership Center. Initial evaluation reports revealed that, indeed, in the lowest performing school district, Orleans Parish, school administrators who undertook professional development through the Center were able to raise levels of student achievement and aggregate scores on the state standardized tests (LEAP) at statistically significant levels in comparison to their peers who did not receive training and their comparable school based on similar SES data.

From the late 90s to the early 2000s, the formative evaluation studies were aimed primarily at *internal* goals: the revamping and refining of the School Leadership Center professional development programs. Katrina, of course, changed that internal orientation, perhaps for the immediate future, if not for the course of its institutional half-life. The focus of research on hence forward, and its professional development menu, is now substantially *externally* driven as a result of the formation of the *Algiers Charter Association*. The goals now are both simple and complex: to raise student achievement to justify the renewal of the state-licensed charters when they come up for renewal in five years, and to execute a curriculum based on world-class standards.

After The Perfect Storm

The State Takeover. Prior to Katrina, the State of Louisiana, Dept. of Education entered into a *Memorandum of Understanding* with the Orleans Parish School Board. The purpose of the Memorandum was to re-delegate, or authorize, the state to manage the $300 million operating budget in the wake of a $30 million deficit, nearly forcing the New Orleans public school district into bankruptcy. The June 2005, Memorandum outlines with some specificity, the areas of fiscal management, which the state would administer, oversee, and ultimately assume public accountability. The means to execute the fiscal management of the Orleans Parish School Board finances would be through a contract to a private accounting firm, the New York-based Alvarez & Marsal (see State of Louisiana, *Memorandum of Understanding*, June, 2005).

Of the eleven fiscal and administrative functions Alvarez & Marsal would manage in behalf of the school district, none specified curriculum and instruction, educational leadership, or professional/staff development (State of Louisiana, Memorandum of Understanding, 2005, p. 4). These functions, which historically had been overseen by the central office and its three geographic area superintendents, apparently, would be seriously compromised owing to staff reduction. Central office would now employ fewer than 70 personnel.

The absence of a coordinated effort in the instructional and supervision of curriculum realm, in effect, helped pave the way for the School Leadership Center to ratchet up efforts. Moreover, when Katrina touched down on August 29, 2006, the School Leadership Center was poised to fill the organizational gap. The contours of the organizational space the Center would fill would divide into two functions. These were curriculum development and educational leadership. These in turn would be mutually informed by the collection and analysis of data from the previous evaluation studies.

<u>The Birth of the Algiers Charter Association.</u> Shortly after the storm, the Orleans Parish School Board in a split 4-2 decision established charter schools in all of the 13 schools scheduled to open on the West Bank of the city. For the time being the school board would retain oversight of the schools; however the intent was to allow each school to function autonomously, with independent operating budgets, and the ability to hire and fire school personnel.[6] Mayor Ray Nagin, who had previously been on record as supporting charter schools for the entire school system, but who was by state law prohibited from maintaining a role in the governance of the public schools in New Orleans, backed the policy to "charter" all of the West Bank schools.

Since the School Leadership Center had been closely involved in providing ongoing professional development and mentoring of administrators in Orleans public schools located in Algiers, it became a relatively simple transition to form an organization to support the fledgling charter district in Algiers.

Overnight, or so it seemed, the school board established the Algiers Charter district and the state legislature virtually eliminated the central office. Five schools on the West Bank (a neighborhood west of New Orleans and across the Mississippi river), five charter schools emerged. Included were three elementary schools and two high schools. The elementary schools were Harte, Behrman, and Eisenhower. The high schools were Walker and Karr, technically a middle school with a ninth grade. At Walker High School, the principal Mary Laurie reopened the school. In December 2006 she passionately greeted her new high school students thusly, and "I apologize for every adult who said you couldn't learn and every school in chaos. We failed them. If we don't acknowledge that, we're never going to change...We've got to get it right. If not this time, when? We will *never* get this chance again" (Ritea, March 12, 2006). The sense of urgency to achieve transformation was striking.

Walker High School in Algiers was previously known for both a strong sports program as well as gang fights (Lauria & Mirón, 2005). In the 1990s one student was shot, apparently a result of gang violence (Miron & Lauria, 1998). At the start of the New Year in January 2006, however, the tone of the student conversations, if not the intensity of fighting, had apparently changed. The principal stated to one of the researcher-consultants, a student reported to me, "Ms. Lorie you *may* want to go next door. They had a fight. But it was nothing." The students resolved the conflict themselves, apparently preventing a more dangerous situation from escalating.

For most empirical researchers, taking individual to advance a particular policy goal or support an educational ideology action is suspect. Perhaps more difficult is social action, which, following Fine (above), is an activist stance in behalf of, or in concert with, the other. The next section analyzed the inherent complexities when educational and social researchers move, conceptually and politically, from an advocacy stance to activism in pursuit of social change.

Part III. Activism And Reflection To Support
School Transformation

On the opening day the research team, which consisted of several nationally recognized researchers who, at one time or another, taught at the University of New Orleans, assumed multiple roles. At varying times throughout the three-day meetings, they were consultants to the School Leadership Center staff, facilitators in the visioning process for school leaders, and providers of technical support for the specifying of learning outcomes.   Day 1 in December 2005 set the political and economic context for Algiers charter schools during the recovery of New Orleans post-Katrina (Bogotch et al., 2006).

The School Leadership Center director, Dr. Brian Reidlinger, indicated to the research and evaluation team that the charter schools fell under the umbrella of the *recovery district* in New Orleans. He emphasized that the newly opened schools in New Orleans, consonant with the spirit of the charter movement and the data supporting increased student achievement when principals underwent professional development with the Center, did not embrace the ideology of embedded failure in the term "recovery district." Rather each of the new principals, and their teaching staff, underwent a rigorous screening and selection process leading to their appointment. For example, only 100 out of the 500 teachers who applied for new positions were hired. They represented a wide spectrum of professional experience and beliefs and a range of ethnicities. They were women and men chosen to lead the educationally refurbished public schools in New Orleans.   Citing the 20 percent hiring rate (and conversely 400 teachers dismissals), Reidlinger signals the quest for excellence via world-class learning standards and the somewhat veiled discourse of privatization. The challenge for the principals, as well as the researchers who posed the abiding question that was to guide the deliberations of the team over the next succeeding sessions, was "can we hold onto the vision of world class schools" and "not get pulled back." The fear was that the school leaders and the teachers would fall back into their comfort zone, and given the huge challenges in simply gearing up to open schools post-Katrina, would not sustain the momentum necessary to achieve lasting transformation.[7] The unspoken fear was that these school leaders would revert to patterns pre-Katrina, the national consensus of which ranked New Orleans near the bottom of urban big city school systems.

Summit I: Setting a Vision for World-Class Schools

At the outset the research team served as consultants, working with the principals of each of the five charter schools to forge a contextual vision specifying what it meant to be a "world class" public school. Based on our combined experiences as participant observers in the continuous process of reforming the New Orleans public schools[8] the qualitative indicators of world-class devised by the new principals generally fell into two categories. These were bread and butter school attributes, largely based on the needs of New Orleans public school children, and more visionary qualities that heretofore were reserved largely for elite public schools in the city. Some of the latter schools were doubtlessly among the best in the state, if not the nation.

"Bread and Butter". The principals believed that teaching and learning in their new schools should be connected to the real life circumstances and needs facing the families and children of those residents who returned to New Orleans after Katrina as well as the expectations of those who desired to return. One of them summarized this perspective from the point of view of quality schools, saying all of the students should "experience a qualitative change from their prior everyday life at their previous schools in New Orleans and "learn what they desired and needed" to survive, but more importantly to thrive in recovering New Orleans post-Katrina. Whether this meant the perceived failings of the public school system or rampant violent crime (Nossiter, 2006), life in New Orleans had to change. Anecdotally it seemed that displaced residents universally did not want to return to business as usual. Widespread media coverage of the events surrounding the planning efforts for rebuilding, for example at the numerous public hearings held in the city and around the southeast region, witnessed scores of people angry at the slow pace of the rebuilding plans (e.g., temporary housing) as well as complaints that the public schools — as governmental entities — lacked adequate curriculum and public accountability in comparison to their counterpart schools in Houston and Atlanta — that returning children to sub par schools was a disincentive. Optimistically, a transformed, world-class system as envisioned by the *Bring Back New Orleans Commission* (2006) was motivation to return. The school leaders in Algiers uniformly welcomed the challenge.

"Beyond Essentials". The following creed exemplified the spirit that the principals sought in their collective labor. "All children would experience success everyday" and I want my students to say "I can't wait to return to school next year" (Bogotch, 2006, field notes).

In a walk through prior to the summit meetings, the following account was recorded:

> I noticed students working in small groups, at centers and at their desks, and students sitting on the carpet in a circle with teachers either on the floor too, or in a small chair. A lot of discussion was going on, the doors to the classrooms were open and the rooms were inviting. I heard teachers encouraging students, gently giving correction, sometimes in private and one on one. [Teachers were teaching].... All students were on task. As I passed through the older students' halls, I saw similar interactions. Teachers were outside of their

doors at the change of class, greeting the students pleasantly. There was the beginning of an altercation between two boys and a teacher stepped in and hugged them both while encouraging them to move on without letting it get out of hand. The students complied with the teacher's request. It just seemed warm and friendly, a please I would not mind sending my kids.

At a deeper level the principals desired that their curriculum would connect their school not only to New Orleans, post-Katrina but indeed to the rest of the world, that is as one researcher noted, both a "sense of self and others." Finally a world-class vision should be made transparent to the school community and converted into a living, organic document. These, then, constituted preliminary elements of what it would mean to establish world-class schools in the Algiers Charter district.

In the brainstorming session with the researchers — as consultants — the collective group of principals desired to create a "wow effect" on opening day.[9] Contextually, this meant the following:

Students would be:

- Engaged in learning from the first moment of instruction;
- Feel special at school;
- Experience a qualitative change from their prior every day life at their previous schools in New Orleans;
- Informally observe the transparent processes of their school;
- Learn what they desire and need.

At the conclusion of this case study I analyze the structural (ideological) constraints that may undermine the transformation process. But first, in the next section, I want to briefly critique the ambitious goals of what I want to call quasi privatization and in a previous case study, "the privatization of the public interest (Mirón, 1992). These ideological on the ground moves in New Orleans, I assert, provide the ideological and social infrastructure leading to "rapid-fire school transformation." Using Fine's three stances (1994) as a heuristic tool I modify her work to the goal of potentially reconstructing schools in New Orleans post-Katrina. Although the following is a critique partially on ideological grounds—I reject the tenets of neo-liberalism that undergirds privatization—my ultimate aim is to move beyond the critique of ideology into the realm of social action to benefit the common good (Worthington, 2006).

    The Spans Of Activist Research, Ventriloquy, Critique, And Reconstruction. On face value, educational leaders in New Orleans had little choice but to do something fundamentally different. Charter schools district wide in a system where only one school had reopened by Thanksgiving out of a total of 120 made the conditions for rapid-fire reform ideal. It did not hurt, moreover, that the federal government promised a grant of up to $20.9 million to launch the massive experiment in school reform (Ritea, 2005). In June, the school district faced a $30 million shortfall pre-Katrina, when the state entered into a *Memorandum of Understanding* with an accounting firm, Alvarez and Marsal, who had offices throughout the world (see above). The district was also in danger of a federal audit of its $300 million operating budget, as auditors had already disclaimed its 2004 financial statements (Alvarez & Marsal, 2004).

    Alvarez & Marsal's proposal to contract out chunks on non instructional services such as cafeterias and food purchasing, payroll, and transportation, pre-Katrina, would of course be strengthened by the waving of union rules granted to the charter district, post-Katrina. Coupled with a neo-liberal ideology that established a free market hiring process for teachers, and a curriculum unencumbered by interference from central office bureaucrats, the 13 charter schools proposed for the unflooded, "high ground" neighborhoods of Algiers, and subsequently, Uptown made criticisms from Interim Superintendent Watson saying that governance reform (charter district) would not alter the system (Ritea, 2005) appear self serving.

As stated, I need not engage in critique from the perspective of critical social theory to observe the inconsistencies between what appear clear moves toward a market-driven model for school reform embedded in the charter schools and the calls for sustained educational transformation from the chair of the education committee of the *Bring Back New Orleans Commission*, (Davis, 2006), Tulane President Scott Cowen. The data can be interpreted at the micro level of individual actors, the policy direction that rebuilding New Orleans leaders had embarked upon (Raffo et al., 2006)

Cowen's dual role as transformation architect and the leader of Tulane University's effort to restructure its institutional mission in the wake of Hurricane Katrina served him well. He had previously consolidated the partnership with Lusher Charter School Uptown and a nearby companion high school, Fortier, with a grant of $1.5 million to the school (Bernofsky, 2006). Thus he appeared to embrace the movement to charter the district. However, the Orleans Parish had voted 4-2 in October to charter all 13 schools on the West Bank. This seemed markedly incon-sistent with the stated process of the education subcommittee of the *Bring Back New Orleans Commission* (2006). This process on face value appeared to call for research, analysis, and evolutionary change leading to sustained transformation. Among other elements, these processes suggested: (1) Conduct case studies of America's top performing schools; (2) Conduct an extensive literature review of best practices of high performing schools; and (3) Conduct a thorough analysis of pre- and post-Katrina school performance and capacity.

At the very least it's clear that the birth of the Algiers Charter District did not align well with the rapid fire pace of the opening of these reconfigured schools in January, and especially with the near overnight decision of the school board and the state to approve the charter licenses for the 13 schools. As we will see in the conclusion this apparent top-down process may have led to the lawsuit by the "People's Hurricane Relief Fund," partly challenging their operation. Moreover the heavy-handed process may make achieving political legitimacy and institutionalizing the governance arrangements problematic in the long term.

In the short term it appears that the process of transformation embedded in the call for sustained change must slow down to address the following: (1) Maximize community, school, and parental input. Non-charter schools in New Orleans such as McMain (Lauria & Miron, 2005), so necessary in this city that needs community centered schools, and Frederick Douglas School have managed to form close bonds with their local communities to create schools that respond to their needs such as the nationally recognized "Students at the Center" writing program. (2) Make equitable the school demographics. It's estimated that as much as 20 percent of the eligible school population (Mirón & Ward, 2006) in New Orleans, a percentage that is overwhelmingly black and poor, is not enrolled in school. It appears that enrollment caps and selective admissions of some of the charter schools such as the quasi-private partnership between Tulane and Lusher (see above) have created this inequity. And (3) in order to gain political legitimacy, and restore good will, the charter schools will need to build alliances with the displaced teacher, the majority of whom were members of the American Federation of teachers. Obviously, this will prove difficult, as one of the prime drivers of the charter school movement was to by pass union rules.

I turn now to the second meeting of the Algiers Charter Association. This meeting highlights the optimistic possibilities for activist research to secure enduring social transformation by focusing on reduction of educational inequality. As we will see, however, this aspiration is fraught with structural, ideological constraints, as well as with ethical dilemmas. Are charter schools en masse in New Orleans, or prime high ground neighborhoods unintentionally reproducing inequality by exclusionary practices that as mentioned, prevented nearly 20 percent of the school age population from entering school on time in January? We do not have space in this study to pursue the ethical questions, but suggest them here as avenues to explore in further research (Mirón & Ward, 2007).

Summit II

The second occasion to employ activist methodology and epistemology arrived one month after the charter schools opened following the holidays. In effect, this was the de facto school reopening in Algiers. Prior to the holidays children were understandably distracted by the hustle and bustle of celebrations, even in devastated New Orleans.

The School Leadership Council director Reidlinger briefed the researcher-consultants with one simple message, an overarching point that he stressed repeatedly with the principals and the assistant principals, the Center's designate school leaders: "You are independent agents." Jokingly he stated that in staff development sessions with the principals, 50 percent of the "central office" was present in those sessions—himself in his accompanying as director of the Algiers Charter Association and a 56 percent time curriculum assistant.[10] The building administrators had direct access to their supervisors for support. The autonomous nature of the charter schools in Algiers, moreover, meant that the principals would be able to hire all new staff and that, although they would be subject to union/district salary scales and benefits, enjoyed flexibility to exceed them (or presumably to lower salaries, though the latter could not be confirmed). Some teachers would be hired in at higher salaries than they were earning pre-Katrina and pre-charter. As I will indicate below, however, the massive dismissal of union teachers, owing to the reduction in the number of schools functioning from over 120 to fewer than 20 would legally jeopardize the autonomy of the five Algiers Charter schools. Its legitimacy would face serious challenges.

At the heart of the school improvement model for the Algiers Charter Association was the principle that *teachers are experts*. This is in line with the first model of reform outlined above. This professional belief — and abiding trust and faith — in classroom teachers was unevenly present in the school district. For example, the selective admissions and citywide access schools (Lauria & Mirón, 2005) employed this belief and tended to act on the principle. The administrators of these high performing schools generally functioned to buffer teachers from bureaucratic encroachment of central office, as well as the pressures from demanding parents, such as those whose families were faculty members from Tulane, or wealthy upper-middle class neighborhoods who sought — and obtained — a world-class education in public, rather than private (or parochial) schools. The latter was the custom of the upper-middle class Protestant and Jewish elite in New Orleans or the Catholic middle class. Among the independent, parochial, and public high schools, these included Newman, Jesuit, and Benjamin Franklin respectively.

School Illustrations. As the researchers-as-consultants transitioned into their technical assistant roles at *Summit II*, the principals and their assistant principals provided specific vision statements. These articulations of their visions of a world class school in-the-making would, in turn, lead to a more focused curricular aims, teaching practices, and a school climate. Each would inspire a transformation in line with the goals of the *Bring Back New Orleans Commission*. For example, one of the challenges post-Katrina was to make

Walker High School safe from violent crime. This early in the transformation process the school had taken a big step toward a safe and trusting climate.

The principal Mary Laurie wanted, above all, for her classroom teachers to "believe in this process" of building capacity, internally for school change, and externally for the fulfillment of the ideological values of the *Algiers Charter Association* to launch world-class public schools. One of the bottom line principles was such that the staff could not maintain a negative school culture. The process of capacity building to support local community development is one theme she would carry with her from previous leadership positions pre-Katrina, and had picked up early in her career from graduate training programs in educational leadership at the University of New Orleans. Her vision for Walker High School was to create a self-reliant school community, one that would work in partnership with neighborhood residents, business leaders, and non-profit community groups. She emphasized outreach to the local community to meet the needs of residents and other key stakeholders. Simultaneously, Laurie would work to make the school community of Walker High School strong, organizationally, culturally, and ultimately spiritually, from within. Her process for change was home grown.

"The Elders". Her staff would "stand on the shoulders of those that came before them," (Mirón, 1996)—the elders of the school and residential community. The elders (senior staff members and 9th grade students) would cultivate in the "youngsters" (beginning teachers and students) the traditions of respect for others, self, and community. In turn the decisions of the school would be conducted with transparence, thus helping to promote trust and confidence. All of these "process values" of educational leadership, values anchored on a conception of leadership as a process of "acting on values" (Mirón, 1997) — all maintained an abiding purpose — finding and speaking with "the common voice." Pre-Katrina, the principal roamed the hallways of

Walker High as a result of school violence. Thus, at the outset the principal sought to create a school culture and identity that would in the future be "more than a police state." This would be accomplished by a couple of simple rules: "no one talks when the speaker speaks" and the elders set the tone for discipline by nudging students who stray from the flock back into the warmth and comfort of the fold.

In summary the bold vision of Walker High School, as well as the wise use of traditions within the African American community, bode well for the possibilities of educational transformation. The possibilities for *action*, moreover, embedded in the guided reflection facilitated by the researchers at the summit meetings of the Algiers Charter Association help establish the conditions for sustained transformation and the realization of meaningful, con-textualized world-class standards in the broader school community in New Orleans. It is apparent that the leaders of the School Leadership Council, and its evolution into an emerging support structure for all charter schools — especially those based on non-selective admissions — could mobilize other communities besides Algiers to move past the status quo. This would be a major achievement in New Orleans. With change, however, there are limits. The balance of this paper examines what I perceive as the major structural limitation to educational transformation—the ideology of equal educational opportunity, a holdover of the civil rights movement and the racial politics of identity and class solidarity (Darder & Mirón, 2006). In the conclusion I briefly return to Fine's (1994) three stances to assess the long-term prospects of social action embedded in activist models of research.

The Politics of Race and Community

The school leaders and the research team identified, on a broad level, a set of educational and institutional constraints that held the potential to severely limit the thrust for transformation. These included the need for clean, inviting school facilities. (Nationally New Orleans schools were not known for their clean, safe buildings. In fact they were widely perceived to be inferior to the worst urban schools systems, for example, Chicago). The leaders worried that the prerequisite intense sense of professionalism may be lacking as the staff geared up to face returning children and families. They were sensitive to traumatized staff. Indeed many of them faced their own existential hurdles, for example replacing the now infamous "FEMA blue roof."

Educational transformation and the quest for world-class standards in New Orleans met a near immediate stumbling block. At the close of *Summit II*, a group known as the "People's Hurricane Relief Fund" filed a class action suit charging the Algiers Charter Schools and others with "refusing to admit students who do not 'meet' the school requirements for admission, even though there is room to accommodate additional children." The suit came on the heels of a conference held in New Orleans the weekend prior, which in part focused on building a national coalition to demand quality education in New Orleans, post-Katrina. The group held loose ties with the Quality Education as a Civil Right (QECR), which was launched in Washington, DC in 2004 (Darder & Mirón, 2006).

Children in high ground New Orleans public schools—Algiers and uptown—were now enrolling in charter schools as the result of the actions taken by the State of Louisiana, Orleans Parish School Board and in part endorsed by the mayor and the *Bring Back New Orleans Commission.* In an article published in the *New Orleans Times-Picayune*, Mayor Nagin was quoted as supporting the move by the school board to establish 13 charter schools on the West Bank of New Orleans—he planned to ask the governor to help him create a citywide charter school system (Ritea, 2005).

Ironically, the press release by the "Advancement Project" and the "People's Hurricane Relief Fund" cited the implicit wishes of the Commission and the mayor to reopen as many public schools in the city as feasible given the massive damage to school buildings, and the enormity of finding temporary housing in the wake of more than 50 percent of the housing stock declared uninhabitable or, worse, incapable of restoration.   In particular the lawsuit alleged that the five Algiers charter schools had denied admission to handicapped children. This charge appeared controversial, as according to the School Leadership Director Reidlinger the special education population exceeded 500, a number that approximated 20 percent of the aggregate school population in Algiers.[11]   Furthermore, the vision of the education subcommittee of the *Bring Back New Orleans Commission* called for networks of charter schools, as well as other flexible, autonomous schools. Purportedly, these clusters of autonomous public schools in New Orleans would be, ideologically, spared of a bloated educational bureaucracy, stifling union rules and hiring practices, and aspire to world-class standards of teaching and learning. So what went wrong? Why the lawsuit by the "Peoples Hurricane Relief Fund"?

There are three plausible explanations why the apparent disconnect between the values of school inclusion explicit in the mission of the *Algiers Charter School Association* to reject selective admissions in favor of open access based on space limitations—and the suit alleging that public school children in New Orleans were denied access to schooling, in effect possibly denying them their civil rights and due process. Each explanation, in turn, points to the ideological constraints on not only the cluster of charter schools in Algiers, but perhaps to the broader transformation movement in New Orleans. These three are: (1) The conflation of east bank admission policies and educational beliefs with West Bank charter schools; (2). The perception that *all* high ground New Orleans charter schools (or magnets), both newly configured or reconstituted, were designed to serve white, middle, upper-middle class students with largely white staff; and (3) The broader struggle for quality schools in New Orleans and across the nation was a struggle both historically rooted in, and therefore must be launched by and for African Americans. I recognize the controversial nature of this conjecture; however I offer it here simply because I believe this is an issue scholars and activists of all colors must reconcile. I hope to address these explanations in a longer study that will focus on the role of the state in establishing a "recovery" district in New Orleans that in effect, took over the district, leaving open in its path a reconfigured school system consisting mainly of charter schools. That study poses the question of the possible denial of citizenship in dispersed New Orleans.

Summary and Concluding Reflections

In summary, activist research in this case study of the *School Leadership Council* and the *Algiers Charter Association* is constrained ideologically and legally. Law suits by the *Peoples' Hurricane Relief Fund* challenge the legality (and ultimately the political legitimacy) of charter schools, and by extension the capacity of their leaders to take social action pointing toward educational transformation and equity for those children left behind. The ideological premise of the lawsuits is based in part on the values of equality and equity for all racial groups, but especially for African America students, who pre-Katrina comprised almost all of the district's enrollment. The values underpinning the lawsuit apparently placed an educational premium on open access to quality public schools.

Returning to Fine (1994; also see Fine, Tuck, & Zeller-Berkman, 2006), I make the following concluding observations. First, the stance of *ventriloquy* is rendered simple in this case study by the descriptive reporting of qualitative data, for example, the specific vision of the world-class schools in Algiers. My colleague for example took meticulous notes at *Summit I*, at times reading them verbatim, to the amazement of the principals and assistant principals. Although it is doubtful that this verbatim reporting will lead to collective action toward equity, I would argue that this research stance may constitute a necessary first step among the educational leaders accustomed to being under siege and flying below radar. It helps gain her or his trust—and importantly provides evidence that people (researchers) are listening.

Secondly, methodologically, *voice* carries the process a step further. It builds upon the trusting relationship—crucial for collaborating with administrators—to establish legitimacy for the researcher to articulate practitioners' sentiments, social reality, and subjectivity. One position is that of an activist-advocate in behalf of equity in admissions that exceeded caps on enrollment previously set (see above). The activist researcher need not act alone. She or he can engage in social activism in solidarity with other researchers, residents, and community activists.[12] The jury is out on whether this advocacy will have an effect on policy and school practices in the charter schools, or whether legal remedies will need to continue in the immediate future.

Thirdly, *activism*, the most politically challenging stance is clearly the most difficult position to negotiate, based on my on-the-ground experience working with the educational leaders in Algiers. The reason is that social action from *outside* is most problematic to negotiate. Compounding this ontological complexity is *distance*, the stance that Fine is the most articulate in criticizing. However, what Fine seems to address is *social*, rather than geographical distance, the problem for which my colleagues and I are confronted — and the politics of knowledge production, which results when distancing occurs. Moreover, the ethics of activism, even when the relationship is participatory action research (PAR) are questionable. Who decides—and how—what social action to take, and who benefits as a result? In this regard, I conclude by quoting one of my colleagues wrestling with this dilemma: "Clearly, without 'good schools,' redefined by New Orleaneans, non-New Orleaneans will not even consider moving here. That is a certainty. So, the future lies with New Orleaneans themselves and with those who have left the city as evacuees" (Bogotch et al., 2006). It is an ethical dilemma stemming from activist research that, I suspect, may last as long as the immediate rebuilding process.

Notes

[1] The author would like to thank Ed St. John for this insight into three views of teachers and teaching in New Orleans.

[2] I thank my dear friend and colleague, the late Dr. Leetta Haynes for this section of the paper. See L. Haynes & L. Mirón, "Action Research, One School at a Time." *Handbook of Educational Administration*, 2007, in press.

[3] As of March 23, there were approximately 900 students living in New Orleans not enrolled in schools. The total estimated enrollment in New Orleans was 9,593 students.

[4] By charter the SLC serves seven (7) "parishes" (Louisiana counties) in metropolitan New Orleans.

[5] A former executive in the old school system, Dr. Smith retired after Katrina. I thank her for her comments on a previous draft.

[6] In total, approximately 3,000 teachers lost their jobs as a result of Katrina and the creation of the clusters of charter schools.

[7] In a nutshell, Mayor Nagin's "Bring Back New Orleans Commission" education subcommittee set forth the following goal for public schools: *Achieve fundamental and lasting transformation.*

[8] Since publication of "A Nation at Risk," the OPSB and its central office had undergone relentless school reform

efforts, embracing a plethora of national as well as homegrown models.

[9] The schools were slated to open just before Winter Break, December 25, and start up again on January 3.

[10] To be accurate the Center employed three full time staff, a substantial percentage drop in proportion to the numbers of central office administrative personnel in the district pre-Katrina.

[11] An article published in *Education Week* described the schools as "a system of schools," rather than a "school system," and enrolled 2,400 students in mid January. "New Orleans Charter Network Gets Under Way." January 18, 2005.

[12] Recently a loosely-knit coalition of researchers, teachers, union representatives, community activists and former New Orleans school district personnel have begun collecting data on the effects of specific charter schools in New Orleans on poor African American children. The coalition has found that there has been a net loss of 43 percent of low income, at-risk students in Orleans Parish. See Charles Hatfield and Associates, L.L.C. (May 1, 2006). Demographic Comparisons of Orleans Public School Students: 2004-05 and 2005-06 (SIS Database); also Luis Mirón, March 2006 and the methods section above.

References

Allen-Haynes, L. (1993). A case study of the Accelerated Schools' school-university partnership model as a change strategy for a college of education's teacher and administrator training programs. Ph.D. dissertation, University of New Orleans.

Alvarez & Marsel Financial Report New Orleans Public Schools. May, 2004.

Argyris, C., & Schön, D.A. (1978). Organizational learning. Reading, MA: Addison-Wesley Publishing Co.

Bernofsky, C. (2006). The Louisiana decision (Part 3, unpublished).

Bogotch, I. (2006). Field notes Algiers Charter School professional development training. January 20, 2006. New Orleans, LA.

Bogotch, I., Mirón, L. Biesta, G. & Reidlinger, B. (2006, April). School effectiveness and its publics: Between global politics and local struggle. Paper presented to the Annual Meeting of the American Educational Research Association. San Francisco, CA. April.

Bring New Orleans Back Education Committee. (2006, January 17). Rebuilding and Transforming: a plan for world-class public education in New Orleans.

Darder, A., & Mirón, L. (2006). Critical pedagogy in a time of uncertainty: A call to action. *Cultural Studies Critical Methodologies*, 6(1), 5-20.

Davis, M. (2006, April 10). Who is killing New Orleans? *The Nation*.

Denzin, N.K., & Lincoln, Y.S. (2003). *Strategies of qualitative inquiry* (2nd ed.). Thousand Oaks, CA: Sage.

Feagin, J.R., & Barnett, B.M. (2004). Success and failure: How systemic racism trumped the brown v. board of education decision. *University of Illinois Law Review*, 2004 (no. 5), 1099-1130.

Fine, M. (1994). Distancing and other stances : Negotiations of power inside feminist research. Gitlin, A. (ed.). *Power and Method.* New York : Routledge.

Fine, M., Tuck, E. & Zeller-Berkman, S. (2006). Do you believe in Geneva? Methods and ethics at the global nexus. Paper presented to the International Congress on Qualitative Inquiry. University of Illinois, Urbana-Champaign.

Friere, P. (1970). *Pedagogy of the oppressed.* New York: Continuum.

Gertz, C. (1983). *Local Knowledge: Further Essays in Interpretive Anthropology.* New York: Basic Books.

Johnson, D.D. & Johnson, B. (2002). *High stakes: Children, testing and failure in American Schools.* New York: Rowman & Littlefield.

Kohn, A. (2000). *The case against standardized testing: Raising the scores, ruining the schools.* Portsmouth, NH: Heinemann.

Kohn, A. (2002). "The five hundred pound gorilla." *Phi Delta Kappan,* 84(2), 113-119.

Lauria, M., & Mirón, L.F. (2005). *Urban schools : the new social spaces of resistance.* New York: P. Lang.

Marsal, A. (April 1, 2006). New Orleans Public Schools Post-Katrina Budget Update: New Orleans Public Schools.

McCarthy, J. (1996). "Reflection: Making learning come alive in accelerated schools." In C. Finnan, E.P. St. John, J. McCarthy, & S.P. Slovacek (Eds.) *Accelerated Schools in action: Lessons from the field,* 293-296. Thousand Oaks, CA: Corwin Press.

Mirón, L. (2007, forthcoming). *A Conception of performative ethnography.* New York and London: Peter Lang Press.

Mirón, L. (1997). *Resisting Discrimination: Affirmative strategies for principals and teachers.* Thousand Oaks, CA: Corwin Press, Inc.

Mirón, L. (1996). *The social construction of urban schooling. Situating the crisis.* Cresskill, NJ: Hampton Press.

Mirón, L. (1992). Corporate ideology and entrepreneurism in New Orleans. *Antipode.*

Mirón, L., & Laria, M. (1998). Student voice as agency: resistance and accommodation in inner-city schools. *Anthropology & Education Quarterly,* 29(2), 189-213.

Mirón, L., & St. John, E.P. (2003). *Reinterpreting urban school reform: Have urban schools failed, or has the reform movement failed urban schools?* Albany: State University of New York Press.

Mirón, L., & Ward, R. (2007). Drowning the crescent city: Told stories of Katrina. *Cultural Studies Critical Methodologies,* 10(10), 1-16.

Mirón, L., & Ward, R. (2006). A first look at the effects of charters on poor students of color: A position paper (p. 4). Urbana: University of Illinois at Champaign-Urbana (unpublished).

Nossiter, A. (2006, March 30). As Life Returns to New Orleans, So Does Crime. *New York Times,* p. 1.

Parker, L. (2003). Critical race theory in education: Posibilites and problems. In M. Peters, C. Lankshear & M. Olssen (Eds.), *Critical theory and the human condition: Founders and Praxis,* pp. 194-198. New York: Peter Lang publishers.

Raffo, C., Dyson, A., Gunter, H., Hall, D., Jones, L, and Kalambouka, A. (2006). Education and poverty: Mapping the terrain and making the links to educational policy. Paper presented to the International Seminar on Education and Poverty. Manchester, UK, March 2006.

Rich, J.M. (1991). *Rationales of educational reform. Urban Education*, 26(2), 149-159.

Ritea, S. (2006, March 12). Learning to Change. *New Orleans Times-Picayune*, p. 1.

Ritea, S. (2005, October 25). Charter Schools Urged for N.O. District; La. Education Chief Cites System's Woes. *New Orleans Times-Picayune*, p. 1.

Ritea, S. (2005, October 19). Board at War Over School Plans. *New Orleans Times-Picayune*, p. 1.

Rizvi, F. (2006). The ideology of privatization in higher education: A global perspective. In D.M. Priest & E.P. St. John (Eds.), *Privatization and public universities.* (65-84) Bloomington, IN: Indiana University Press.

St. John, E.P., Griffith, A.I., & Allen-Haynes, L. (1997). *Families in Schools: A Chorus of Voices in Restructuring.* Portsmouth, NH: Heinemann.

State of Louisiana.   (June 2005). Memorandum of Understanding. In Department of Education (Ed.) (p. 12).

Worthington, S. (2006).   Inquiry, equity, and integration: Education and applied social science for the public good.   Presentation to the College of Education, University of Illinois, Urbana-Champaign. March 28.

CHAPTER 9

PROFESSIONAL DEVELOPMENT IN STUDENT AFFAIRS: FROM LEARNING ABOUT DIVERSITY TO BUILDING JUST COMMUNITIES

Kimberly Kline

There is a challenge when preparing student affairs professionals to practice in and encourage diversity within a critical mass (Flowers & Howard-Hamilton, 2002; King, 2001). While graduate courses in student affairs graduate programs rely on theories of student development, they overlook the professional development of student affairs practitioners-in-training. Students learn about theories and research on college students and administration, but do not have ample opportunities to reflect upon and integrate those theories into practice (Nottingham, 1998). In many cases, social justice issues are treated at an espoused level, but insufficient attention is given to the practice of social justice in student affairs administration. To understand and resolve this dilemma, it is important to focus on research that creates paths toward actionable change within student affairs preparation programs. Specifically, action-based inquiry in the classroom provides concrete communication tools for student affairs practitioners to ease the challenge in a campus environment to engage in dialogue with individuals who are different from them.

317

Copyright ©2007 AMS Press, Inc. All rights reserved.

This chapter describes an action experiment which suggests that understanding individual social action theories is intrinsic to building a community that supports diversity. Habermas (1990, p. 58) theorizes that "communicative action" provides a process by which groups of individuals can build understanding. To overcome the gap between theory and practice, graduate students reflected on action theories — in relation to social justice issues — both inside and outside of the classroom. Habermas's theory of communicative action, and Schön's theory of reflective practice (1983), can inform new approaches to social justice education and practice in student affairs.

In this study we examined ways in which student affairs graduate students learned action theories, reflected on their own practices, and dealt with social justice issues in their professional practice. We examined whether there is evidence of change in perceptions, understanding, and/or action as a consequence of a course with this focus. An additional question asked whether the action experiment would result in evidence of change in students' attitudes about social justice issues in student affairs. The study was based in a one-semester course in a student affairs master's program at "Midwest University." The course addressed the dilemma of integrating social justice content, using a theory of action approach (Argyris, Putnam, & Smith, 1985; Argyris & Schön, 1974) to help students better understand how they acted or believed that they should act in various professional situations. The action experiment employed classroom research, a Freirian pedagogical approach, and a case study methodology within the course. I co-taught the course and acted as a participant-observer in the research process, working collaboratively with the instructor and students.

Background

The Framework: Theories of Action

Argyris and Schön's theory of professional effectiveness and Habermas's social critical theory provided the design for the study. Theories of action illuminated how the assumptions people make influence their actions in the situations they encounter in day-to-day life or professional practice. Argyris and Schön explained two types of theories of action: *espoused theories and theories-in-use.* "When someone is asked how he would behave under certain circumstances, the answer he usually gives is his [sic] espoused theory of action for that situation...however, the theory that actually governs his actions is his theory-in-use" (Argyris & Schön, 1974, pp. 6-7). A person's espoused theories and her theories-in-use contribute to how she makes meaning of everyday professional situations. While Argyris and Schön have defined a theory of action in professional settings as being closed and goal-oriented (Model I) or open to conventions about intent in situations (Model II), they do not explain what determines or defines effective action. Their models assume an implicit notion of effectiveness. They assume: (1) the intent of all action is to be "effective," and (2) parties involved share an understanding of the action's purpose. Often, the purpose of the action either was not defined, or there was dissention in agreement of what the aim of action should consist of. Their theory of professional effectiveness contains assumptions about organizational effectiveness, and these assumptions must be questioned. In the following paragraphs I provide an overview of Argyris and Schön's (1974) theory of action, along with its strengths and limitations as a professional development tool within a student affairs course. Habermas's notion of social critical theory will also be discussed.

Argyris and Schön (1974) discuss an individual and organizational theory of action in their text *Theory in Practice: Increasing Professional Practice.* In *Theory in*

Practice, Argyris and Schön suggest that individuals function in an organization or in life from a set of underlying assumptions about how the world and how the individuals' relationships within that world work. They propose that an individual's theory of how the world works, or her "theory of action" guides the individual's behavior in an organization.

Argyris and Schön divide individual behavior in two basic categories. They purport that most individuals and organizations function within a Model I framework. This model is based on the "theories-in-use" observed by Argyris and Schön in researching organizations and individuals within them. Argyris and Schön define theories-in-use as "general characterizations of how theory applies to human interactions" (1974, p. 37). Observing one's theories-in-use is a difficult concept for an individual to embrace. Argyris and Schön differentiate between the theory an individual espouses about how organizations and individuals should work and the theory that individuals actually use in real-life situations. They suggest there is a substantial gap between an individual's "espoused theory" and the theory or theories that they actually use. Argyris and Schön find that many individuals may espouse Model II values such as providing workers or even their friends and family with free and informed choices and valuing personal causality; however, they believe that most individuals function in the controlling, defensive, low-risk, rational ways associated with Model I. Life experience teaches us to think abstractly, quickly, "on our feet." We are rarely encouraged to stop and reflect on how or why we reacted to a particular situation in a particular manner. A crucial skill in developing an awareness of our own theories-in-use is "describing (our) directly observable behavior" (Argyris & Schön, 1974, p. 38).

Argyris and Schön developed Model II to describe theories-in-use that they observed in subjects within their studies that are "free of the disfunctionalities of Model I" (1974, p. 85). Argyris and Schön claim that their research supports a great need for a model of theories-in-use "that reduces the negative consequences of Model I and increases growth, learning and effectiveness" (1974, p. 85).

Argyris and Schön (1974) note that frequent incongruities exist between espoused theory and theories in use within a discipline of study (p. 174). Most student affairs preparation programs include a set of theories, coupled with issues of professional practice. What is absent at times is the testing of these theories and issues in student affairs courses that involve students. The theories are simply presented, rather than designing forums for dialogues about how students believe that the theories may or may not work in practical settings. Upcraft notes "discussions...and inclusion of theory and reactions to it in courses in student affairs graduate programs" could provide a strategy for better linking theory to practice within our field (1994, p. 441).

Social Critical Theory of Habermas as a Framework for Analysis

Jurgen Habermas is a German philosopher who is often referred to as the contemporary representative of the "Frankfurt School" of philosophy (Blackburn, 1994). During the 1930s, the philosophical approach of the Frankfurt school began to receive attention in the United States, particularly when placed in the context of social issues. This philosophical approach became known as critical theory, and "...described any attempt to understand practices of criticism, interpretation, and historical understanding of social action, including especially that of writing" (Blackburn, 1994, p. 89). Critical theory philosophers researched contradiction in social arrangements in which certain groups are excluded from power or from full access to information. Early critical theorists included Hegel and Marx, and later Habermas, who based his work out of the hermeneutics tradition.

The hermeneutics tradition developed from text interpretation and is particularly concerned with interpreting the meaning of an experience or writing in the framework of the participant. Hermeneutics considers facts without meaning to be incomplete. In the positivist/naturalist tradition, methodology is key to producing valid knowledge; while in the hermeneutic tradition, knowledge comes from the interpretation within the context of the author's intent (Patterson, Watson, Williams, & Roggenbuck, 1998). In *Moral Consciousness and Communicative Action* (1990), Habermas goes beyond the positivist/naturalist tradition and the hermeneutic tradition to examine a discourse ethics based theory of communicative action. He "...attempts to connect discourse ethics to the theory of social action via an examination of research in the social psychology of moral and interpersonal development" (Habermas 1990, p. ix).

The work of Jurgen Habermas is particularly important to this study because of his concern for and work with discourse ethics. Using discourse ethics, or more specifically, the process of communicative action within a classroom setting, can provide students with opportunities to challenge their internal biases that they bring to a conversation with another individual.

It is important to note that Argyris and Schön's Model I and Model II theories fall short in reaching what Habermas refers to as an ideal "speech situation" for a statement to be true (Habermas, 1990, p. 135). Habermas believes that the ideal speech situation is the basis for the "ideas of rationality, freedom, and justice, as well as the idea of truth" (Argyris, Putnam, & Smith, 1985, p. 75). The dilemma with Argyris and Schön's Model I and Model II theories of action is that Model II is oriented toward effectiveness, which is goal-based. It does not consider gender, race, or socioeconomic status, influence-situated expectations, or goals. Alternatively, social justice issues can create a division among individuals within a group unless they have the communication skills to discuss those issues in a free and open environment. Habermas's concept of social critical theory was used in this study to build an understanding of whether or not Argyris and Schön's method of teaching professional education can be used to better understand social critical issues.

Student affairs masters programs validate the importance of moral and interpersonal development. This is reflected in many student and cognitive developmental theories in most curricula. What is missing in this curriculum, however, is a process that teaches individuals to work as social agents with students in their professional practice. While Argyris and Schön's theory of professional development was central to this course, the framework of Habermas's social critical theory is necessary for analyzing the changes evident from the research conducted during the course. Argyris and Schön's theory of professional development, coupled with Habermas's concept of social critical theory through communicative action, provides a basis for analysis. The goal is to better understand whether or not bridging the gap between theory and practice can be realized in a classroom such as the one created for this experiment.

Reflective Practice in Student Affairs

Reflection is defined as "a process or activity that is central to developing practices" (Dewey, 1933, 1938; Leitch & Day, 2000, p. 180). Arlin (1990) and Csikszentmihalyi and Sayers (1995) associate reflection with thinking and purport that it involves the cognitive processes of "problem finding" and "problem solving" (Leitch & Day, 2000). King and Kitchener adopted Dewey's (1933, 1938/1960) notion that "reflective judgments are made to bring closure to situations that can be characterized as 'uncertain,' where there is uncertainty about a solution" (Evans, Forney, & Guido-DiBrito, 1998, p. 162).

Schön is credited with bringing reflection into the forefront of educational practice through the term *reflective practitioner* in his 1983 text of the same title. In this text, Schön expands upon Dewey's (1933) concept of thinking-in-action. Schön (1983) distinguishes between two types of reflective thinking: reflection-on-action and reflecting-in-action. Russell and Munby (1992) define reflection-on-action as the "systematic and deliberate thinking back over one's actions" (p. 3). Reflection-in-action conversely "is a way of making explicit some of the tacit knowledge embedded in action so that the agent can figure out what to do differently" (Argyris, Putnam, & Smith, 1985, p. 51). The "agent" or practitioner in a real-time situation will stop and reconstruct an actual situation in order to better understand and learn from it.

Why introduce reflective practice into a student affairs course? A positivist stance suggests that one cannot measure the success of the student affairs apprentice until she has experienced academe as a professional. One can argue, however, that a student affairs curriculum is merely theory that cannot be transferred into practice until the novice professional is immersed in the full-time workplace. Nottingham (1998) in her chapter *Using Self-Reflection for Personal and Professional Development in Student Affairs* suggests that the use of self-reflection as described by Russell (1993) in teacher education programs "...is very appropriate for professional development in student affairs, in that learning in both areas is a process of being told what to do, watching others, and doing" (Nottingham, 1998, p. 74). Richardson (1990) notes that Zeichner (1983) and Gore (1987) describe many teacher education programs as being technical in nature, and that the elements of thinking like a teacher and making sense of one's practice are missing (Schön, 1987). This tested practice, derived from teacher education, strongly supports the argument for deliberate infusion of reflective practice and the use of action theories into student affairs master's programs. Such infusion provides student affairs master's students with a learning laboratory in which they can learn to better navigate the unique environment of a university. Moore (1991) notes "Rarely are student affairs professionals — or university administrators in general, for that matter — formally trained in organizational behavior and the political dimension of organizational life ... most of us learn about institutional politics through experience, often at high personal costs ..." (p. 2).   This gap contributes to the failure of many young, promising student affairs professionals.

Ramaley (2000) suggests that change within an organizational structure such as a college or university must begin with its leader providing an experimental mode through which the leader both models and encourages public learning.   Ramaley (2000) suggests four approaches to achieve public learning within an institution: 1) the leader should instill a discipline of reflection and a culture of evidence;   2) the leader should create "new patterns of conversation that encourage and support the involvement of everyone in defining the issues that will be important in building the organization" (p. 79); 3) adopt a philosophy of experimentation within the institution, and 4) "...create new ways to facilitate access to information, so that everyone can make informed choices" (p. 80).   Providing student affairs master's students with the tools and the confidence to participate in public learning can raise the level of influence that the student affairs profession has on an institution and transform an organization into a community of learners.

Social Justice Issues in Student Affairs Programs

More recently, American student affairs masters programs have made honest attempts to consciously incorporate cognitive-structural theories, human development theories, and postmodern writings in a diverse approach to student development.   In many cases these attempts have resulted in students leaving such preparation programs with a sense of hierarchy when it comes to "isms" that different societal groups face.   Frequently lacking are (1) a deliberate introduction and immersion in the actual discourse among students and instructors and (2) the purposeful infusion of social justice issues into discourse and reflective practice.

In this study the term "oppression" was used to describe issues of social injustice in which a group of student educators can work together towards a socially just world. Bell (1997) defines oppression as:

> ...the pervasive nature of social inequality woven through social institutions as well as embedded within individual consciousness. Oppression fuses institutional and systemic discrimination, personal bias, bigotry, and social prejudice in a complex web of relationships and structures that saturate most aspects of life in our society (p. 4).

Social justice education courses evolved during the late 1960s and 1970s. Only more recently, however, have some forerunners in this field of study stated the need for a theory synthesizing the literature and historical experiences of both the oppressed and dominant groups to date. Bell (1997) draws on the work of Freire (1970) to identify the need for a praxis process. Praxis includes both theory and practice as "intertwining parts of the interactive and historical process" of an individual. (Bell, 1997, p. 4). During the curriculum intervention, students developed their own professional praxis. This exercise introduced the social justice theory of oppression to students as a choice to include or exclude social justice praxis within their individual professional praxis.

The coupling of social justice educative practices and action theories in a student affairs classroom allowed participants to experiment with critical theories, and test the linkages between student affairs practice and social justice in an applied setting. Both aspects are crucial to the level of preparedness of the entry-level student affairs practitioner, as well as their perceptions of that preparedness.

It is important to examine aspects of student development theory to help the student affairs practitioner-in-training more fully understand what they, and other students, are experiencing. More recent studies have reported, however, that this area of theory has not concerned itself with concepts such as social status, positionality, or different life experiences (Bidell & Fischer, 1992; Rogoff, 1984; Rogoff, Gauvain, & Ellis, 1984; Bell, 1997). Attempting to provide an engaging and safe environment for the study participants, the instructors adopted Bell's principles (1997) outlined as an adaptation of the current body of social justice education practice. They include the following:

1) Balance the emotional and cognitive components of the learning process;
2) Acknowledge and support the personal (the individual student's experience) while illuminating the systemic (the interactions among social groups);
3) Attend to social relations within the classroom;
4) Utilize reflection and experience as tools for student-centered learning;
5) Value awareness, personal growth, and change as outcomes of the learning process (p. 30).

Bell's concepts of social justice were introduced in this course. The course dealt with the intersection between social justice and action science, and students were encouraged to reflect critically and openly about their own assumptions regarding social justice issues.

A Model of Social Justice Development for the Student Affairs Scholar/Practitioner-in-Training

As the semester unfolded, a framework emerged illustrating what each student experienced in the course. The student is referred to in this model as "the student affairs practitioner-in-training," and a picture of this model is provided on page 330.

In interviewing each student, it became clear that students had pre-existing attitudes toward the discussion of diversity issues in the classroom. As illustrated in the model below, these pre-existing attitudes can be attributed to three factors: (1) past classroom experience; (2) their perceptions of social justice issues and (3) socioeconomic class. The model then notes the student beginning the professional development in student affairs course.

During the semester-long course, students were exposed to social justice texts, dialogues and theories of action so that they could experience new methods and approaches to discussing difficult issues. In addition, students reflected verbally in class and in their written assignments. The teaching team utilized action science as a process for co-constructing a communicative classroom setting among the instructor, teaching fellows and students.

Student reactions fell into two primary categories: resistance towards discussing diversity issues and open conversation. As mentioned in chapter two, open conversations regarding issues of social justice and learning theories of action, and considerable resistance to these issues took place simultaneously. Eight of the nine participants initially expressed frustration, anxiety and sometimes anger about being asked to discuss diversity issues "again." These participants attributed their initial resistance to both personal and prior educational experiences, though most of these eight students reported they resisted the professional development course based on past educational experiences or courses at the master's level.

The study's first goal was to find out how student affairs master's students learn action theories through the use of action science. To answer this question, I researched types of scholarship currently being utilized in student affairs classrooms. The landscape is currently changing within the student affairs field. An emerging paradigm is taking shape, with an increasing number of scholar/practitioners within student affairs who consistently argue for scholarship that is constructed through a postmodern lens. Research within our field should be conducted in ways that allow emerging scholars and practitioners to seek alternate truths. With an ever-changing college population, it is the only appropriate tack to take as we sail into new waters.

Using action theories such as Argyris and Schön's Model I and Model II theories of action (Argyris & Schön, 1974) and concrete exercises within student affairs preparation courses present our students with opportunities to (1) liberate themselves through self-discovery and (2) practice "dry runs" of some political situations that they are likely to encounter as new professionals.

The Intervention: A Social Constructivist and Liberatory Approach to Learning

The study examined student experiences in a graduate class using Argyris and Schön's theory of professional effectiveness to critically examine literature on social justice. The classroom experiment addressed the use of social justice issues in the classroom and in student affairs practice. The course readings on social justice for the course were used to facilitate conversation and provide opportunities for students to co-construct meaning of social critical issues in professional practice. Vigorous discussion and collaborative projects encouraged participation by students. Argyris and Schön's theory of professional effectiveness and case method were utilized so that participants could publicly test their assumptions.

Argyris and Schön point out a positive consequence of openly discussing incongruencies between espoused theory and theory-in-use within a professional preparation curriculum: "Faculty might be encouraged to conduct research or to guide others to do so in order to reduce the gap between espoused theory and theory-in-use. This would make the kind of learning necessary to minimize self-sealing processes and maximize double-loop learning more likely in the academic setting" (Argyris and Schön, 1974, p. 176). The course content provided an opportunity to examine whether Argyris and Schön's approach to professional education can

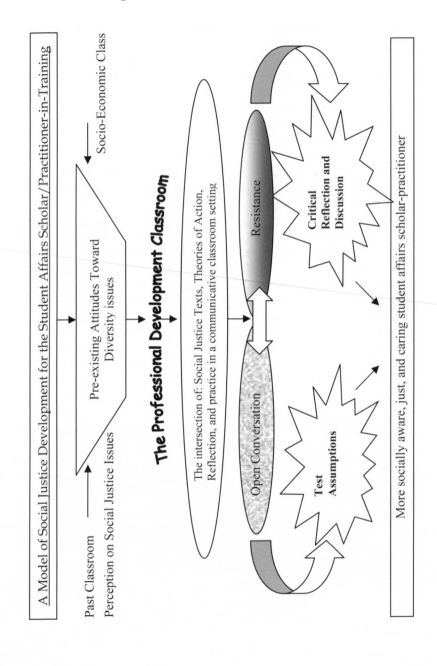

A Model of Social Justice Development for the Student Affairs Scholar/Practitioner-in-Training

Socio-Economic Class

Pre-existing Attitudes Toward Diversity issues

Past Classroom Perception on Social Justice Issues

The Professional Development Classroom

The intersection of: Social Justice Texts, Theories of Action, Reflection, and practice in a communicative classroom setting

Resistance

Open Conversation

Critical Reflection and Discussion

Test Assumptions

More socially aware, just, and caring student affairs scholar-practitioner help students build a better understanding of social critical issues.

Habermas's social critical theory was used to analyze the changes in students' perceptions. Specifically, I explored ways in which individuals can have distorted views of their theories of action and issues of social justice, and how "removing distortions in our understanding of ourselves" can help bring about more a more equitable discourse in the workplace (Blackburn, 1994, p. 165). The data collected in this study was utilized to examine the concepts of Argyris and Schön's theory of action, and Habermas's social critical theory. The teaching team for this course tried to create an environment where participants could co-construct both an individual and community-based understanding of professional practice. In my role as a participant-observer, I assumed a dual role of observing how students learned about theory, while simultaneously learning about the meaning of theory from examining their experiences. In an effort to be purposeful in achieving a co-constructed environment and to maximize my understanding, I drew from the work of Stage et al. (1998) and their recommended conditions for educators employing beliefs of social constructivism in the classroom. These conditions include:

- Students' active involvement in the social processes of the classroom;
- Emphasis on the critical role of peers, in particular more skilled students, in promoting understanding;
- Enculturation of students into the community of the particular academic discipline or profession;
- Emphasis on the common construction of knowledge that results when students involved in an activity negotiate their individual accounts and arrive at some level of agreement;
- Overt use of the sociocultural context to promote learning;

- Use of relevant situations in which students are called upon to solve dilemmas; and
- Appreciation of multiple perspectives (p. 40).

These conditions helped me to constantly filter my observations through a social constructivist lens.

Spring's (1994) interpretation of Freirian-type dialogues of teachers facilitating in the classroom were also used in my role. Freire suggests that it is important for dialogues to first take place frequently among teachers who work with similar types of students. In this study, the teaching team had a unique opportunity to observe and reflect on one group of students. Spring suggests that in Freirian dialogues, learning takes place on three levels. "On one level, the teachers learn about their surrounding world. On another level, they learn how they themselves think about the world. And, finally, they learn why they think about the world the way they do" (Spring, 1994, p. 160). In creating a socially constructed classroom, the teaching team was able to (1) learn about some of the challenges that participants in the professional development course faced; (2) learn about where each teacher stood on some of these issues and problems that the participants brought forward, and (3) through reflection, think about how we personally would act if placed in a certain professional situation and use some of these reflections in purposeful ways. Primarily, reflections were used to create and engage our students in new dialogue to find their professional voices and philosophies in student affairs. Weekly scheduled meetings between the teaching team, and several additional conversations with and without our students sparked realistic and sometimes difficult dialogues for the group. The teacher continuously encouraged the teaching team to inform the class, encouraged the class to inform us, and suggested that we reflect upon our practice as co-constructors of knowledge in the student affairs field.

We looked for evidence of change or learning using the aforementioned constructs, and findings indicate that although most participants resisted the introduction of social justice issues into a course on professional development, they came to understand how reflective practice could help them deal better with the difficult issues they faced in their practice.   Participants were mainly concerned with being better prepared to survive the political environments in universities, but were unsure of how to acquire the necessary skills. They were interested in theory, but found it difficult to distinguish action theories from other learning theories such as psychosocial developmental theories. Practical exercises, such as the professional dialogues and professional praxis paper, combined with reflection, helped students to better link action theories to practice.

As an action researcher, I dually acted as a participant-observer over a four-month period, working collaboratively with the instructor and students. The professor introduced me as an action researcher and a teaching fellow who would not be leading group discussions because of human subject guidelines, but who would be a participant/observer in the course. Also, one other teaching fellow was introduced and the professor shared his expectations for this course, including the importance of confidentiality of class discussions. This dual role ultimately worked well, because it provided countless opportunities for interventions between the participants, the professor, the other teaching fellow, and me. I was able to provide information to the professor and teaching fellow on insights gained from the one-to-one interviews.   Though the individual's anonymity was protected, I would share suggestions, praises, or frustrations shared by students in the course. Simultaneously, I worked to gain the trust of course members.   As the semester progressed, many interventions and insights were well received when I provided them to the class. This is not to suggest that participants always agreed with my observations. The more that they trusted the process, the more the participants shared. It was not that we working to build a "perfect classroom," but rather we were all ultimately working to build a safe classroom where ideas could be debated critically. Thus, professional development in a student affairs course was conceived.

Course Structure

The master's level course was structured similarly to a course previously taught at the doctoral level, in that it was frontloaded with the appropriate amount of readings and assignments for a two-credit master's level course. The second half of the course was more loosely structured, and students were provided with theory, practical information, and insights via an open dialogue format. Exercises and tools were also included to mold the structure of the second half of the course to best meet the needs of the entire class. Confidentiality and group process guidelines were outlined during the first class, and students were encouraged to give both themselves and others full value in subsequent course discussions. The professor conveyed a message that all participants in the course (i.e., ten students, the two teaching fellows, and the professor) were considered equal. The professor had certain responsibilities, such as being the lead discussant for course literature, but the group was jointly responsible for the direction that the course took.

Assignments. Three different types of written data were analyzed in an effort to provide a rich description of the participants' voices as they made meaning of their experiences throughout the semester of the professional development course.

Professional Dialogues 1 and 2. Two assignments titled *Professional Dialogue 1 and 2* are examined. In these two assignments, students selected a dialogue they had in a professional situation and were comfortable sharing with the group. It could have been an intervention recalled from the past or a hypothetical intervention. The students were given the following instructions:

1) *Context:* Describe the context for the dialogue (the participants and the situation in which the dialogue occurred, or that they expect could occur);

2) *Dialogue:* Record (or recollect) the statements made by you and the other(s) involved in the dialogue (parenthetically or beside each statement record your interpretation of what the speaker meant). Record a minimum of two pages of the dialogue using this format. It is generally appropriate to disguise the name(s) of the other participant(s) in the conversation by using pseudonyms.

3) *Analysis:* Reflect back on the dialogue. Identify the underlying assumptions you held about effective action based on the Argyris and Schön text.

The data collected and synthesized through the professional dialogue assignments was used to answer research question one: "How do student affairs masters students learn action theories?" as well as question two: "How does the use of action theories in a student affairs master's course on professional development enable students to make meaning of their experiences both inside and outside of the classroom?" In addition, this assignment gives students an opportunity to experiment with Model I and Model II behavior. This pertains to the second professional dialogue in particular, since the class members participated in a classroom exercise before they completed the second dialogue. The class processed each other's professional dialogues in small groups using Model I and Model II Elements of Theory: students are able to take the knowledge gained through the first exercise into the writing of their second dialogue. The researcher could compare any insights gained between assignment one and assignment two.

Group Project. During the course, groups were formed to work on collaborative projects. These group projects were mini "action experiments" that enable members of the class to practice aspects of action science. The projects involved collaboration on the development of the design, working together on the experiment, and collaborating on the presentation of results and insights.

The data collected through the group project will help to shed some light on question two: "How does the use of action theories in a student affairs master's course on professional development enable students to make meaning of their experiences both inside and outside of the classroom?" It also allowed me to discern any patterns of practice or patterns of reflection related to the setting of goals and the variables of Model I and Model II (Argyris & Schön, 1974).

Praxis Papers. Students were asked to compose a *Praxis Paper* that discusses the evolution of their professional praxis. This paper was based on the course readings, outside readings, course discussions, and their own reflections. The students were given the following instructions by the professor:

1) *Understanding of Professional Practice* — a discussion of historical practice, focusing on your personal theories in use (referencing your first two assignments and the small group discussion of these assignments, your group project, and other recollections of your prior professional practice).

2) *Envisioning New Forms of Praxis* — develop a practical vision for how you might transform your professional praxis, either as an individual practitioner, or as a member of a community of practitioners.

3) *Action Steps* — identify a set of action steps you can take as you attempt to move toward your vision of your future praxis.

4) *Appendices* — append supporting materials, including your first two dialogues and copies of relevant journal entries.

5) *References* – use APA style for the texts you used in the paper.

The requirements of the praxis paper provided a built-in source of data for this study. Analyzing the praxis papers gave me the ability to gain insight into all three research questions via another form of data. Future ideas for research emerged through the praxis papers as well.

Method

Participants

Nine of the ten students (five women and four men) who enrolled in the course have participated in the study. The participants ranged in age from 22 to 53, and while a few students had several years of experience in student affairs, the majority of participants had two to four years of primarily paraprofessional experience. Some participants self-identified themselves during the first interview session in terms of ethnicity, regionality, religious affiliation, type of student, and sexual orientation. For example, one participant has self-identified as Latin American, one has self-identified as a "Southerner" and another as Jewish. Three students have identified themselves as being "non-traditional students" ranging in age from 44 to 53 in the midst of career changes. And one student self-identified as being gay, while another self-identified as being bisexual.

Interviews

Data collection included interviews with participants enrolled in the professional development course in the spring semester of 2002. Students who enrolled in the professional development course chose whether to participate in the study, and the course professor had no knowledge of which students participated. Participants were asked to agree to two one-to-one interviews, each lasting no longer than two hours. The first set of face-to-face interviews occurred midway through the semester and the second set of interviews took place via telephone during the summer following enrollment in the course The goal of each set of interviews was to give the student an opportunity to reflect upon his or her experiences within the course.

Using the semi-structured interview format, I framed the interviews with Model II behavior as an interviewer that would produce valid information, test the interviewees' assumptions and produce more directly observable data for myself and the interviewee. This interviewing method was used by Argyris (1993) in the text *Knowledge for Action*. For instance, if an interviewee stated: "I wish to provide as much information as necessary for my staff to be successful in their jobs," I would respond with the question: "Can you provide an example of a situation where you provided a staff member with valid information and the result was successful?" This not only allowed me to obtain additional data, but also gave both myself and the interviewee insight into how they perceived their success upon reflection.

Findings

The semester-long classroom research study was an enlightening experience. Most participants expressed extreme anxiety and frustration over openly discussing social justice and other difficult issues. The participants admitted these feelings only after there was an "intervention" of sorts, initiated by the professor and teaching fellows. Students were not willing to share their thoughts or participate in one particular class meeting, and the professor and teaching fellows believed that they must "walk the walk" to provide the class with valid information regarding their observations, in the spirit of the action theories that they were presenting. The spontaneous intervention took many class participants by surprise, and several shared their disbelief that such a dialogue had been initiated. As students in the class felt more comfortable, they started to test assumptions and communicate more openly about assumptions. This was accomplished in most cases through critical reflection and discussion. The act of reflecting critically and testing assumptions in a public setting appeared to be the catalyst for some to move beyond their personal biases towards individuals who were different from them. In the social justice development model that I offer, this state of being is referred to as "a more socially aware, just and caring student affairs scholar-practitioner."

In and out of the classroom, many students have spoken of their extreme frustration and at times anger regarding the way that their preparation program had handled the teaching of multicultural issues. Some students were also frustrated with the way that the professional development course was structured, as evidenced by some of the reflections of participants in this chapter. As the participant-observer and action researcher, I was told privately on several occasions, and observed publicly through the class meetings (during the second half of the semester) that they simply could not believe that the professor really wanted them to test their assumptions publicly. Data eventually captured in interviews, self-reflection, and group exercises supported a shared belief that initially, they did not feel safe discussing social justice issues freely. As the semester unfolded, however, students spoke more openly and with more frequency. Some students who at first appeared to be comfortable in discussing charged issues increasingly delved into more personal and difficult issues. By the eighth week of the semester, and specifically after the class "intervention," seven of the nine students who previously were silent in class were beginning to share their thoughts with minimal to no prompting. The action experiment topics chosen by the participants in this study also indicated the types of topics that the overall class felt comfortable discussing.

This leads us to the other two research questions that were put forth in this study: (1) How well prepared were student affairs master's students to deal with issues of social justice in their professional practice? And (2) How does the use of action theories in a student affairs master's course on professional development enable students to reflect and make meaning of their experiences, both inside and outside the classroom? As indicated by the voices of the participants in this study, students viewed their experience with the structure, content, and overall experience within the professional development course in a variety of ways (pseudonyms are used). Zoe provides a reflective example of her experiences within the course. She states:

> I do think—like the way the course has gone, and I mentioned this before, in the beginning (the professor) was just lecturing and I was just sitting there and I was just like oh, man. He was very, very theoretic (al) on how he presented things. And then the course got better when we started doing our dialogues. Then the material that we were reading was kind of really brought to life and I could see the connections between the dialogues and Model I and Model II. And then these last two weeks, having something to go by—the personal experiences that we're sharing and an article to discuss. I really enjoyed this because you hear other people's opinions. But as far as things that I would recommend members of the course address, I think we should continue sharing our personal experiences, discussing and relating the course material to it. But then maybe taking it to the next

level as far as what do we do with this discussion—
you know asking really the practice.

Zoe indicates that she was uncertain as to the direction
that the course would take. She uses words such as
"theoretical" and indicates some discomfort when
participating in a course when the material being presented is
entirely theoretical. Zoe does note a difference in attitudes
regarding the course material once concrete assignments,
such as the professional dialogues, and later the topical
discussions on functional areas of student affairs bringing the
readings (the theoretical) "to life." It should be noted that
Zoe's interview took place in March, two months into the
course and semester. Some participants who were interviewed earlier in the semester were not as accepting of the
course material as those participants interviewed mid-
semester. In all cases, the interviews were used to inform the
teaching teams' work. There were several times when the
teaching team received feedback that was utilized to adapt
the course to the needs of the class. Yolanda provides an
example of this feedback that was utilized. She states:

> And the social justice piece, I don't feel like I've
> been given a clear connection. I understand to be a
> better professional you need to understand the
> background of people that you're talking with, your
> background, whatever. I had to force myself to
> make that connection. I don't feel like it's been
> made, and I feel like we're reliving our diversity
> class, which is not, I don't think, what the goal was.
> And I think what happened was I don't think you
> guys had any clue about all and everything we
> brought into that.

Interviews like Yolanda's influenced the evolving
design of the course. The input was critical in co-
constructing meaning for both the teaching team and the

students. Opinions varied, as is noted by this next quote by Max, who quotes:

> Without talking too long, I think the other thing is the open dialogue we have in the class. I enjoy it. It feels like a safe place. I think it's healthy for some of the people attending the class. I think I've gotten past that; so I don't think it's as healthy for me. This class has proved to me that if you put people in a class and I think you could sprinkle any type of diversity into this class, you would have the same approach, you would have open dialogue, feel safe when you start—it just seems there's a lot of goodness there because I know that I'm more likely to speak up for some of these diversity issues and bring some of this into the open to talk about in this class than I am in other classes...I bring it up in another class—it's almost like throwing a piece of me into a fish tank of piranhas just to get rid of the part and then by the time you can get in there to pull whatever's left out, it's just like going in all these different directions. Well, you know about personal politics. In here, I think it's good because I know people in this class really well. And I know that things that they talk about in this class are not what they talk about in other classes; and I know what ends up happening is people start to assume a problem that these people that are in our class who never talk about that stuff in other classes are just racist, or just apathetic towards diversity issues, or they're apathetic towards multi-cultures without questioning their assumptions about really why. And it makes me feel good about humanity because we see certain people in our class bring real issues to the table; but it's because we can talk about it. And it's not like anybody raises their voices in the class; it's just really calm. I'm just like—I know

how I feel about this and I'm going to say it today.
And that may or may not make sense.

An analysis of the data in this study provides evidence
that critical reflection encouraged by the teaching team,
through the use of action science, eventually created open
conversation. That is not to say that all of the participants
always took part in this open conversation. During the first
half of the semester in particular, some participants expressed
that they did not believe the conversation was open. Or,
more dramatically, the silence in the classroom would speak
for itself. The conversation during the second half of the
semester was much more open. Participants began to take
most to all of the responsibility for co-creating dialogue in
the class, and would challenge one another more to test their
assumptions if a particular conversation was being conducted
at a superficial level.

Social justice texts, along with theories of action,
reflection and practice were introduced into our experimental
classroom setting. These theories and texts alone did nothing
to bring about open conversation and/or resistance,
particularly given the pre-existing attitudes towards diversity
that participants brought to the classroom. It was only when
the theories and texts that were introduced were filtered
through an action science process of acting on assumptions,
reflecting upon those assumptions, and then publicly testing
the assumptions that some of the barriers of resistance began
to break down. Just as the action science process leads an
individual towards better understanding of her place in the
world, participants began to test their own assumptions and
critically reflect and discuss how they could work toward a
better understanding of their own professional practice
within the context of the professional development
classroom.

Conclusions

The purpose of this study was to examine ways in which
student affairs graduate students learn action theories, reflect
on their own practices, and deal with social justice issues in
their professional practice.   The primary intent of this
examination was to explore whether or not students could
build new understandings of themselves and their
professional field through the practice of "communicative
action" that Habermas (1990) refers to in situated contexts.
Habermas's concept of social critical theory was used in this
study to build an understanding of whether Argyris and
Schön's method of teaching professional education can be
used in turn to build an understanding of social critical issues
within the student affairs classroom.   The study also
examined how students' assumptions about social critical
issues might influence their actions in professional practice.

There is a dilemma with Argyris and Schön's Model I
and Model II theories of action because their ideal
professional setting is one that is oriented toward
effectiveness, and this is a goal-based objective. A goal-
based objective of effectiveness does not distinctly consider
gender, race, socioeconomic status, influence-situated
expectations, or goals. One might ask, "Effective for
whom?" Even though Argyris and Schön suggest that Model
II values the valid sharing of information and joint decision
making, there are still a set of "criteria" framing Model II
behavior that runs the risk of maintaining a win/lose reality,
regardless of wanting a win/win situation to occur.
Conversely, dealing with and discussing social justice issues
in a setting that is not safe and open to the sharing of valid
information can result in the silencing of voices rather than
co-constructing meaning as a group. It was only through the
coupling of Argyris and Schön's theory of professional
development, with Habermas's concept of social critical
theory through communicative action that this study

attempted to provide one way to bridge the gap between theory and practice.

This study and the social justice development model offer implications for teaching where social justice is a focus. There are implications for other student affairs courses, as well as for courses addressing social critical topics. In addition to offering courses that deal with notions of oppression, it is just as important to provide students with some of the necessary tools that they will need to confidently participate in discussions regarding oppression and other professional challenges that they will face on a daily basis.

A review of the literature in student affairs, as well as from the participants in this study clearly shows that an educational philosophy is something that is welcomed and needed within student affairs preparation programs and courses. What remains unclear, however, is how an educational philosophy might be integrated into the student affairs field. A review of the praxis papers by participants in this study revealed that students struggled to describe who they were as professionals, and why they made professional decisions. In some cases, particularly where social justice issues are concerned, many participants felt uncomfortable because they were not accustomed to a classroom forum in which challenging others and being challenged was perceived as being safe. It is important to ask: Is the student affairs profession providing the foundation necessary for student affairs practitioners-in-training to become successful agents of social change? Is that even the responsibility of student affairs preparation programs? These questions warrant further research consideration by student affairs scholar/practitioners.

Situated pedagogy (Friere, 1987) suggests that students be presented with critical issues that may be most difficult for them to perceive. In the professional development course, students were presented with a syllabus situated within a critical framework. For some of the participants in the study, issues such as actionable knowledge and social justice were difficult concepts to grasp and discuss openly. Much of the second half of the semester was dedicated to issues, projects and dialogues that the students were experiencing at the time in their respective workplaces. It can be compared to Freire's definition of dialogic education "that is situated in the culture, language, politics and themes of the students" (Shor & Freire, 1987, p. 104). Students were first uncomfortable with the class format, and some of the topics were more difficult for them to perceive. For many participants, "social connectedness and mutual responsibility" were initially not part of their reality. As the semester progressed, however, the students became much more comfortable with the class format. Attitudes and behaviors of the class changed from the beginning of the course to the end of the course. Five of the nine participants exhibited a form of liberation by speaking without inhibition to share their attitudes with the class. There appeared to be a correlation between the student's awareness level and her ability to speak calmly and listen intently to others in the class. In this sense, the course succeeded to instill confidence in students by practicing the act of communicating with their colleagues on difficult issues. All nine participants in this study showed evidence of being more socially aware at the end of the semester as opposed to the beginning of the semester. They developed a more just attitude towards each other and in their professional practice.

Co-constructing an educational philosophy in a critically reflective course such as the professional development course may give students in preparation programs the confidence that is necessary to achieve individual critical consciousness. Indeed, this educational philosophy could be used to ground the framework of an overall student affairs preparation program. Helping future student affairs scholar-practitioners to achieve greater individual levels of consciousness could in turn open up opportunities for practitioners everywhere to engage in inclusive dialogues.

These dialogues can only help to model caring behavior for our students who are in need of such positive role modeling.

REFERENCES

Argyris, C. (1993). *Knowledge for action.* San Francisco: Jossey-Bass Publishers.

Argyris, C., Putnam, R., & Smith, D. (1985). *Action science.* San Francisco: Jossey-Bass Publishers.

Argyris, C., & Schön, D. (1974). *Theory in practice: Increasing professional effectiveness.* San Francisco: Jossey-Bass Publishers.

Arlin, P. (1990). Wisdom: the art of problem finding. In R.J. Sternberg (Ed.), *Wisdom: its nature, origins and development.* Cambridge: Cambridge University Press.

Bell, L. (1997). Theoretical foundations for social justice education. In M. Adams, L.A. Bell, and P. Griffin (Eds.), *Teaching for diversity and social justice: A sourcebook.* New York: Routledge.

Bidell, T. & Fischer, K. (1992). Beyond the stage debate: Action, structure, and variability in Piagetian theory and research. In R.J. Sternberg and C.A. Berg (Eds.), *Intellectual development.* New York: Cambridge University Press.

Blackburn, S. (1994). *The oxford dictionary of philosophy.* New York: Oxford University Press.

Blimling, G. (2001). Uniting scholarship and communities of practice in student affairs. *Journal of College Student Development, 42*(4), 381-396.

Csikszentmihalyi, M. & Sawyers, K. (1995). Creative insight: the social dimension of a solitary moment. In R.J. Sternberg and J.E. Davidson (Eds.), *The nature of insight.* London: MIT Press.

Dewey, J. (1938). *Experience and education.* New York: Collier Books.

Dewey, J. (1933). *How we think.* Boston: D.C. Heath.

Evans, N., Forney, D. & Guido-DiBrito, F. (1998). *Student development in College: Theory, research and practice.* San Francisco: Jossey-Bass Publishers.

Evans, N. & Reason, R. (2001). Guiding principles: A review and analysis of student affairs philosophical statements. *Journal of College Student Development, 42*(4), 359-377.

Flowers, L.A., & Howard-Hamilton, M.F. (2002). A qualitative study of graduate students' perceptions of diversity issues in student affair preparation programs. *Journal of College Student Development, 43*(1).

Freire, P. (1985). *The politics of education: Culture, power and liberation.* S. Hadley, MA: Bergin & Harvey.

Freire, P. (1970). *Pedagogy of the oppressed.* New York: Herder and Herder.

Gore, J. (1987). Reflecting on reflective teaching. *Journal of teacher education, 38*(2), 33-39.

Habermas, J. (1990). *Moral consciousness and communicative action.* Cambridge, MA: MIT Press.

King, P. (2001). On expecting more of ourselves: A reply to "guiding principles: a review and analysis of student affairs philosophical statements" by Nancy J. Evans with Robert Reason. *Journal of College Student Development, 42(* 4), 378-80.

Leitch, R. & Day, C. (2000). Action research and reflective practice: towards a holistic view. In C. Day, J. Elliott, B. Somekh, R. Winter and K. Green (Eds.), *Educational action research: An international journal, 8* (1), 179-193.

Moore, P. (1991). *New directions for student services: Managing the political dimension of student affairs, 55.* San Francisco: Jossey-Bass.

Nottingham, J. (1998). Using self-reflection for personal and professional development in student affairs. In W. Bryan and R. Schwartz (Eds.), *New directions for student services: Strategies for staff development: Personal and professional education in the 21st century.* San Francisco: Jossey-Bass Publishers.

Patterson, M., Watson, A., Williams, D., & Roggenbuck, J. (1998). A Hermeneutic approach to studying the nature of wilderness experiences. *Journal of Leisure Research, 30* (4), 423-452.

Ramaley, J. (2000). Change as a scholarly act: Higher education research transfer to practice. In A. Kezar and P. Eckel (Eds.), *New directions for higher education: Moving beyond the gap between research and practice in higher education.* San Francisco: Jossey-Bass Publishers.

Richardson, V. (1990). The evolution of reflective teaching and teacher education. In R. Clift, W. Houston, and M. Pugach (Eds.), *Encouraging reflective practice in education: An analysis of issues and programs.* New York: Teachers College Press.

Rogoff, B. (1984). Introduction: Thinking and learning in social context. In B. Rogoff & J Lave (Eds.) Everyday Cognition: Its Development in Social Context. Cambridge, MA: Harvard University Press, p 1-8.

Rogoff, B., Gauvain, M., and Ellis, S. (1984). Development viewed in its cultural context. In M. Bornstein and M. Lamb (Eds.), *Developmental psychology: An advanced textbook.* Hillsdale, NJ: Lawrence Erlbaum.

Russell, T. (1993). Reflection-in-action and the development of professional expertise. *Teacher Education Quarterly, 20*(1), 51-62.

Russell, T. & Munby, H. (1992). *Teachers and teaching: from classrooms to reflection.* New York: Falmer Press.

Schön, D. (1983). *The reflective practitioner.* United States: Basic Books Inc.

Schön, D. (1987). Educating the reflective practitioner: Toward a new design for teaching and learning in the professions. San Francisco: Jossey-Bass.

Shor, I. & Freire, P. (1987). *A pedagogy for liberation: Dialogues on transforming education.* S. Hadley, MA: Bergin & Harvey.

Spring, J. (1994). *Wheels in the head: Educational philosophies of authority, freedom, and culture from Socrates to Paulo Freire.* New York: McGraw-Hill, Inc.

Stage, F. Mueller, P. Kinzie, J., & Simmons, A. (1998). *Creating learning centered classrooms: What does learning theory have to say?* ASHE-ERIC Higher Education Report, Vol. 26, no. 4.

Upcraft, M. (1994). The dilemmas of translating theory to practice. *Journal of College Student Development. 35,* 438-443.

Zeichner, L.M. (1983). Alternative paradigms of teacher education. *Journal of Teacher Education,* 34 (3), 3-9.

CHAPTER 10

SCHOOL REFORM, SCHOLARSHIP GUARANTEES, AND COLLEGE ENROLLMENT: A STUDY OF THE WASHINGTON STATE ACHIEVERS PROGRAM[1]

Edward P. St. John and Shouping Hu

While there has been substantial debate in the policy literature about the potential effects of early guarantees of student aid and of high school reform on college enrollment rates, no prior research has compared the effects of the two types of interventions on college enrollment rates for high school students. This void should not come as a surprise given that few interventions combine both reforms in high school preparation and early guarantees of student financial aid. Since there is a lingering debate in the education policy literature about the two approaches to improving college access, it is important to consider how both types of reforms link to college enrollment before we attempt to make causal inferences.

The Washington State Achievers (WSA) Program, funded by the Bill & Melinda Gates Foundation, may be the only large scale reform that can be used to study these questions simultaneously. Five-hundred students from 16 funded schools received WSA scholarship (WSAS) guarantees immediately after being included in the program

351

Copyright ©2007 AMS Press, Inc. All rights reserved.

in 2002, with awards being given during the senior year. The same number of students in the subsequent high school cohorts received aid guarantees in the 11th grade. In addition, the high schools were funded for a three-year planning process followed by implementation of comprehensive school-wide reforms in 2005. WSA provides grants to these high schools to support high school restructuring, including implementation of small schools within high schools and expansion of international baccalaureate (IB) and other advanced high school courses. There were changes in courses offered at WSA schools during the planning period so school reforms may have had an effect on enrollment even before implementation of the new high school models. Since the aid guarantees were implemented for students enrolling in college in the fall of 2002 and there was improvement in offering of advanced courses by the fall of 2004, both types of reforms could have influenced college enrollment rates for high school seniors in these schools. However, the fact so many features were included in the design of this reform, it has proven difficult to evaluate the effects of specific program features on preparation and enrollment.

This chapter examines the enrollment effects of WSA using surveys of high school seniors in WSA schools and comparison schools, along with follow-up telephone surveys in the fall after their senior years to check on college enrollment status. Our objective is to examine how receipt of WSA scholarships (WSAS) was associated with college enrollment. Surveys of four senior classes of students in WSA and comparison high schools were conducted by a research team at the University of Washington: one survey in 2000 (before WSA) and surveys of the first three WSAS cohorts (2002, 2003, and 2004). First, as background, the WSA program is situated within the current debates about public policy on college access. The research approach, findings, and conclusions follow.

Background

It is important to consider the roles of both financial aid and academic preparation in analyses of college enrollment. Studies of Indiana's Twenty-first Century Scholars Program reveal that providing guarantees of financial aid to low-income students in 8th grade substantially improved the odds of their applying for and enrolling in college (St. John, Musoba, Simmons, Chung, Schmidt, & Peng, 2004) and equalizes the odds of persistence for low-income students who gain access through the program (St. John, Gross, Musoba, & Chung, 2006). This research evidence suggests that providing financial guarantees can improve the odds of preparation and enrollment. However, the relative effects of aid guarantees and high school courses have not been previously examined. The WSA program provides a natural experiment that can be studied to test these relationships.

The WSA Program

In 2002 the Bill & Melinda Gates Foundation initiated a comprehensive intervention program that combined high school reform with an early aid guarantee program. The Washington State Achievers Program, administered by the Washington Education Foundation, provided grants for school restructuring to 16 high schools with high rates of students on free and reduced lunch, as well as a limited number of annual guaranteed grants to 500 low- and middle-income students each year. The grant awards were implemented in 2002 with award guarantees being made to students in the senior classes. The balanced access model (St. John, 2003) illustrates the major features of the WSA Program (Figure 1).

The left hand side of the figure illustrates the school reform features of the GMS programs. Funding was provided to the 16 high schools to support restructuring large high schools into smaller schools that share the same facilities, along with expansions of International Baccalaureate (IB).

Figure 1
A BALANCED APPROACH TO COLLEGE ACCESS AND SUCCESS: LINKING K-12 AND POSTSECONDARY POLICIES TO PREPARATION, COLLEGE CHOICE, AND PERSISTENCE

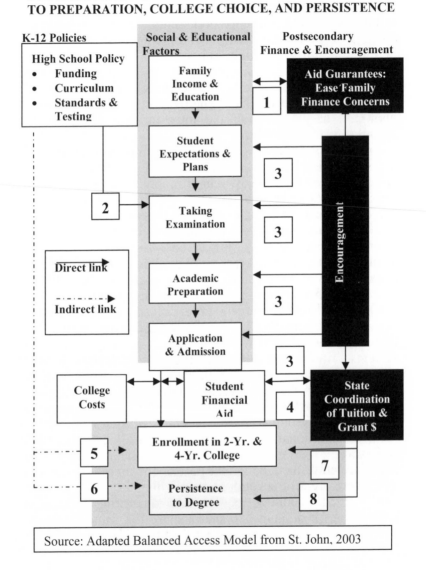

Source: Adapted Balanced Access Model from St. John, 2003

The restructuring of the schools can have a direct influence on preparation through the courses students complete (advanced placement [AP] and /or IB), In addition other forms of student engagement introduced in the reform, such as mentoring, can influence college enrollment. In addition, the school reform can have an indirect influence on college enrollment through high school completion and more advanced steps related to preparation, including college application and so forth. Participating schools received funding for school reforms in 2001, so the graduating class of 2002 was the first to have some indirect benefit of the school reform, given the implementation time.

The right hand side of the figure illustrates the role of the scholarship program administered by WEF. The WEF selected 500 students each year from the 16 high schools. In 2000 students were selected from the senior class, early in the school year. In subsequent years they were selected from the junior class. In 2000 it was not possible for the program to influence curriculum, but it could influence the more advanced steps, including applications for college and student aid (St. John & Hu, 2006). Students were selected for the WSAS from among the qualified applicants using William Sedlacek's noncognitive criteria (Sedlacek, 2004; Sedlacek & Sheu, 2006). Students from families earning less than $50,000 per year were qualified. The early analyses of selection reveal that among applicants, student with more engaged parents and students of color were more likely to be selected (Emeka & Hirschman, 2006). The WEF provides mentors from within the school and community to work with the selected group. Thus, students selected for WSAS receive additional encouragement. The encouragement provided WSAS recipients, like the financial support, can influence enrollment and other postsecondary outcomes.

There are also several ways in which the WSA program can influence college choice and academic success in college. A prior study found that having more grant aid available improved the odds of enrollment in four-year

colleges and private colleges for students in the 2000 cohort
of WSAS students, controlling for other factors related to
family background and preparation (St. John & Hu, 2006). It
is also possible that GMS can influence engagement in
academic and community activities in college, as well as
persistence and degree completion. The WEF provides
mentors for recipients who enroll in college, as noted on the
left side of the figure, a factor that can further influence
academic success in college.

This study focuses on the enrollment effects of gains in
preparation (linkages 2 and 5 in Figure 1) and of scholarships and early encouragement (linkages 3 and 7). Increased
availability of AP/IB courses can have a direct effect on the
percentage of students completing these courses (linkage 2)
and an indirect effect on increasing enrollment through
preparation. Through high school reform we could expect:
(a) an increased percentage of students completing AP/IB
courses; and (b) an increased enrollment rate for students
completing AP/IB. Both the comparison and WSA schools
could have *a* (improved rates of completion of AP/IB
courses) and *b* (improved enrollment rate rates). We also
need to consider the fact that in WSA schools: (c) recipients
of WSAS may be more likely to take AP/IB courses because
they think they will be able to pay for college; and (d)
students who received the additional award may be more
likely to enroll in college (linkage 5). Within econometric
research it is common to think (linkage 4) about *d* (receipt of
aid as having an effect on enrollment). However, in WSA,
students who receive aid guarantees also receive
supplemental mentoring and encouragement to take
advanced courses (represented by the "encouragement" box)
so the indirect effects of WSA on course completion could
be attributable to encouragement as well as to the aid
guarantee and the actual differential in aid awards
attributable to the program (linkage 7). In this study we
attempt to build an understanding of these effects by
considering these different linkage structures using both

descriptive statistics and logistic regression analyses. Our purpose is to illuminate the linkages rather than to measure causal effects.

A Natural Experiment

Although WSA was not designed using random assignment of scholarships within WSA schools or matched comparison schools, a natural experiment has evolved. Charles Hirschman, a sociologist at the University of Washington, had conducted a survey of all Tacoma high school seniors in 2000, a study that included nearly equal numbers of both WSA schools and other high schools. There were SES differences between the two sets of schools, but this survey did provide a cohort that was followed into college. After its staff found out about the Tacoma study, which had been funded by the Pew Foundation, the B&MGF provided support for the follow-up telephone survey in the fall of 2000 to determine whether students had enrolled in college. In addition, B&MGF helped support a follow-up survey of students in 2002 in Tacoma and an expanded sample of WSA and comparison schools in 2003 and 2004.

In combination these surveys provide samples that can be used to examine both the effects of receipt of WSAS on college enrollment, comparing the 2000 and 2002 cohorts, and of the effects of school reform, comparing the expanded surveys for 2003 and 2004. Students in these latter two cohorts received benefits of the school reform process, in the form of increased opportunity to take advanced courses, but the full reforms had not yet been implemented. With the UW surveys it is possible to examine trends in enrollment across all four cohorts, but the question about advanced courses was added to the survey for cohorts after 2000.

This study builds an understanding of the effects of the reforms using a three-step analytic process. First, the trends in rates of college enrollment and enrollment in advanced courses are examined across comparison and WSA schools, building a descriptive understanding of the extent of change in access to advanced courses and college enrollment. Second, logistic regression analyses are used across the cohorts and with pooled cohort data to estimate the effects of advanced high school courses and scholarships on college enrollment. The discussion of the findings focuses on understanding the linkage structures, rather than making attributions about program effects. We take the step because it is important to rethinking the linkage structures between reform efforts and intended outcomes as an intermediate step before evaluating effects.

Research Approach

Unlike experiments that use random assignment of treatment—an approach that can assess using comparison of means—natural experiments require sound logical models that control for other variables that are logically related to intended outcomes. In this study, the intended outcome was enrollment. To the extent that the treatment and comparison schools are similar, we can examine enrollment rates and make informed judgments about the relationship between treatments and effects. However, from prior research we know that the schools have different SES characteristics (Emeka & Hirschman, 2006; St. John & Hu, 2006), so simple comparisons have limited utility. At a minimum we know we must control for SES related variables when making comparisons.

In addition, we had two treatment variables in the naturally occurring experimental study: a limited number of WSAS awards were given to students in the junior years (treatment 1) across three cohorts; and school reform went into effect in their final year of the study. Since we have information on two cohorts from Tacoma high schools, one before the scholarships were implemented (2000) and the other the year after (2001), we could compare the rates of enrollment in the two sets of schools, controlling logically for SES difference (i.e., the higher SES schools had a higher base enrollment rate in 2000). While this method can be informative for thoughtful reflection on scholarships, it is not of much use for the analysis of the second treatment since there were changes in the rates at which students took AP/IB courses in both sets of high schools. A simple comparison of rates across schools is not workable.

Rather than rely on simple comparisons—or the more complex, but similar method of effect size analyses—this study uses a mixed methods approach. We compare rates of enrollment and of completion of advanced high school courses, conduct logistic regression methods, and compare regression results with changes in rates, to build an understanding of the two types of treatments. Before describing these three steps in the analysis, we describe the logical model used in the regression analyses.

Logical Model
The logical model (Table 1) for the logistic regression analyses of enrollment viewed enrollment as a function of:

- WSAS (recipients, applicant non recipients in WSA schools compared to students in comparison schools)
- Family background (race/ethnicity, gender, family support, parents' education, home language);
- High school experience (high school grades, AP/Honors/IB courses taken); and
- Aspirations.

The variable coding for the model is described in Table 1. Dichotomous variables were used to make discrete comparisons, such as male compared to female. When possible and appropriate, dichotomous coding was used so that simple comparisons could be made. Design sets of variables were used to examine the effects of variable sets when more complex comparisons were needed. For example, we compared three types of students in WSA schools (WSAS recipient, WSAS applicant-non-recipient, and

WSAS non-applicant in WSA schools compared to being from a comparison school). Design sets were also used for race/ethnicity, high school grades, and aspiration. In addition, a continuously coded composite variable was constructed for family support.

Table 1 Variable Coding for Enrollment Model

VARIABLE	Coding/ Comparison
WSA	**Design Set**
Non-applicants in WSA Schools	Comparison School.
Aid Applicants but Non-Awardees in WSA Schools	Comparison School
Aid Awardees in WSA Schools	Comparison School
Gender	**Dichotomous**
Men	Women
Ethnicity	**Design Set**
African American	White/Other
Hispanic	White/Other
Asian American	White/Other
American Indian	White/Other
Parental Education	**Dichotomous**
Father's Education (BA or Higher)	Less than BA
Mother's Education (BA or Higher)	Less than BA
Family Support	**Continuous**
Family Support	Composite score
Family Structure	**Dichotomous**
Living with Both Parents	Other Living Arrangement

Table 1 Variable Coding for Enrollment Model, cont.

Home Language	Design Set
Other than English	English spoken
Missing report	English spoken
Cumulative Grade	**Design Set**
Mostly A	Mostly B
Mostly C	Mostly B
Mostly D	Mostly B
Education Aspiration	**Design Set**
High school or less	Four-year or higher
Less than two-year college	Four-year or higher
Two-year college	Four-year or higher
Advanced Courses	**Dichotomous**
Taken or planned	No advanced courses
Cohort	**Design Set**
2003 Cohort	2002 Cohort
2004 Cohort	2002 Cohort

Logistic regression models were used in the second step of the analysis using a two-step sequence. In the first step the design set of variables was used to compare three categories of students in WSA schools (successful scholarship applicants, unsuccessful applicants, and non-applicants) to students in comparison schools. In the second step all of the additional variables were added to provide an analysis of the effects of WSAS with controls for other variables influencing scholarships.

Three sets of logistic regression models are presented. The analysis of the 2002 cohort examines the effects of WSAS the first year of implementation. The analyses of the 2004 cohort provide information on the effects of WSAS and of advanced high school courses the year after the high school reforms were implemented. And analyses of the combined 2002, 2003, and 2004 cohorts provide additional information on the effects of WSAS and high school courses. Since WSA was not awarded in 2000 and the questions about advanced high school courses were not asked of this group, we could not complete a similar analysis of this cohort, although descriptive statistics for this group are presented in the appendix, along with similar data for the other three cohorts.

Analysis Methods
As a first step in this study we examine trends in enrollment rates at WSA schools compared to non-WSA schools, comparing enrollment rates for 2000, 2002, 2003, and 2004. In addition, for WSA schools we consider trends in college enrollment rates for each of the three categories of students within WSA schools: WSAS recipients, applicants/non-recipients, and non-applicants. In addition we examine trends in taking advanced course for these groups for 2002, 2003, and 2004. The descriptive statistics for each of the cohorts are presented in the appendix.

Second, the two-step logistic regression analyses present both the odds ratios and delta-p statistics (change in probability measures) for each of the analyses. Three levels of statistical significance are presented (.001, .01, and .05) for the independent variables. Delta-p statistics were calculated using a method recommended by Petersen (1985). In addition, three model indicators are presented: -2 Log L, Cox & Snell R2 (a pseudo R2), and chi square.

The final step in the analyses examines the change in rates relative to the delta-p statistics for the independent variables related to SES. This method of comparison provides a means of assessing the relative adequacy of different methods of measuring the effects of reforms implemented as natural experiments.

Limitations

The survey response rates and methods limit the generalizations that can be made from this study. Charles Hirschman and his colleagues survey all high school students in their senior cohorts. About 75 percent of the students in the high schools responded to the two stage surveys (Emeka & Hirschman, 2006). However, given that the schools were not randomly selected and not all WSA schools were sampled, no attempt is made here to generalize beyond the populations studied.

Further, the survey did not ask questions about family income. Since family income and parents' education are highly correlated as part of socioeconomic status (Becker, 2004), the reader is reminded that both fathers' and mothers' education are general SES measures and, as such, include some income effects.

Finally, no attempt is made here to adjust for selection, so no claims can be made about causality. While we use the term "effects" in the discussion of statistical relationships, we do not mean to imply causality in this discussion. We know from prior analyses that variables related to both family background and family support were associated with both application to and selection for WSAS (Emeka & Hirschman, 2006). We do include these selection related variables in the logistic regression models and step in those and other independent variables as a means of exploring these effects of selection. We did not make any further attempt to control for selection.

We also recognize that in analyses of college enrollment decisions, inclusion of variables related to high school experiences, like high school courses, introduce measurement problems. For example, social background variables are linked to access to advanced math courses (St.

John, 2006). Therefore it is not possible to fully distinguish the effects of social background from these school variables.[2] However, the alternative of specifying school comparison variables within models that control only for SES (e.g., Herting, Hirschman, & Pharris-Ciurej, 2006), makes it impossible to distinguish the effect of specific intervention features, like high school courses or aid guarantees, from other school effects, like change in school culture or increases in college knowledge that result from school reforms. In this study we attempt to distinguish among the different program features within a comprehensive reform. While our approach may be imperfect, we conclude this method provides more insights than the alternative of considering school effects along with SES.

Findings

Descriptive Statistics and Trends

While our focus in this study is on the effects of financial aid and high school reforms on enrollment rates, it is also important to consider other trends in other descriptive statistics.

Enrollment Rates

The trends in college enrollment rates (Figure 2) should be considered as two distinct transitions, given the differences in the sample populations for the first two and second two cohorts. The same schools were included in the 2000 and 2002 surveys, so it is possible to consider change in transitions rates after implementation of WSAS in 2002, compared to an earlier period. In addition, the larger cohort of schools was surveyed in 2003 (the year before school reforms) and 2004 (the first cohort to benefit from reforms). The comparison between 2003 and 2004 provides a lens of effects of the high school reforms.

Between 2000 and 2002, the percentage of students enrolling in the Tacoma area WAS schools increased from

55.5 percent to 59.3 percent, a 3.8 percentage point increase. However, during the same two year period, the college enrollment rate for the respondents in the non-WSA schools in Tacoma increased by 4.9 percentage points, from 64.4 percent to 69.3 percent. So even after implementation of the WSAS the gains in enrollment rates in the WSA schools were less than those in the non-WSA schools. It is possible that other factors related to differences in either SES or preparation explain the larger gains in non-WSA schools, but it is not possible to assess differences without controlling for these variables.[3]

It is evident from these analyses that in 2002 the WSAS recipients enrolled in college at a substantially higher rate than either non-recipients or non-applicants, but it is not possible to discern useful information about the effects of the WSA awards from this type of information. In fact it is not clear from these analyses whether other factors related to selection (i.e., background and family support variables) explain variation in the outcome (i.e., enrollment rates).

In the larger sample of schools, there were also improvements in college enrollment rates between 2003 and 2004, the two years before the small school reforms were implemented in WSA schools. The improvement in the enrollment rate for students in all schools was 3.4 percentage points, from 67.6 percent to 71.0 percent, while the non-WSA schools improved enrollment rates by 2.2 percentage points (from 75.0% to 77.2%) and by 3.7 percentage points in WSA schools (from 57.6% to 61.3%).

A closer look at the subpopulations within WSA schools reveals that the non-applicants for WSAS enrolled at about 50 percent in both 2003 and 2004, but that both WSAS recipients' and non-recipients' enrollment rates improved. While WSAS recipients had higher enrollment rates in 2004 than applicant non recipients (88.7% compared to 71.6%), the applicant non-recipients experienced the largest gain in enrollment rates across years. Applicant nonrecipients for WSAS had a 12.2 percentage point gain in enrollment rate (from 59.4% for the 2003 cohort to 71.6% for the 2004 cohort), compared to a gain of only 4.4 percentage points for WSAS recipients (from 84.4% to 88.7%).

Advanced HS Courses

Could school reforms help explain the slightly larger improvement in 2004 compared to 2003 for WSA schools compared to the comparison schools? Trends in the rates of completion of advanced high school courses provide some evidence related to this question (Figure 3). However, both WSA and comparison schools showed improvement in the percentage of students who completed advanced courses.

The percentage of students in the 2004 cohort, 52.4 percent, was 6.3 percentage points higher than for the 2003 cohort (46.1%). The rate of increase in completion of high school courses was slightly higher for non-WSA schools: a 6.3 percentage point gain in non-WSA schools (from 50.8% for the 2003 cohort to 57.1%) and by 5.2 percentage points in WSA schools (from 39.8% to 45.0%). Therefore the changes in completion of advanced courses per se do not appear to be the explanation for the larger gains in college enrollment rates for WSA schools.

The breakdown of course taking by the three categories of students within WSA schools does not clarify the trends. The percentage of WSAS recipients with advanced courses did increase, from 58.1 percent for the 2003 cohort to 71.8 percent for the 2004 cohort, suggesting that the supplemental encouragement they received may have influenced course completion during their senior year. However, the percentage of WSA applicant non-recipients who completed advanced courses remained stable at about 40 percent, even though this group increased most substantially in enrollment rates. The non-applicants, the groups within WSA schools to experience the least gain in enrollment rates between 2003 and 2004, had a larger gain in completion of advanced courses (from 34.9% in 2003 to 37.3% in 2004) than the non-recipient WSAS applicants.

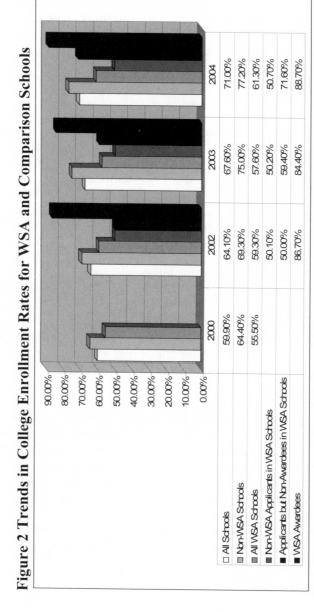

Figure 2 Trends in College Enrollment Rates for WSA and Comparison Schools

	2000	2002	2003	2004
All Schools	59.90%	64.10%	67.60%	71.00%
Non-WSA Schools	64.40%	69.30%	75.00%	77.20%
All WSA Schools	55.50%	59.30%	57.60%	61.30%
Non-WSA Applicants in WSA Schools		50.10%	50.20%	50.70%
Applicants but Non-Awardees in WSA Schools		50.00%	59.40%	71.60%
WSA Awardees		86.70%	84.40%	88.70%

Note: Enrollment rates for 2000 and 2002 are for Tacoma area schools. Enrollment rates for 2003 and 3004 add additional WSA and comparison schools.

Trends in rates of advanced-course completion in relation to trends in college enrollment do not provide a particularly compelling explanation for changes in enrollment rates between 2003 and 2004. There was more improvement in completion of advanced courses in non-WSA schools, but these schools had more modest enrollment gains.

Differences in Student Background
The relationships between student aid, high school courses, and college completion are most appropriately interpreted in relation to student background variables that influence all of these outcomes. The four appended tables provide descriptive statistics broken down by school type for each year, as well as for the three groups within the WSA schools for 2002, 2003, and 2004. Two factors merit consideration.

First, there were substantial differences in variables related to SES status for WSA schools and non-WSA schools. The students in non-WSA schools were more likely to be whites, to have parents with college degrees, to speak English at home, and to have both parents at home. These differences were evident for the initial samples in 2002 and 2003, and for the expanded sample. Our argument is that it is inappropriate to consider the role of preparation or high school achievement without considering these other factors.

Second, there were some very modest changes in aspirations and other intermediate indicators of enrollment within WSA schools, but these indicators also changed in comparison schools. For example, a comparison of the 2003 cohort (Table A.3) and the 2004 cohort (Table A.4) shows slight improvement in aspirations to attain a four-year degree for seniors in WSA schools, from 61.2 percent in 2003 (Table A. 1) to 62.6 percent in 2004 (Table A.2). However, there was an even greater change in these variables within the comparison schools, from 71.8 percent in 2003 (Table A.1) to 75.5 percent in 2004 (Table A.2).

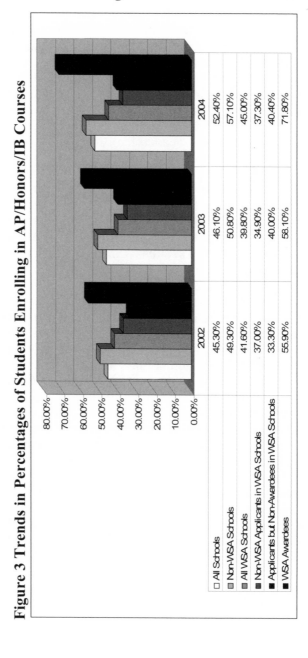

Figure 3 Trends in Percentages of Students Enrolling in AP/Honors/IB Courses

	2002	2003	2004
☐ All Schools	45.30%	46.10%	52.40%
Non-WSA Schools	49.30%	50.80%	57.10%
All WSA Schools	41.60%	39.80%	45.00%
Non-WSA Applicants in WSA Schools	37.00%	34.90%	37.30%
Applicants but Non-Awardees in WSA Schools	33.30%	40.00%	40.40%
WSA Awardees	55.90%	58.10%	71.80%

Logistic Regression Analyses

Logistic regression analyses provide a means of examining the effects of one set of variables on an outcome controlling for other variables related to the outcome. This type of multivariate analysis is especially important in studies of enrollment because students have the freedom to make choices about college if they have the financial resources and are academically prepared. Both preparation and finances influence ability to enroll, but the individual maintains some degree of discretion over enrollment.

While college admissions and selectivity play a role in gaining entry to four-year colleges, virtually any high school graduate in the state of Washington can enroll in a two-year college. Therefore, using enrollment in any college as an outcome mitigates this discretionary role of college admission decisions in the present study. Therefore we can consider the direct effects of high school courses and aid guarantees on enrollment (linkages 5 and 4 from Figure 1). However, to more fully understand the role of preparation and finances in the enrollment process, it is also important to consider opportunity to enroll in four-year colleges, or college choice, a step not taken in this paper.

The analysis of the combined cohorts (Table 2) revealed a somewhat more complex pattern. Not only were more variables significant in both models, but there were significant differences across cohorts in the second model. This analysis included the cohort variables in the second model. Students in the 2004 cohort had higher odds of college enrollment than students in the 2002 cohort, while there was not a significant difference between the 2003 and 2002 cohorts. Being in the 2004 cohort rather than the 2002 improved the odds by the otherwise-average sample member by 28 percentage points. This cohort effect is independent of

Table A.1 Comparison of Student Characteristics and Other Indicators in 2003

VARIABLE	Value	All Schools	Non-WSA Schools	WSA Schools			
				All WSA Schools	Non-Applicants of WSA	Applicants but Non-awardees of WSA	Awardees of WSA
Education Aspiration	To Attain a 4-year Degree	67.3%	71.8%	61.2%	54.3%	62.9%	86.0%
	No	32.7%	28.2%	38.8%	45.7%	37.1%	14.0%
Education Expectation	To Attain a 4-year Degree	61.2%	67.3%	53.0%	45.7%	54.1%	80.1%
	No	38.8%	32.7%	47.0%	54.3%	45.9%	19.9%
Lost Aspiration	Lost Aspiration	7.1%	5.1%	9.8%	10.7%	10.0%	6.5%
	No	92.9%	94.9%	90.2%	89.3%	90.0%	93.5%
Financial Aid Application	Applied for Financial Aid	43.8%	44.3%	43.1%	31.8%	48.8%	81.2%
	No	56.2%	55.7%	56.9%	68.2%	51.2%	18.8%
Education Plan After High School	Planning to Continue Education	75.2%	79.5%	69.3%	63.1%	71.2%	91.4%
	No	24.8%	20.5%	30.7%	36.9%	28.8%	8.6%
College Enrollment Rate	Attending any type of college	67.6%	75.0%	57.6%	50.2%	59.4%	84.4%
	No	32.4%	25.0%	42.4%	49.8%	40.6%	15.6%

Table A.1 Comparison of Student Characteristics and Other Indicators in 2003, cont.

Gender	Men	46.6%	45.6%	47.9%	49.3%	47.6%	43.0%
	Women	53.4%	54.4%	52.1%	50.7%	52.4%	57.0%
Ethnicity	African American	12.4%	8.9%	17.1%	14.7%	19.4%	24.2%
	Hispanic	9.5%	7.5%	12.3%	12.8%	11.2%	11.3%
	Asian American	16.3%	14.0%	19.3%	15.4%	30.0%	24.2%
	American Indian	3.9%	2.3%	6.0%	6.5%	5.3%	4.8%
	White	57.9%	67.2%	45.3%	50.6%	34.1%	35.5%
Father's Education	Lower than Four-year College	68.9%	58.9%	82.4%	80.2%	85.9%	87.6%
	Four-year College and higher	31.1%	41.1%	17.6%	19.8%	14.1%	12.4%
Mother's Education	Lower than Four-year College	72.4%	63.6%	84.2%	83.2%	87.6%	84.9%
	Four-year College and higher	27.6%	36.4%	15.8%	16.8%	12.4%	15.1%
Family Support	Family Support	6.76	6.92	6.54	6.47	6.50	6.8
Family Structure	Living with Both Parents	58.2%	63.0%	51.8%	53.9%	54.7%	41.4%
	No	41.8%	37.0%	48.2%	46.1%	45.3%	58.6%

Table A.1 Comparison of Student Characteristics and Other Indicators in 2003, cont.

Home Language	Other than English	22.7%	16.4%	31.2%	26.8%	47.1%	33.3%
	No	77.3%	83.6%	68.8%	73.2%	52.9%	66.7%
Cumulative Grades in High School	Mostly A	24.0%	28.8%	17.6%	16.4%	12.7%	26.3%
	Mostly B	45.5%	45.4%	45.5%	41.8%	51.6%	54.3%
	Mostly C	26.9%	23.0%	32.1%	35.8%	32.1%	18.3%
	Mostly D	3.6%	2.8%	4.8%	6.0%	3.6%	1.1%
AP/Honors/IB Courses	Taken or Taking	46.1%	50.8%	39.8%	34.9%	40.0%	58.1%
	No	53.9%	49.2%	60.2%	65.1%	60.0%	41.9%
% of Sample		100%	57.5%	42.5%	28.3%	6.8%	7.4%
N		2,516	1,447	1,069	713	170	186

Table A.2 Comparison of Student Characteristics and Other Indicators in 2004

VARIABLE	Value	All Schools	Non-WSA Schools	All WSA Schools	WSA Schools Non-Applicants of WSA	Applicants but Non-awardees of WSA	Awardees of WSA
Education Aspiration	To Attain a 4-year Degree	70.4%	75.5%	62.6%	54.1%	69.7%	84.6%
	No	29.6%	24.5%	37.4%	45.9%	30.3%	15.4%
Education Expectation	To Attain a 4-year Degree	64.0%	69.9%	54.6%	46.7%	56.0%	78.5%
	No	36.0%	30.1%	45.4%	53.3%	44.0%	21.5%

Table A.2 Comparison of Student Characteristics and Other Indicators in 2004, cont.

Lost Aspiration						
Lost Aspiration	7.5%	6.2%	9.5%	9.4%	14.7%	6.7%
No	92.5%	93.8%	90.5%	90.6%	85.3%	93.3%
Financial Aid Application						
Applied for Financial Aid	45.4%	43.5%	48.5%	35.9%	56.9%	82.6%
No	54.6%	56.5%	51.5%	64.1%	43.1%	17.4%
Education Plan After High School						
Planning to Continue Education	76.0%	79.1%	71.1%	63.1%	75.2%	93.8%
No	24.0%	20.9%	28.9%	36.9%	24.8%	6.2%
College Enrollment Rate						
Attending any type of college	71.0%	77.2%	61.3%	50.7%	71.6%	88.7%
No	29.0%	22.8%	38.7%	49.3%	28.4%	11.3%
Gender						
Men	44.9%	44.6%	45.4%	48.5%	41.7%	37.6%
Women	55.1%	55.4%	54.6%	51.5%	58.3%	62.4%
Ethnicity						
African American	11.2%	7.3%	17.2%	16.7%	14.7%	20.0%
Hispanic	7.7%	5.5%	11.1%	12.1%	11.0%	8.2%
Asian American	15.7%	13.1%	19.9%	15.1%	28.4%	30.3%
American Indian	4.3%	3.4%	5.8%	6.1%	8.3%	3.6%
White	61.1%	70.7%	46.0%	50.0%	37.6%	37.9%
Father's Education						
Four-year College and higher	32.8%	43.7%	15.6%	16.9%	11.0%	14.4%
Lower than Four-year College	67.2%	56.3%	84.4%	83.1%	89.0%	85.6%

Table A.2 Comparison of Student Characteristics and Other Indicators in 2004, cont.

Mother's Education	College and higher	28.1%	37.0%	14.1%	15.6%	10.1%	11.8%
	Lower than Four-year College	71.9%	63.0%	85.9%	84.4%	89.9%	88.2%
Family Support	Family Support	6.79	6.97	6.49	6.36	6.70	6.78
Family Structure	Living with Both Parents	61.3%	65.8%	54.3%	53.8%	59.6%	52.8%
	No	38.7%	34.2%	45.7%	46.2%	40.4%	47.2%
Home Language	Other than English	22.1%	15.5%	32.4%	28.5%	40.4%	40.0%
	No	77.9%	84.5%	67.6%	71.5%	59.6%	60.0%
Cumulative Grades in High School	Mostly A	23.0%	25.3%	19.3%	16.4%	21.7%	26.7%
	Mostly B	48.3%	50.9%	44.3%	41.1%	45.3%	53.3%
	Mostly C	24.6%	20.3%	31.4%	35.6%	31.1%	19.0%
	Mostly D	4.1%	3.5%	5.0%	6.9%	1.9%	1.0%
AP/Honors/IB Courses	Taken or Taking	52.4%	57.1%	45.0%	37.3%	40.4%	71.8%
	No	47.6%	42.9%	55.0%	62.7%	59.6%	28.2%
% of Sample		100%	61.0%	39.0%	25.9%	4.7%	8.4%
N		2,331	1,423	908	604	109	195

WSA, but could be related to an overall improvement in college preparatory courses in 2004 (as noted in Figure 3).

In both the first and second steps, receipt of WSAS was positively associated with enrollment while being a non-WSAS applicant was negatively associated with enrollment (Table 2). Applying for WSAS and not receiving the award was negatively associated with enrollment when other variables were controlled for. There is strong evidence that the background variables are associated with selection for WSAS (Emeka & Hirschman, 2006), so the combined model controls for selection process. Once the negative consequences of not being selected were partially controlled for, the non-selection was neutral. In this final model, the receipt of WSAS improved the odds of enrollment for the otherwise-average sample member by 21 percentage points.

Several of the background variables were also associated with enrollment. Hispanics and American Indians were less likely than whites to enroll. Having either fathers or mothers with college degrees was positively associated with college enrollment.[4] The composite family support variables were positively associated with college enrollment. Students who lived with both parents had substantially higher odds of enrolling in college. The composite measure of family support also had a substantial positive association with college enrollment. However, controlling for preparation and other factors, expecting to attain less than a four-year degree was positively associated with college enrollment.

High school preparation variables also had a substantial and direct association with college enrollment. Students with low grades were less likely to enroll than students with B-grades, whiles students with A-grades were more likely to enroll. Taking an advanced course (AP/IB) had a positive association with college enrollment, increasing the odds of enrollment by 16.6 percentage points.

TABLE 2 Coefficient Estimates from Logistic Regression Model for College Enrollment for All Samples of WSA Students and Students in Comparison Schools

VARIABLE	Coefficients	Odds Ratio	Delta -p	Sig.	Coefficients	Odds Ratio	Delta -p	Sig.
WSA			-				-	
Non-applicants in WSA Schools	-1.075	.341	-.182	***	-.606	.546	0.116	***
Aid Applicants but Non-Awardees in WSA Schools	-.588	.555	-.078	***	-.134	.874	0.128	
Aid Awardees in WSA Schools	.843	2.322	.131	***	.939	2.558	0.210	***
Gender								
Men					-.084	.920	0.221	
Ethnicity								
African American					-.157	.855	0.171	
Hispanic					-.334	.716	0.205	**
Asian American					.046	1.047	0.171	
American Indian					-.709	.492	0.253	***
Parental Education								
Father's Education					.182	1.200	0.342	*
Mother's Education					.345	1.411	0.290	***
Family Support								
Family Support					.353	1.424	0.358	***

TABLE 2 Coefficient Estimates from Logistic Regression Model, cont.

VARIABLE	Coefficients	Odds Ratio	Delta -p	Sig.	Coefficients	Odds Ratio	Delta -p	Sig.
Family Structure								
Living with Both Parents					.511	1.667	0.479	***
Home Language								
Other Than English					-.024	.976	0.280	
Cumulative Grade								
Mostly A					.404	1.498	0.093	***
Mostly C or Below					-.615	.541	0.358	***
Education Aspiration								
Lower than Four-Year					.758	2.135		***
College							0.181	
AP Course								
Taken or Taking					.697	2.008	0.166	***
Cohort								
Year of 2003					.150	1.161	0.033	
Year of 2004					.219	1.245	0.280	*
-2 Log Likelihood	6,813.7				5,422.0			
Cox & Snell R²	.067				.266			
Chi Square	401.3				1,793.0			

Note: *** $p<0.001$, ** $p<0.01$, * $p<0.05$.

Given the substantial cohort effect for 2004 in the analysis for the three cohorts, a 28 percentage point difference in odds (Table 2), we also examined enrollment by students in the 2004 cohort (see Table 3). The analyses of the 2004 cohort showed background variables had a similar set of associations with enrollment by the cohort. However, compared to the analyses of the three cohorts (in Table 2), the analyses of the 2004 cohort reveals a slightly smaller delta-p (18.5. percentage points) for WSA and for advanced courses (11.6 percentage points). Perhaps the overall positive effect of being in the more progressive cohort—what we might call gains associated with the college going culture— offset specific effects of advanced courses and aid guarantees.

Conclusions

This chapter has examined the effects of improvements in preparation, financial aid guarantee, and other effects of school reform on college enrollment decisions. The WSA program provided guaranteed scholarships for low-income students in a select group of high schools. There was also improved availability of advanced preparation courses during the period studied. The analyses indicate a small improvement in college enrollment rates in WSA schools as a consequence of the intervention. However, since comparison schools had a wealthier population and also had substantial improvement in advanced courses, the enrollment rate at WSA schools increased at only a slightly higher rate than non-WSA schools. We examined the relationship between reforms using descriptive statistics and logistic regression analyses, as well as by comparing the two forms of analyses.

Table 3 Coefficient Estimates from Logistic Regression Analysis of College Enrollment by Students in the 2004 Sample

VARIABLE	Coefficients	Odds Ratio	Delta -p	Sig.	Coefficients	Odds Ratio	Delta -p	Sig.
WSA								
Non-applicants in WSA Schools	-1.208	.298	-.293	***	-.580	.559	-.141	***
Aid Applicants but Non-Awardees in WSA Schools	-.381	.683	-.092		.102	1.107	.023	
Aid Awardees in WSA Schools	.797	2.219	.158	***	.973	2.647	.185	***
Gender								
Men					-.250	.778	-.059	*
Ethnicity								
African American					.007	1.007	.002	
Hispanic					-.132	.876	-.031	
Asian American					-.023	.977	-.005	
American Indian					-.711	.491	-.174	**
Parental Education								
Father's Education					.270	1.310	.060	
Mother's Education					.444	1.559	.095	**
Family Support								
Family Support					.385	1.470	.083	***

Table 3 Coefficient Estimates from Logistic Regression Analysis, cont.

VARIABLE	Coefficients	Odds Ratio	Delta -p	Sig.	Coefficients	Odds Ratio	Delta -p	Sig.
Family Structure								
Living with Both Parents					.566	1.761	.118	***
Home Language								
Other Than English					-.056	.945	-.013	
Cumulative Grade								
Mostly A					.325	1.384	.071	
Mostly C or Below					-.629	.533	-.153	***
Education Aspiration								
Lower than Four-Year					.841	2.320		***
College							.165	
AP Course								
Taken or Taking					.554	1.741	.116	***
-2 Log Likelihood	2,497.0				1,975.3			
Cox & Snell R²	.072				.265			
Chi Square	165.4				687.1			

Note: *** *p*<0.001, ** *p*<0.01, * *p*<0.05.

The logistic regression analyses revealed anticipated relationships between predictor variables and enrollment. Both advanced courses and aid guarantees were positively associated with enrollment, along with SES indicators and other variables. However, while we did not complete a causal analysis, it appears the number of new students who enrolled was small: the total number of students enrolling in 2004 over the rate of the prior year was about 30 students. The logistic regression analyses suggest that WSA awards did have an influence on enrollment, controlling for student academic preparation.

The process of evaluating educational reforms is complex. Substantial revision in educational programs coupled with improvement in financing of students results in modest changes in overall rates. Some students who would have enrolled without aid received aid, so not all awards resulted in new enrollment. Some WSAS students would have taken advanced courses without the additional support, but the awards also encouraged some students to take advanced courses. Nevertheless there was an apparent gain in enrollment attributable to the intervention and the number of students predicted from analyses of the intervention for one cohort (2003) provided reasonable predictions of change in enrollment behavior for the next year (2004). We conclude that these methods provided a workable approach to assessing the impact of education and finance reforms.

Notes

[1] This study was prepared with financial support from the Bill & Melinda Gates Foundation using surveys conducted by Charles Hirschman of the University of Washington. Charles Hirschman and Stephen Thorndill (the Washington Education Foundation) provided a thoughtful review of earlier drafts. The financial support, data access, and reviews are sincerely appreciated by the authors. However, the analyses and interpretations are the authors' and do not reflect policies of points of view of any of these contributing organizations.

[2] We thank Charles Hisrchman who noted this problem in a review of an earlier version of this paper and we note the problem.

[3] Given the very substantial differences in SES across the two types of schools, it makes little sense to impute effect sizes to determine the significance of these differences.

[4] The reader is reminded that family income and parents' education are highly correlated. These variables serve as proxies for SES.

References

Becker, W.E. (2004). Omitted variables and sample selection in studies of college-going decisions. In E.P. St. John (Ed.), *Readings on equal education: Vol. 19. Public policy and college access: Investigating the federal and state roles in equalizing postsecondary opportunity* (pp. 65-86). New York: AMS Press, Inc.

Choy, S.P. (2002). *Access & persistence: Findings from 10 years of longitudinal research on students*. Washington, DC: American Council on Education.

DesJardins, S.L., & McCall, B.P. (2006). The impacts of the Gates Millennium Scholars Program on selected outcomes of low-income minority students: A regression discontinuity analyses. Presented at the Student Financial Aid Research Network, Providence, RI, July 2006.

Emeka, A., & Hirschman, C. (2006). Who applies for and who is selected for Washington State Achievers Scholarships? In E.P. St. John (Ed.), *Readings on equal education: Vol. 21. Public policy and equal educational opportunity: School reforms, postsecondary encouragement, and state policies on postsecondary education* (pp. 167-194). New York: AMS Press, Inc.

Herting, J.R., Hirschman, C., & Pharris-Ciurej, N. (2006). "The Impact of the Promise of Scholarships on College Ambitions, Preparation, and Enrollment: A Preliminary Evaluation of the Washington State Achievers Program." Revised version of a paper presented at the 2005 APPAM meetings.

Petersen, T. (1985). A comment on presenting results from logit and probit models. *American Sociological Review, 50,* 130-131.

Sedlacek, W.E. (2004). *Beyond the big test: Noncognitive assessment in higher education.* San Francisco: Jossey-Bass.

Sedlacek, W.E., & Sheu, H.B. (2006). Early academic behaviors of Washington State Achievers. In E.P. St. John (Ed.), *Readings on equal education: Vol. 21. Public policy and equal educational opportunity: School reforms, postsecondary encouragement, and state policies on postsecondary education* (pp. 195-210). New York: AMS Press, Inc.

St. John, E.P. (2006). *Education and the public interest: School reform, public finance, and access to higher education.* Netherlands: Springer Academic Press.

St. John, E.P. (2003). *Refinancing the college dream: Access, equal opportunity, and justice for taxpayers.* Baltimore: Johns Hopkins University Press.

St. John, E.P., Gross, J.P.K., Musoba, G.D., & Chung, A.S. (2006). Postsecondary encouragement and academic success: Degree attainment by Indiana's Twenty-First Century Scholars. In St. John, E.P. (Ed.), *Readings on equal education: Vol. 21. Public policy and equal educational opportunity: School reforms, postsecondary encouragement, and state policies on postsecondary education* (pp. 257-291). New York: AMS Press, Inc.

St. John, E.P., & Hu, S. (2006). The impact of guarantees of financial aid on college enrollment: An evaluation of the Washington State Achievers Program. In E.P. St. John (Ed.), *Readings on equal education: Vol. 21. Public policy and equal educational opportunity: School reforms, postsecondary encouragement, and state policies on secondary education* (pp. 223-270). New York: AMS Press, Inc.

St. John, E.P., Musoba, G.D., Simmons, A.B., Chung, C.G., Schmit, J., & Peng, C.J. (2004). Meeting the access challenge: An examination of Indiana's Twenty-first Century Scholars Program. *Research in Higher Education, 45*(8), 829-873.

Part IV

Conclusions

CHAPTER 11

CONFRONTING EDUCATIONAL INEQUALITY: LESSONS LEARNED

Edward P. St. John

The Chapters in Volume 22 of *Readings on Equal Education* have addressed issues related to educational with a focus on strategies for improving equal opportunity and diversity. This goal is appropriately characterized as an activist agenda, made necessary by the devaluing of equity issues within the mainstream discourse of educational policy (St. John, 2006b). However, while some researchers are exposing the nature of inequality and a few are taking advocacy positions aimed at reducing inequality, this does not mean that such academic work lacks the objectivity necessary for high quality research. In fact the opposite appears to be the case because public policy in education has been captured by interests that privilege wealthy students over low-income and working-class students. This problematic situation is made worse by the inability of many policy makers to deal with issues of race in policy and practice. Exploring the theme "confronting inequality" can help situate the need for retheorizing and activist inquiry in education.

Confronting Inequality

First, *educational policy in the U.S. has been in the midst of a swing away from principles of equity and justice for more than two decades.* For decades educational policy

387

Copyright ©2007 AMS Press, Inc. All rights reserved.

research has taken place within a context of increasing inequality. The educational reforms initiated during this period have emphasized excellence—a term that is a code word for test scores—and undermined equal access to quality education, a conclusion evident in research on market reforms, like charters (Eckes & Rapp, 2006) and vouchers (Metcalf & Paul, 2006). Policies that emphasize testing are at the very core issue of the accountability and excellence movements in education, complicating efforts to reduce inequality in educational opportunity. The claim of conservative education reformers has been that outcomes matter but funding does not (Finn, 1990), while the research contradicts this claim, especially with respect to educational achievement by high school seniors (Musoba, 2006). These conclusions, reached in the last volume of REE (St. John, 2006b), are accentuated by the research presented in the preceding Chapters. Consider these findings that emerge from the research studies in this volume:

- Working students achieve as well, with respect to class grades, as other students, but students who work more than 20 hours a week are less likely to complete their degrees within the same time periods as other students (Perna, Cooper, & Li, Chapter 4). This finding reinforces the conclusion reached in the reanalyses of the National Educational Longitudinal Survey (NELS) in the previous volume of REE: low-income students were more likely to still be enrolled after 8 years of college than to have dropped out (St. John & Chung, 2006).
- State merit grant programs undermine racial diversity in enrollment opportunity, including higher education desegregation plans (Inoue & Geske, Chapter 4), a finding that further illuminate the tragedy of the rush to merit grants in the southern U.S. (Heller & Marin, 2002, 2004).

- Inequalities in educational opportunity are underemphasized in most of the literature on the public good in higher education (Pasque, Chapter 2) because the arguments about the public good are used to rationalize public spending on higher education. It is little wonder that state funding for student grants have not kept pace with rising college costs within states (Heller, 2006a).
- Low tax rates within states are significantly associated with the rise in the percentage of college costs paid by students (Fisher, Chapter 6). The shift toward privatization can be characterized as a global ideological shift (Rizvi, 2006) that is causing major adaptations within public universities (Priest & St. John, 2006). These developments, especially the shift away from need-based grants within public universities (Hossler, 2006), can further undermine equal educational opportunity.

Second, *it is increasingly necessary to reframe policy and practice in education to make visible the inequalities that face practitioners and researchers.* Researchers are increasingly confronted by the problem of having to reframe theory in order to make visible the inequalities evident in educational practice. Consider the following examples of retheorizing in this volume:

- Tierney and Venegas (Chapter 1) focus on the need to consider how students, parents, and educators learn about student financial aid. Even if perfect information were available, there are still many barriers facing low-income students. For example, many of the students studied by Tierney and Venegas (2006) have low incomes, some may not have filed tax returns, and may be in the country illegally. Yet these families face the same challenge to apply for college and student aid as wealthier families. Their cultural ecology model (Chapter 1) could be useful in illuminating the complexity of the aid process.

- There are alternative ways to structure student aid programs to encourage families to fill out financial aid applications. If for example, families were notified that they were eligible for aid based on their tax returns or their applications to free and reduced lunch (Heller, 2006b), then the mysteries of aid could be demystified for low-income families. Such practices could move the U.S. closer to the goal of providing access to higher education as a basic right, as recommended in the last volume of REE (St. John, 2006b). Such adaptations of current policies and programs would be a radical departure from current practice.

- The Bill & Melinda Gates Foundation's Washington State Achievers (WSA) Program represents a comprehensive way to structure an early intervention program to encourage access (St. John & Hu, 2006). It provides support for school reform to provide a better quality of courses, mentoring for students, and guarantees of student aid for students selected for this aid. Yet since the scholarships are limited, an increasing number of students in the WSA schools graduate prepared for colleges but lack the financial support of their peers selected for the scholarships. Thus, even the generosity of a wealthy foundation has a limited capacity to address inequalities when student aid is not adequate to ensure prepared, low-income students can afford to pay for continuous enrollment. The options, including working during college, can impede educational opportunity as Perna and colleagues demonstrate (Chapter 4).

- The analysis of students' voices about graduate education (Chapter 3) illustrates some of the ways student financial aid extends aspirations. Students who had not expected to enroll in graduate school did so when they received aid. The funding helped them to realize new possibilities. This adds substance to Tierney and Venegas' argument that information on student aid could expand postsecondary aspirations by students in high schools, especially if there is sufficient student aid available to them.

Third, *many of the current approaches to student aid and educational reform undermine long-standing social and political obligations to equalize educational opportunity.* While there has been an erosion of policies that promote equal opportunity, such as affirmative action polices in California and Washington, the efforts to desegregate schools and colleges have a constitutional basis. However, Inoue and Geske (Chapter 5) have added substantially to understanding how the movement toward merit aid has undermined the intent of desegregation in one state:

- Soon after agreement to a desegregation plan in Louisiana, the state passed a new merit aid program (known as TOPS).
- The distribution of the TOPS program favored Whites over African Americas because of the emphasis on test scores—without considering unequal access to advanced high school courses (the primary predictor of these scores)—many African Americans had the necessary GPA but not the ACT sores.
- The distribution TOPS awardees undermined desegregation of the state's land grant university, Louisiana State University. LSU was more racially segregated after the implementation of TOPS, undermining the intent of the desegregation plan.

Such a pattern of contradictory policy decision making and implementation is not new in either state of federal or state policy. The general pattern of emphasizing merit grants in the 1990s (Heller & Marin, 2002) followed federal action implementing loans over need-based grants (Hearn & Holdsworth, 2004; St. John & Wooden, 2006), a policy emphasis that followed the redirection of need-based aid to middle-income students after the passage of the Middle Income Student Assistance Act in 1978 (St. John & Byce, 1982).

This pattern of implementing new policies that undermine earlier programs that focus on equal education opportunity is visible across K-12 (St. John & Mirón, 2003) just as it is in higher education. In K-12 the direction of policies on Title I (Wong, 2003) and comprehensive school reform (St. John, Manset-Williamson, Chung, Musoba, Loescher, Simmons, Gordon, & Hossler, 2003) have labeled schools as failing and forced reform models onto schools. While the failure of desegregation seems to have been related to white flight rather than the implementation of other policies (Orfield & Eaton, 1996), the evolution of education policy has not help move education closer to the intent of desegregation.

Fourth, *the overemphasis on policies and practices that contradict the intent of equality opportunity means that finding a balanced approach in policy and practice may require taking an activist approach.* If our goal is to find a better balance in policy between emphases on excellence and equity, then it may necessary to take an activist approach in both policy and practice. This is the issue addressed by Mirón (Chapter 8) in his work in New Orleans Schools and by Kline (Chapter 9) in her action research on education for student affairs professionals. Mirón had to face up to a policy emphasis on new market approaches as he emphasized social equity and carism in his interventionist efforts. For Kline, the question was how best to design instruction to encourage students to test their own assumptions, as a step toward encouraging diversity. Both of these activist researchers were seeking to find more balance in a system that was out of balance.

In past issues of *Readings on Equal Education*, researchers have examined programs like the Gates Millennium Scholars (GMS) program (Hurtado, Nelson Laird, & Perorarzio, 2004; Sedlacek & Sheu, 2004; Wilds, 2004) and Washington State Achievers (WSA) programs (Emeka & Hirschman, 2006; Sedlacek & Sheu, 2006) that were designed to overcome structural barriers to access. GMS provided large grants to low-income, high-achieving students of color, enabling many to attend and persist in high-prestige, private colleges (St. John & Chung, 2004). The WSA program in contrast, supported high school reform and student aid, a dual approach to enabling low-income student to prepare for and enroll in four-year colleges (St. John & Hu, 2006).

Three of the Chapters extend understanding of the role of comprehensive programs that including school reforms and student aid as means of promoting college access. Wooden (Chapter 7) examined how schools reproduce inequality and ponders the ways reforms that include school restructuring might transform these patterns. In Chapter 10, Shouping Hu and I examine how school reform leads to improvement in access to advanced courses, as an enhancement of the effects of student aid. Finally, the analyses of graduate student voices (Chapter 3) reveals how the receipt of student aid not only removes barriers to access, but also enables students to dream beyond their aspiration, reversing the widely observed pattern of declining aspirations for minority students (Carter, 2002; Hearn, 2001).

While WSA and GMS were major programs funded by the Bill & Melinda Gates Foundation, the actions taken by Kline and Mirón were individual actions, taken to seek and promote social justice and educational opportunity. In both cases the researchers reflected on their own assumptions as they worked with people who held different views to create new opportunities. In this case, researchers cannot assume they have all the answers; rather they have the opportunity to pose new interventions that could change practice. In both cases, the action researchers sought to find evidence that could help inform practices.

The idea that activism is necessary to bring balance to the current system differs in some basic ways from the making arguments about creating a different types of organization or policies. The focus sometimes shifts to focusing on how to make current policy work better for those who are lease advantaged by the system now in place. Regardless of the strategies being used in educational policy and practice, it is important to reflect on whether all have equal opportunity to prepare and whether all who are equally prepared have equal opportunity to enroll in college. If either the opportunity to prepare for advanced education in the basic (k-12) system or to participate in the advanced system is unequal, then some type of intervention is necessary. The emphasis on equal distribution of rights must be balanced with commitment to remedy unequal access to that right (St. John, 2006a). This argument is implicit and Rawls's *Theory of Justice* (2001) and is directly applied to education as Amy Fisher reminds us (Chapter 6).

Lessons Learned

Inequality is not new, nor has it been remedied in education. For a brief period in the 1970s educational opportunity in the U.S. was more equal than it was before that period or than it has been since (St. John, 2003). Nearly three decades have passed since the equal educational opportunity goal of the Great Society was partially realized through implementation of the *Elementary and Secondary Education Act* and the *Higher Education Act*. A decade after implementation of this legislation, in the middle 1970s, major progress was evident, especially in enrollment rates across diverse racial/ethnic groups (St. John, 2003). This historical blip on the trend line of persistent inequality in equal educational opportunity is noteworthy because it serves as a reminder that greater equality is possible through interventions in policy and practice.

We are now in a period of history in which the dominant policies—the accountability and market models that are so widely advocated and used—undermine the older role of policy in promoting uplift of aspirations and attainment for students who start out with fewer resources and less opportunity. As a conclusion I suggest lessons learned that can inform a new generation of research and practice that focusing on contending with—and potentially reducing— inequalities in educational opportunities.

Lesson 1: The predisposition of policy toward excellence, economic-development, and market rationales makes it difficult to voice concerns about inequality. Arguments used to rationalize reforms promote economic development. *Excellence* for all has become coded language for redirecting school reforms from promoting equal opportunity to serving middle-income students. *Economic development* is used to rationalize redirecting resources from colleges and universities as a means of saving taxes. *Market* models provide means to restratify, if not to resegregate, education.

Collectively the Chapters in this volume further illuminate the problem. Consider Inoue and Geske's study of student merit grants and desegregation in Louisiana (Chapter 5): the implementation of the state's merit program undermined the intent of the state desegregation plan. At a macro level, Penny Pasque's analysis of the literature provided a compelling portrayal of the policy argument emphasizing economic rationales over humanistic rationales of the public interest. At the micro level, Kline's classroom experiment illuminated how the predisposition of graduate students closed off consideration of race, at least at the start of their graduate course. When we consider the role of these predispositions toward self-interest of monetary and education privilege, it is easier to understand how privatization of higher education could have resulted from the decline in tax rates (Fisher, Chapter 6).

Lesson 2: Make sure that available resources are used to promote equal opportunity. Tierney and Venegas (Chapter 1) propose a cultural ecology model for examining how information of resources might help students envision new pathways to educational opportunity. Their argument that culture plays a role in this reproducing unequal opportunity is illuminated by the findings of other studies in the volume. Perna, Asha, and Li (Chapter 4) provide further descriptive evidence of the ways excessive work during college limits opportunity. They argue that colleges should make sure working students find out about available student aid. Wooden (Chapter 7) examines students' experiences in a urban high school, providing further evidence that counselors make tracking decisions that make it more difficult for students to realize their educational dreams. His findings illustrate that process of providing better information to minority students may start with deeper changes in the system of high school counseling. The study of Achiever high schools suggest that school restructuring, coupled with mentoring and student aid (Chapter 10), can have a positive influence on expanding opportunity, enabling students from less affluent schools to keep up with students from more affluent schools in preparation and enrollment. This supports the notion that while researchers and activists make linkages between resources and need, they need to have reasonable expectations about the extent of reform that is possible at any point in time.

We should keep in mind that when the language of "every child" is used to argue for reform, an implicit argument is being made in opposition to targeting resources to students with the highest need. An effort must be made to connect low-income students with available resources, especially resources that are targeted on low-income students. This lesson may extend beyond information about student aid to the general problem of how to reassert social justice considerations into the policy discourse on educational policy.

Lesson 3: School reform can create opportunities to improve academic preparation and access. Wooden's study of the urban high school (Chapter 7) illuminates the values of social uplift are still alive and well, as least in one urban high school. The African American tradition of education emphasized carism and cross generation uplift, the core values of equal opportunity. Wooden illustrates that these values are still deeply held among African American high school students, but are limited in the structure of schools. This is a contrast to the study of Washington State Achievers where an apparent effort was made to improve schools and there was evidence of improved access (Chapter 10).

Lesson 4: It is difficult to maintain a focus on equal opportunity when policy emphasizes markets. The two studies of the public good—Pasque's literature review and Fisher's regression analyses—reveal that a set of forces promoting privatization of higher education are well established. Pasque (Chapter 2) illustrates that arguments about the public good are not frequently centered in the logic of equal opportunity. Fischer (Chapter 6) illustrates that when state contexts are taken into account (i.e., the fixed effects regression model) the difference attributable to political ideologies fade and the role of taxes shine through as the most important force in privatization of public colleges. Privatization drives up college costs, which puts college further out of the reach of college prepared students from low-income families. The fact the providing financial aid enables qualified students to aspire higher illustrates too that spiral of rising costs causes problems with inequalities (Chapter 3).

Lesson 5: Changing attitudes involves creating space for open discourse. Kline (Chapter 9) demonstrates that creating discursive space in the classroom enables students to test predispositional assumptions and take new forms of action. She observed resistance among graduate students to open discourse and to the principles of social justice. Student projects tested assumptions about inequality by trying out new strategies as part of a class project. In a different situation, as an activist researcher, Mirón (Chapter 8) influenced policy by engaging in the policy discourse within the governance of New Orleans schools after Hurricane Katrina. In both cases, finding the discursive space—creating the room to test out new assumptions—made differences in the forms of action taken. In contrast, closed thinking is typical of academic action, which generally sets out to state and prove positions. Academic strategic action of the classical type has less chance of providing opportunities to explore and test alternative, competing assumptions, which is necessary to change attitudes and create new forms of action that integrate concern about justice.

This notion of discursive space also applies to policy research. Arguments about education for all and research that focuses on the correlates of achievement are used to rationalize the new economic and excellence policies in education (St. John, 2006a). This problem was addressed in REE volume 19, which examined how the federal government misused statistics (Becker, 2004; Heller, 2004) to build the case that the access problem was due to poor preparation when the statistics in the report demonstrated that nearly half of the college prepared low-income students in the class of 1992 did not have the opportunity to enroll in four-year colleges (Fitzgerald, 2004; Lee, 2004). The claims that underlie conservative education policies are research based, justified by research that tests a narrow set of explanations without considering the alternatives. Better balance is needed in research, just as it is in educational policy.

Lesson 6: It is crucial to reassert equal opportunity as a rationale for reform as having equal value with the dominant rationales of excellence and economic development. Economic rationales are frequently used to argue for education reform. For example, the Spellings Commission (U.S. Department of Education, 2006) argued that the value of education was the reason college access should be expanded and did not adequately address inequalities in the opportunity for prepared, low-income students to enroll. Mirón (Chapter 8) demonstrates one means of asserting equity issues into the policy discourse, through advocacy in the policy decision process. The Bill and Melinda Gates Foundation demonstrated another in the Washington State Achievers Program (Chapter 10): initiating a new comprehensive reform that might serve as a model for other reforms in schools and public agencies. However, these actions further illustrate the problem facing the reformer, be they individuals or large foundation — the normal course of action in educational policy and practice has undervalued principles of justice and social change by giving preference to economic rationales for change. The major challenge for advocates of social justice is to discover new and better ways to bring concerns about social equity into the discourse economic, social, and educational policies.

References

Becker, W.E. (2004). Omitted variables and sample selection in studies of college-going decisions. In E.P. St. John (Ed.), *Readings on equal education: Vol. 19. Public policy and college access: Investigating the federal and state roles in equalizing postsecondary opportunity* (pp. 65-86). New York: AMS Press, Inc.

Carter, D.F. (2002). College students' degree aspirations: A theoretical model and literature review with a focus on African American and Latino students. In J. Smart (Ed.), *Higher education: A handbook of theory and research.* Bronx, NY: Agathon Press.

Eckes, S., & Rapp, K. (2006). Charter school research: Trends and implications. In E.P. St. John (Ed.), *Readings on equal education: Vol. 21. Public policy and equal educational opportunity: School reforms, postsecondary encouragement, and state policies on postsecondary education* (pp. 3-36). New York: AMS Press, Inc.

Emeka, A., & Hirschman, C. (2006). Who applies for and who is selected for Washington State Achievers Scholarships? In E.P. St. John (Ed.), *Readings on equal education: Vol. 21. Public policy and equal educational opportunity: School reforms, postsecondary encouragement, and state policies on postsecondary education* (pp. 167-194). New York: AMS Press, Inc.

Finn, C.E., Jr. (1990, April). The biggest reform of all. *Phi Delta Kappan, 71*(8), 584-592.

Fitzgerald, B. (2004). Federal financial aid and college access. In E.P. St. John (Ed.), *Readings on equal education: Vol. 19. Public policy and college access: Investigating the federal and state roles in equalizing postsecondary opportunity* (pp. 1-28). New York: AMS Press, Inc.

Hearn, J.C. (2001). Access to postsecondary education: Financing equity in an evolving context. In M.B. Paulsen & J.C. Smart (Eds.), *The finance of higher education: Theory, research, policy, and practice* (pp. 439-460). New York: Agathon Press.

Hearn, J.C., & Holdsworth, J.M. (2004). Federal student aid: The shift from grants to loans. In E.P. St. John & M.D. Parsons (Eds.), *Public funding of higher education: Changing contexts and new rationales* (pp. 40-59). Baltimore: Johns Hopkins University Press.

Heller, D.E. (2006a). Early commitment to financial aid. *Applied Behavioral Scientist.* 49(12): 1719-1738.

Heller, D.E. (2006b). State support of higher education: Past, present, and future. In D.M. Priest & E.P. St. John (Eds.), *Privatization and public universities.* (11-37) Bloomington, IN: Indiana University Press.

Heller, D.E. (2004). NCES research on college participation: A critical analysis. In E.P. St. John (Ed.), *Readings on equal education: Vol. 19. Public policy and college access: Investigating the federal and state roles in equalizing postsecondary opportunity* (pp. 29-64). New York: AMS Press, Inc.

Heller, D.E., & Marin, P. (Eds.). (2004). *State merit scholarship programs and racial inequality.* Cambridge, MA: The Civil Rights Project, Harvard University.

Heller, D.E., & Marin, P. (Eds.) (2002). *Who should we help? The negative social consequences of merit scholarships.* Cambridge, MA: The Civil Rights Project, Harvard University.

Hossler, D. (2006). Student and families as revenue: The impact on institutional behaviors. In D.M. Priest & E.P. St. John (Eds.), *Privatization in public universities: Implications for the public trust.* Bloomington, IN: Indiana University Press.

Hurtado, S., Nelson Laird, T.F., & Perorarzio, T.E. (2004). The transition to college for low-income students: The impact of the GMS Program. In E.P. St. John (Ed.), *Readings on equal education: Vol. 20. Improving access and college success for diverse students: Studies of the Gates Millennium Scholars Program* (pp. 155-182). New York: AMS Press, Inc.

Lee, J.B. (2004). Access revisited: A preliminary reanalysis of NELS. In E.P. St. John (Ed.), *Readings on equal education: Vol. 19. Public policy and college access: Investigating the federal and state roles in equalizing postsecondary opportunity* (pp. 87-96). New York: AMS Press, Inc.

Metcalf, K.K., & Paul, K.M. (2006). Enhancing or destroying equity? An examination of educational vouchers. In E.P. St. John (Ed.), *Readings on equal education: Vol. 21. Public policy and equal educational opportunity: School reforms, postsecondary encouragement, and state policies on postsecondary education* (pp. 37-74). New York: AMS Press, Inc.

Musoba, G.D. (2006). Accountability v. adequate funding: Which policies influence adequate preparation for college? In E.P. St. John (Ed.), *Readings on equal education: Vol. 21. Public policy and equal educational opportunity: School reforms, postsecondary encouragement, and state policies on postsecondary education* (pp. 75-125). New York: AMS Press, Inc.

Orfield, G., & Eaton, S.E. (1996). *Dismantling desegregation: The quiet reversal of Brown v. Board of Education.* New York: Free Press.

Priest, D., & St. John, E.P. (Eds.) (2006). *Privatization in public universities.* Bloomington, IN: Indiana University Press.

Rawls, J. (2001). *Justice as fairness: A restatement.* Cambridge, MA: Belknap Press of Harvard University Press.

Rizvi, F. (2006). The ideology of privatization in higher education: A global perspective. In D.M. Priest & E.P. St. John (Eds.), *Privatization and public universities.* (65-84) Bloomington, IN: Indiana University Press.

Sedlacek, W.E., & Sheu, H.B. (2006). Early academic behaviors of Washington State Achievers. In E.P. St. John (Ed.), *Readings on equal education: Vol. 21. Public policy and equal educational opportunity: School reforms, postsecondary encouragement, and state policies on postsecondary education* (pp. 195-210). New York: AMS Press, Inc.

Sedlacek, W.E., & Sheu, H.B. (2004). Correlates of leadership activities of Gates Millennium Scholars. In E.P. St. John (Ed.), *Readings on equal education: Vol. 20. Improving access and college success for diverse students: Studies of the Gates Millennium Scholars Program* (pp. 249-264). New York: AMS Press, Inc.

St. John, E.P. (2006a). *Education and the public interest: School reform, public finance, and access to higher education.* Dordrecht, The Netherlands: Springer.

St. John, E.P. (Ed.) (2006b). Readings on equal education: Vol. 21. *Public policy and equal educational opportunity: School reforms, postsecondary encouragement, and state policies on postsecondary education.* New York: AMS Press, Inc.

St. John, E.P. (2003). *Refinancing the college dream: Access, equal opportunity, and justice for taxpayers.* Baltimore: Johns Hopkins University Press.

St. John, E.P., & Byce, C. (1982). The changing federal role in student financial aid. In M. Kramer (Ed.), *Meeting student aid needs in a period of retrenchment* (pp. 21-40). New Directions for Higher Education, No. 40. San Francisco: Jossey-Bass.

St. John, E.P., & Chung, C-G. (2006). Postsecondary access and attainment: Reanalysis of the National Education Longitudinal Study. In E.P. St. John (Ed.), *Readings on equal education: Vol. 21. Public policy and equal educational opportunity: School reforms, postsecondary encouragement, and state policies on postsecondary education* (pp. 295-340). New York: AMS Press, Inc.

St. John, E.P., & Chung, C-G. (2004). The Impact of GMS on financial access: Analyses of the 2000 cohort. In E.P. St. John (Ed.), *Readings on equal education: Vol. 20. Improving access and college success for diverse students: Studies of the Gates Millennium Scholars Program* (pp. 115-153). New York: AMS Press, Inc.

St. John, E.P., & Hu, S. (2006). The impact of guarantees of financial aid on college enrollment: An evaluation of the Washington State Achievers Program. In E.P. St. John (Ed.), *Readings on equal education: Vol. 21. Public policy and equal educational opportunity: School reforms, postsecondary encouragement, and state policies on postsecondary education* (pp. 211-256). New York: AMS Press, Inc.

St. John, E.P., Manset-Williamson, G.M., Chung, C-G., Musoba, G.D., Loescher, S., Simmons, A.B., Gordon, D., & Hossler, C.A. (2003). Comprehensive school reform: An exploratory study. In L.F. Mirón & E.P. St. John (Eds.), *Reinterpreting urban school reform: Have urban schools failed, or has the reform movement failed urban schools?* (pp. 129-154). Albany, NY: SUNY Press.

St. John, E.P., & Mirón, L.F. (2003). A critical-empirical perspective on urban school reform. In L.F. Mirón & E.P. St. John (Eds.), *Reinterpreting urban school reform: Have urban schools failed, or has the reform movement failed urban schools?* Albany, NY: SUNY Press.

St. John, E.P., & Wooden, O.S. (2006). Privatization and federal funding for higher education. In D.M. Priest & E.P. St. John (Eds.), *Privatization and public universities.* (38-64), Bloomington, IN: Indiana University Press.

Tierney, W.G., & Venegas, C. (2006). Fictive kin and social capital: The role of peer groups in applying and paying for college. *Applied Behavior Scientist.* 49(12): 1687-1702.

Wilds, D.J. (2004). Foreword. In E.P. St. John (Ed.), *Readings on equal education: Vol. 20. Improving access and college success for diverse students: Studies of the Gates Millennium Scholars Program.* New York: AMS Press, Inc.

Wong, K.K. (2003). Federal Title I as a reform strategy in urban schools. In L.F. Mirón & E.P. St. John (Eds.), *Reinterpreting urban school reform: Have urban schools failed, or has the reform movement failed urban schools?* (pp. 55-76). Albany, NY: SUNY Press.

U.S. Department of Education. (2006) *A Test of Leadership: Changing the Future of U.S. Higher Education,* Washington, DC: authors.

INDEX